A SPECK IN THE OC
I n d e

Foreward   2

1. *A Scenic Heaven of which man had made a hell.*   4
2. Blues, Natives, Hawks and Rhadegunds   24
3. Dipping through the Tropics   32
4. What does a DC Do?   42
5. The Kedong Massacre   64
6. Looking each other in the eye   72
7. Not fair dealings   86
8. New boy at the office   100
9. Baby Taylor's mosquito   114
10. The position isn't easy or comfortable   118
11. The domestic round the common task   126
12. *A very gay, a very gallant and a very much misunderstood community.*
                                                               138
13. A story of courage   148
14. Service in the outposts   156
15. Comrades in arms   192
16. Transplanting English law to far off lands   200
17. We and They   220
18. The leopard murders of Opobo   236
19. *Sing a song of prices*   248
20. Tax collecting and touring   260
21. Uhuru!   268

Notes and Bibliography   290

ILLUSTRATIONS

Swahili Trader	4
Hal Williams, Cambridge	24
Building the East African Railway	32
Railway map, Sudan	40
Village meeting, Tana River, Kenya	42
Resolving a border dispute, Kenya.	46
Hal Williams, tea party in Kakamega, Kenya.	62
Map,. British East Africa	64
Sir Frederick Jackson	66
Masai Moran	69
John Ainsworth	71
Arthur Collyer photographing tribesmen	72
Arthur Collyer, 'The DC'	86
Arthur Collyer's safari notes	89
Maps Masai Areas,	91,92 & 98
Arthur Collyer's porters	93
Masai family, 1908	94
Masikonde and family	96
Arthur Collyer and Freize	99
Hal Williams with Italians	100
Letters from Mullens & Reece	106,108 &109
Map Sierra Leone	114
Clarence Buxton	118
Agnes Budge and children's party	126
Sue and Veronica Williams and friends	128
Hal Williams and Sir Phillip Mitchell	129
DC's House, Southern Sudan	131
Joy Williams	133
Kakamega Hospital	137
Settlers' tea party	138
Margaret and Olive Collyer	143
Olive Collyer's headstone	147
Pat O'Dwyer at Cambridge	148
J.A.G. McCall on duty	156,187,200,207,236,148
Hal and Joy Williams	184
Andarobo	220
Sunflower plant, Uganda	251
H.M. The Queen	268
Letter from Paul Mboya to Hal Williams	289

A SPECK IN THE OCEAN OF TIME
FOREWARD

The picture on the cover of this book is from a tapestry and like every tapestry, it is indistinct. History is also like that but the furore about whether or not Britain should have ruled an empire, has offered some an opportunity to rework the whole picture of British colonial history in Africa. Academics, politicians and others have taken advantage of a hazy knowledge of that immense and mysterious continent and many have jumped on the grievance or guilt band wagon. The men who carried out the day to day work serving as colonial administrators have largely been discounted, sometimes maligned.

Some of the stories in this anecdotal history are taken from books that have been written, but the principal protagonists are people whose stories have not been published. It is therefore a collation of the many strands and threads that made up the lives and work of those who served Africa administrating such disparate places as Gwandu, Kiambu or Moyamba.

Nearly thirty years ago, the idea was born that I should write down their stories, before they and their wives faded away largely forgotten by history. What did these men and women do on a day to day basis for the people of Africa? What problems did they face and how did they resolve them? In the background there are some of our own recollections growing up as children of an administrator in Kenya. A trifle misty the overall picture may be but like the tapestry, we remember a simpler and gentler Africa than we see today.

I would like to thank all those who with unstinting generosity have entrusted me with their stories. There are few main contributors to this book with whom I did not communicate either personally or with their children. I acknowledge with enormous gratitude all those who have given it its anecdotal richness and I greatly esteem their contribution - to the book, yes - but most of all to Africa.

The picture on the cover is a tapestry designed by Miss Edith Weisman and embroidered by Miss Rickman of the East Africa Women's League. Completed c 1962. Mrs Jeannie Davis believes that she knew them when she was a child in the 1950s. *"They were known as The Ladies, and they lived in a mission station at Weithaga. They were not missionaries but taught women to cook and, embroider. I never discovered why they were there. They had 25 different varieties of fruit in their lovely garden, and made delicious Cape gooseberry jam. One of them wore very dumpy hats."*

A Swahili (Zanzibari) trader in Uganda. Taken from *The Uganda Protectorate* by Sir Harry Johnston, published in 1902

Chapter 1

A SCENIC HEAVEN OF WHICH MAN MADE A HELL.
Margery Perham

Africa. The very word throbs with adventure and derring-do. Explorers battling with the unknown; Zulu impis well drilled and terrible; elephant under the fever trees trumpeting a warning. And for those of us who once lived there, the word creates a turmoil of pictures and emotions similar to the memories of a past and passionate love affair. The physical beauty of the place is impossible to forget. As I look back on my childhood I see immense blue skies, plains of golden grasses as far as the eye can see, conical huts surrounded by fields of waving maize and millet, papyrus floating islands travelling serenely on the blue waters of Lake Victoria, rolling hills eight thousand feet above sea level where we used to gallop, steep thickly forested gullies where black and white colobus monkeys played like glossy flying carpets over ice clear forest streams: dusty deserts, snow-capped mountains, casuarina trees soughing in the sea breezes, sweltering drives through rolling thorn scrub: an impossibly, hauntingly lovely continent often richly endowed with productive soils and a benign climate.

But nestled in her lusty beauty Africa's children have so often lived in terrible misery.

Throughout her history African kingdoms have prospered and then faded away before they could settle into civilisations. Trade would flourish; gold to the Pharaohs, ivory and spices to Europe, slaves to desert sultanates, Greece and Rome and, much later, to America. Powerful kings, chiefs and sheikhs rose out of the brief order and prosperity and their courts were pompous and splendid. Art flourished in some places and many fine examples exist in museums and galleries such as the wonderfully fashioned heads from Ife dating perhaps as far back as the 12th century and the fabulous Benin bronzes made in the sixteenth century.

It seems that steady progress and prosperity was elusive and all too often the powerful chiefs and their people degenerated into depravity. The history of Africa, from what we can gather, was a rollercoaster of riches and famine, of peace and desperate tragedy.

Many of Africa's people were cut off from the ebb and flow of learning by the continent's vastness. In most parts of sub-Saharan Africa, before the latter part of the nineteenth century, the wheel, currency and the written word were unknown. Interior travel was limited and boats were small and frail, not designed for journeys but for fishing close to shore.

The population was often also badly weakened by malnutrition and animal-borne diseases, some of which lodged in their bloodstreams for life. In East Africa, for example, they had to contend with malaria, sleeping sickness, black-water fever, leprosy, yaws, intestinal parasites, dysentery and bilharzia. And in West Africa can be added to that list, sickle cell, river blindness and a louse-borne disease known as relapsing fever.

Famine was a constant threat. Sir Frederick Jackson wrote: *My personal experiences of famines* [in East Africa] *were few I am glad to say.* But he then went on to say that during a famine in the coast regions in 1883, *children were sold into slavery by their parents.* And another in Kamassia in 1896 where, *of course, it was the women and children who suffered the most; they do so every time, and the worst offenders in getting more than their fair share of the little food there was were the young men of warrior age.*

6

In Ukamba in 1899, he noted *"a very bad and ever memorable* [famine, where] *the starving women and children were dreadful to look upon.*

It would be unreasonable to assume that these famines were a phenomenon only of the nineteenth century. One must suppose that they occurred before the African dawn of history.

There is an interesting pointer to the physical damage caused by generations of disease and malnutrition in a book written by my great aunt, Margaret Collyer, who went to Kenya in 1915. She refers to the small stature and weakness of the Kikuyu peoples who could not be employed in heavy work such as road-building. The Kikuyu probably lacked protein because they had difficulty in keeping cattle. The hubristic Masai, believing that God had ordained that all cattle should be theirs, could not tolerate others keeping them. This meant, it is believed, that the Kikuyu were reduced to hiding any livestock they were able to keep and subsisting on mainly vegetables. The work that required powerful man-power was given to what were then known as the "Kavirondo" – now the Luo - people who had always lived off the bounty of Lake Victoria. Today, the Kikuyu are tall, lithe, strong and sometimes competing successfully with the best of the best in the athletics field.

Sleeping sickness wrought havoc in some populations. A species of tsetse fly is responsible for this disease which induces a hopeless and fatal torpor in a victim. In Uganda between 1901 and 1906, 200,000 people died in an epidemic wiping out whole villages.

The tick and tsetse fly were also a constant menace to the domestic animals upon which the people relied. The mightiest tribe to hold sway in Kenya's rich grazing fiefdom which stretched over mountain and plain was the Masai. (Now-a-days known as the Maasai.) This nomadic people relied exclusively on the food produced by cattle, sheep and goats and they measured their wealth by, as well as bartered with, their livestock. Perhaps it had happened before – perhaps even many times – but in 1890 an epidemic of rinderpest swept through all Africa. Nearly all the Masai cattle died. Smallpox followed the rinderpest. Influenza followed the smallpox. Some believe as many as three quarters of the tribe died.

Taking advantage of the weakened Masai, reduced to mere *"tattered bands,"* their ancient adversaries, the Kikuyu and the Kamba, seized their opportunity for revenge for the countless times the Masai had pillaged their villages. They swooped upon the defenceless Masai manyattas (homesteads), killed the old, keeping some as slaves and selling the young to Swahili traders. The Masai, when they could, retaliated by wholesale massacres such as formerly they had never committed.

As if these dangers and disasters were not enough for the African to contend with in his life, witchcraft and the occult dogged the daily lives of many villages and made it problematical trying to get through each day. Cut off from the rest of the world, generation after generation, it is easy to see how fear of evil spirits could hobble innovation and everyday activities, while also leaving them open to exploitation by the more intelligent members of the community.

It was a constant lottery for a person to know when he or she had transgressed. It might be that their sin was as commonplace as stepping on a bone that had been chewed the previous night. The witchdoctor was often all-powerful and could bring his enemies to book by instilling great fear. In some parts of Africa there were trials for misdemeanours and they could be grim. In Cameroon *trial by ordeal took place deep in the forest and the wretched wrongdoer was made to drink a deadly draught of poison concocted from powdered sasswood. If he or she vomited, acquittal was declared but, of course, if the poison stayed down guilt and death followed."*

"It was dangerous for a man to have more than others, to attract attention to himself, for that meant the attention of sorcerers, black magic men – witch-doctors as we incorrectly say – ... and the whole race of cheats and extortioners, who have, from the Stone Age, kept African man and woman in abject, shivering terror and subjection.

Fear of the occult shackled innovation and continued into the twentieth century. An example of this is given in Margaret Collyer's autobiography where she describes a chilling ceremony which took place on her farm in the early 1920's in order to discourage the petty thieving that plagued her early farming efforts. Her headman, Kago, first called a council which deliberated all day *when not a stroke of work was done.* In the evening Miss Collyer handed over to them an old sheep. The ceremony, *whatever it was going to be, was to take place next day, when again no work would be done. It was all very sinister.*

The drumming that night being worse than usual, I could not sleep at all and went to Kago's tent to find out what it was all about, and whether I could witness the happenings on the morrow. At first he would not hear of my being present; no white man had ever been allowed at any of these ceremonies, and he evidently did not think it very safe. The sacrifice was to take place in the forest, where a clearing had already been prepared for it. On second thoughts Kago said I could go with him, but that we must both hide in a deep ditch near the spot, I being made to promise that, whatever I saw, I would not cry out or say a word to stop the proceedings.

[That evening] it was eerie waiting in the gloom of the trees listening to the muffled beat of drums as the procession solemnly and slowly approached the forest edge. For a time it halted while the shrieking women were dismissed and the drums stilled. Now they came on again, marching silently; except for an occasional snapping of a dead stick, there was no sound to indicate that upwards of thirty men were within a short stone's throw of our sanctuary. So silently did they come that I was wondering what had happened to them, when the lamb and elders suddenly appeared and took the centre of the leaf-strewn stage. After these followed, in single file, the procession of the morans, who squatted in a circle round the three principle actors in this dramatic scene.

How I wished I understood the Kikuyu tongue, for two long speeches were delivered by the elders, each in turn standing up during the course of his oration.

... For the next half hour I was forced to witness the most dreadful cruelty it has ever been my lot to imagine. The sheep was thrown on its side. One man pulled back the head, the other with a knife slit the skin between the bones from chin to joint of jaw, then drew the tongue down through the cut. Each warrior in turn

was called up, and on taking the oath, bit off a portion of the living tongue. Then the legs of the animal were broken with sticks, each man repeating the following words (or as near as I can translate them) – 'As I break the bones of this sheep, so may I be broken if I steal while on this white woman's farm.' After having smashed all the sheep's legs to pieces, it was killed by cutting the throat.

Also in her book, Margaret Collyer demonstrates the power of suggestion still retained in the African mind in the early 20th Century. On her fledgling farm in the 1920's the men had completely run out of their staple, maize meal or *posho*. *The men struck work and for a day I was left to herd the cattle myself.* She sent Kago to the nearest township of Gilgil to buy *posho* and while he was gone she took on two strangers who had strayed on to the farm. When Kago returned Miss Collyer told him she had written on two extra men, *thinking he would be pleased to have the extra help. He did not enthuse at all and when again the following morning no one turned out to work I got on my toes and wished to know the reason for it. Kago drew a long face and said, 'It is because you have written on two 'Ndea' – a witch-doctoring tribe that the Kikuyu were afraid of.*

After trying to insist that everyone went back to work, and meeting with *that silent resistance so characteristic of the Kikuyu tribe* she gave way and dismissed the two men. *At that particular moment I missed a hammer I needed and enquiring what had become of it, I was told that it was in the hut of the strangers. Every man in turn refused to fetch it for me. Kago acted as spokesman and said the hammer could not be collected as the 'Ndea' had put a bad snake to guard the door of their hut so that nobody could pass in.*

'Well' I said 'I must get that hammer myself since you are all afraid of a snake.' And I proceeded to walk towards the hut with the men following behind at a respectful distance. Just as I reached the door, Kago seized my arm and pulled me back, crying, 'The snake will get you! Don't you see it with his head up ready?' Of course there was no snake. I then faced the crowd and told them to look straight at me. As soon as all eyes were on mine, I repeated twice, very slowly and distinctly, 'There is no snake here,' and after a minute or two I bade them look again. This time they saw nothing, and I walked into the hut and brought out the hammer.

10

Cannibalism was another bloody cloud under which certainly some African men, women and children had had to live. Sir Bryan Sharwood Smith, who was in the Nigerian Colonial Service, describes an evening in the twenties which he spent with the old men of North Eastern Cameroon, their tongues loosened by the palm wine they were drinking by the fire.

We were talking about the days when the ritual consumption of human flesh was a part of their daily life ... As I displayed interest, the old men ... began to describe in grisly detail, exactly how these things had been arranged. The ... condemned were secured, head downward, between two upright stakes, their limbs spread-eagled. Beneath them burned a slow smoky fire. Around, in anticipation, squatted the elders, each with his back against an upright slab of rock in the position to which his status entitled him. As life passed, boiling palm oil was introduced into the body, from above – I had heard enough.

Given the fears, the diseases and the perils, it is understandable that progress in Africa often faltered.

During the 19th century a great many, perhaps even the majority, of the ordinary men and women of Africa were so weakened and dispirited that they were wide open to violation. And violated they were by the *great African catastrophe*.

Slave trading and slave taking were rampant throughout most of Africa. For centuries slave traders fed the greedy markets of North Africa, the Middle East and southern Europe, and latterly of course the Americas and the Caribbean. In East Africa Arab and Swahili slavers armed pugnacious tribes and encouraged them to prey upon the weak who would then be walked to the coast, shipped to Zanzibar and sold in the slave market there. One such slaving chief, Mponda, who was also known as Mlosi (The Sorcerer) had his headquarters in what is southern Malawi today where the river Shire leaves Lake Malawi, and he commanded its exit with his guns. He called himself the Sultan of Nkonde but in fact he was a Swahili and he sucked the life blood out of the peaceful and prosperous Nkonde people.

It is hard to imagine what it was like to walk mile upon thirsty, lonely mile with a heavy forked branch or gori stick fixed around the neck. But a record of a visit to an old slave halt in Kitale in Kenya in 1905, described by an old man who had served with Arab slavers brings home something of the stark reality.

A Sudanese, Mbarak, worked for Captain Meinertzhagen in his old age and he took the Captain to visit the halt. ... *a double stockade* [encircling] *an area of about 4 acres on a slight rise, with open ground for about 200 yards on all sides and a glorious view of* [Mt] *Elgon to the west and of the Cherangani Hills to the East. Old Mbarak became quite excited when he found himself back in his old haunt and took me round the stockade, explaining what went on in every corner of the camp. The main gate was on the south of the stockade, the latter being made of solid wooden uprights woven together with thorn and smaller branches ... Mbarak showed me where the Arabs slept near the entrance, where the girls were kept, where boys were kept and where they were castrated, and where the men were kept constantly shackled in eights to a heavy log by iron chains ... Castrated boys were the best looked after as they were the most valuable but ... over 50% died before reaching the coast; the girls were not shackled but went free and were raped both at night and all through the day whenever the caravan halted.*

Zanzibar was the centre of the East African trade and one historian describes the island as: *carrying the mark of Cain. The harbour and its beach were studded with whatever bloated corpses or part-corpses might have escaped the attention of the sharks – affording ... sights ... sufficient to shock even those who have been familiar with the dissecting-room. For murder was endemic on the island, and the harbour served as a convenient repository for the bodies of men, women and children who came to unwitnessed but grisly ends in the unlit alleys after night-fall. These unfortunates were usually the victims of lawless slave traders from Arabia and the Persian Gulf known locally as 'Northern Arabs' and dreaded by the townspeople. Not content merely with the human cargoes they could pick up in Zanzibar's open market, these slavers would scour the city at night, seizing anyone careless enough to go into the streets without an armed escort. Those who resisted got the blade of a jembia between the ribs and were pitched into the harbour. The submissive ones were bound and gagged, taken to caves along the shore and later transported secretly to the slave dhows.*

The Sultan of Zanzibar would have considered it a bad year if his annual income from duties on the slave traffic fell below one hundred thousand US dollars which is calculated at more than ten times that today.

Along the East African coast, as early as 1876 the British were busy trying to stop slave trading with the Royal Navy chasing slaving ships in and out of the estuaries and inlets.

The Nigerian Handbook published in 1953 notes that between 1788 and 1847, over 5 ½ million people suffered the tragedy of slavery, while their brothers who sold them were no more concerned than those who employed them. In 1849 John Beecroft, governor of Fernando Po, off West Africa, was appointed Consul and Agent for the Bights of Benin and Biafra. His job was to regulate the local lawful trade between the Ports of Benin, Brass, New and Old Calabar, Bonny, Bimbia and the Cameroons. Despite this and the addition of a United States Naval patrol on the West Coast, the slave trade intensified in Lagos in 1859 which led to the Treaty of 1861 by which Lagos was ceded to the British Crown.

The suppression of the slave trade was a slow business both in West and in East Africa where the hinterland was also a source of rich pickings. How men, women and children fell prey to the Swahili and Arab traders who captured and brought them to market in Zanzibar is told to Frederick Jackson by one escapee. Jackson, was one of the earliest Europeans to penetrate the area. The escapee's name was Bahati (Fortune) and she came from what was then known as Ketosh, around the north eastern spur of Lake Victoria, known then as the Kavirondo Gulf.

Frederick Jackson was camped at Machakos in 1889 on his way to Uganda from the coast. He wrote:

A Kavirondo slave woman came into camp, having run away from the caravan of Abdulla bin Hamid near Nzawi. She had been captured in Ketosh, and as she had heard we were going to Kavirondo, she asked to be taken back to her own country. Her request was at once granted, and after an issue of cloth to hide her nakedness, she was handed over to the tender care of old Sadi. Her name was Bahati.

When Jackson arrived in the country of the Ketosh he said that *numerous ruined, burned and abandoned villages bore testimony to the handiwork and treachery of the Mombasa slaver, Abdulla bin Hamid and that prince of rogues, fat Sudi of Pangani.*

It would appear that for many years past the Ketosh had been the happy hunting ground of the Swahili and Arab traders, particularly on those occasions when they arrived from Karamojo via Baringo after an unsuccessful quest for ivory and with plenty of trade goods on hand; or when the easy acquisition of a batch of slaves was too tempting to forego on their leaving Mumia's on their way coastwards. In either case their tactics were the same ...

Having arrived at a village, and after accepting the proffered hospitality of a portion of [the population] the black-hearted ruffians would in due course announce that they required a large stock of food for their coastward journey, and that they were prepared to pay double the market price in order to obtain it quickly. The ruse, of course, attracted women and children from far and wide.

Jackson explained that in the meantime, as a further blind, they told the villagers that it would be necessary for them to move camp outside the village and make a boma or stockade, in order to prevent the porters from running away on the day of their departure.

The people came into sell their produce on the appointed day and when they were all in the stockade, the gates were locked; *the women and children were seized and any man who offered resistance was shot. Old Bahati told us that was the way she was taken captive.*

On the western side of Africa, Abeokuta was a market centre for a similar ocean-going slave trade. To the north, in Zaria, there was a second slave trade which was in Hausa and Fulani hands, supplying the Mediterranean and the Middle East by way of the overland desert route. Witness to this in 1902 was a company of British soldiers, led by Captain Lugard, who were powerless to prevent *hundreds of slaves being hawked about in the streets in irons or a tribute of a 100 being sent off to Sokoto.* The girls were worth about five pounds and the boys were valued at six pounds.

Sir Bryan Sharwood Smith records:

The powerful chiefdoms in the Western Sudan — that vast belt of scrubland and savannah that stretched for hundreds of miles from Lake Chad — constantly preyed upon the weaker tribes. Many treated the border areas of their chiefdoms as no better than a breeding ground for slaves. Whole towns and villages were razed to the ground, the inhabitants being either slaughtered or carried into captivity.

The pagan tribes in the forest country north of the Niger suffered from the ravages of Umaru Nagwamatse, son of the fifth Sultan of Sokoto. District Commissioners in the first half of the twentieth century used to encounter buried in the bush, the crumbling ruins of the towns and villages that Umaru and his successor had pillaged in their search for slaves. These beleaguered people had to till their farms in fortified villages but were forced also to send tribute to Sokoto in an effort to ensure protection.

It is odd but true that inter-tribal slave raiding seems to be more acceptable to us today as we beat our breasts over our own part in the infamous intercontinental slave trade. But surely the former can have been scarcely less terrible for the people involved.

In East Africa it is difficult to know exactly the scale of inter-tribal slave raiding but in 1933 Hal Williams, served the British Administration in the northern Kenya desert, known then as the NFD (Northern Frontier District.) His *Handing Over Report* describes at length the nine tribes which inhabited or wandered through the area that the young District Officer administered.

One tribe was the Gurreh, a mainly light-skinned people who were strict Muslims and who roamed between *Abyssinia and British Territory."* Another tribe, the Gurre Murre, were *"an agricultural tribe of negroid origin, the greater number of whom are resident in Abyssinia or Italian Somaliland. They were at one time slaves of the Gurreh.* Hal Williams, also

15

added that they were fine fighters and noted archers. They also brewed a particularly potent alcoholic beverage from the dom palm, which was the downfall of many an askari (soldier.)

It is not outside the bounds of possibility that there were some quiet corners of Africa, free of slave raiders, or tribal raiders, the kind of idyll of peaceful prosperity that many people nostalgically imagine the whole continent to have been. We hope so, but the picture does not suggest this. Whisking ourselves north of Kenya's NFD to the Sudan, life for the average man and woman throughout history must have been at best tough, but often desperate.

General Gordon described the Sudan as *a useless possession, ever was so and ever will be so. Larger than Germany, France and Spain together, and mostly barren it cannot be governed except by a dictator who may be good or bad ... No one who has ever lived in the Sudan can escape the reflection on what a useless possession is this land. Few men also can stand its fearful monotony and deadly climate.*

Allan McCall, a one-time Director of Agriculture in the Sudan, wrote: *Before the outbreak of the Mahdi's rebellion in 1881 the total population*[of the Sudan] *was calculated as having been 8,500,000 (in a country of 1,000,000 square miles: the largest country in Africa.) Of these, some 3,500,000 were killed by famine and disease, and some 3,250,000 in battle and tribal strife between 1882 and 1898.*

In about 1822, when Muhammed Ali, an Albanian employed by the Sultan of Turkey, fought his way to supreme power as 'Pasha of Egypt', he needed money and slaves. He decided to invade Sudan and by the middle of the nineteenth century he was more or less in control of the country. Government was chaotic. In 1839 the number of slaves led away into captivity was at least 200,000. Conditions were appalling.

By 1869 the power of the slave traders had become so great that they were practically independent kinglets, with armed forces at their call, flouting the authority of Khartoum. This was a state of affairs that Ismail Pasha, who had become Khedive of Egypt in 1863, could not brook, and a policy of reform was initiated. On this occasion the agents were Europeans and their efforts were genuine. What these few British, Swiss, Austrians, Italians, Danes and others could do, they did. [However] the vast distances, difficulties of communications, the climatic conditions, the general confusion prevailing and, above all, the calculated obstructiveness of a venal official staff, rendered their task a hopeless one.

Slavery of any kind was certainly an opportunity for the powerful to get rich quick. From the sixteenth to the nineteenth centuries European slaving ships were particularly active along the West African coast and there are families in Europe and in Africa today whose fortunes are based on the slave trade. However, in Britain attitudes began to change. Sir Thomas Fowell Buxton, (1786 – 1845) a vigorous and prominent anti-slavery campaigner, wrote *The Bible and the plough must regenerate Africa*. Lugard, who was later to become known as the founder of the Colonial Service in Africa, said *We have thus a duty of expiation to perform towards the African"* and he believed that he could think of *no juster cause in which a soldier can draw his sword* than in the fight against slavery.

The abolition movement in Britain achieved success in 1807 with the Abolition of Slavery Act which made it a felony for any British ship to engage in the 'carrying trade'. From that date the West Coast of Africa was patrolled by the Royal Navy. Known as the coffin squadron, these ships and their crews faced determined opposition. Skirmishes at sea and diseases from the land took a heavy toll; and the valiant contribution of those naval crews to peaceful trade has been all but forgotten.

Slaves were still taken and traded but Lagos was the last major stronghold of slavers and was captured by the Royal Navy in 1851. However, domestic slave owning continued in Africa into the 1920's and some District Commissioners had the task of giving them their freedom when they asked for it. In Eastern Kordofan in the Sudan, when a slave petitioned to be free he was either sent to special villages designated to freed slaves or an effort was made to reconcile him with his master on the basis of a free servant because the erstwhile slave was often very much depended upon to water the flocks and herds.

Poor beautiful Africa! Distance and difficult terrain kept her out of the currents of knowledge, diseases weakened her people, famine depopulated her, fear of the supernatural hobbled so many of her tribes and slavery created a massive brain drain.

In the nineteenth century communications in Europe and the Americas improved apace. By the second half of the century it was a natural progression that Europeans would be reaching Africa and striking inland. During this period there was in Europe what some describe as a mini-ice age, when extreme cold caused great hardship and famine. One August in Scotland, farmers were walking on ice above the standing wheat fields. Perhaps this acted as a spur but whatever the reasons, some headed for Africa. Some among them were men with avarice and power on their minds. *The adventurers and speculators into whose hands Africa would fall if the great governments abandoned the continent.*

In 1903 a man called Gibbons, together with 30 armed Swahilis, had installed himself in an area south east of Mount Kenya where he had hoisted the Union Jack, and was busy collecting a hut tax, and extorting ivory and fourteen year old girls from the local population. The colonial administration charged him and packed him home in chains. Besides Mr Gibbons, a major Kikuyu chief called Karurie had much of his vast wealth – he lived in splendour with 39 wives and 60 children – lifted off him by a certain Mr Bryce who offered to take his store of ivory to the coast to sell. That was the last time the chief saw the ivory or Bryce.

Captain Lugard was shocked in East Africa when a wandering gold prospector advised him *'On the first signs of insolence or even familiarity, kick them under the jaw (when sitting) or in the stomach. In worse cases shoot and shoot straight, at once.' More pernicious advice than his, given to an intending traveller ... I cannot conceive,* wrote Lugard.

Some early adventurers exploited Africans' vulnerability but it would be inaccurate and unfair to put down the British colonial enterprise solely to exploitation and aggrandizement. Morris tells us in his book *Pax Britainnica* that, *the Dualla chiefs of the Cameroons repeatedly asked to be annexed, but the British either declined or took no notice at all.*

Lord Lugard can be accurately described as the father of the British Colonial Service in Africa. His biographer, Margery Perham, also made it her life's work to study the British Colonial administration. She accuses early British governments of being more interested in spheres of influence in Africa than in annexation. She cites the example of the country then known as Nyasa but which is Malawi today. The Swahili and Arab slavers in this area were extremely powerful and some of the British traders wanted the newly-arrived Captain Lugard to lead an expedition to take them on. However, the Prime Minister, Lord Salisbury, *would neither send an expedition to Nyasa, nor annex it, nor declare it British territory. He went so far as to say "We cannot begin a crusade into the interior.*

It was also an unenthusiastic British government which had watched the financial failure of Sir William McKinnon's Imperial British East Africa Company and it was with reluctance that it bowed to clamour demanding that it take up the reins of government over East Africa in 1895. These demands were motivated by altruism and religion as well as by trade and expansionism. And this latter reason, although perhaps muddled by today's thinking, was not necessarily vainglorious or unworthy.

The cost of colonialism was no snip. Less than a decade after the Union Jack had been run up over British East Africa, The Governor of Kenya, Sir Charles Eliot, told Lord Delamere that Kenya alone was costing the British tax payer two hundred and fifty six thousand pounds per annum and there were ten other major colonies to finance.

Without integrity we had no right to be there.

Loveluck

This broad brush history gives some idea, I hope, of the general state of Africa at the end of the nineteenth century. Waiting in the wings were the young men who were to spend their working lives serving Africa; serving the people of Africa and trying to create an atmosphere of peaceful security in which they could prosper.

These sons of Britain were not blimps sporting large moustaches, carrying bullwhips in one hand and gins and tonics in the other, as portrayed by some creators of modern faction, but they were graduates from the finest British universities or they were survivors of distinguished military service.

Many of them were keen sportsmen; indeed the Sudan Political Service had the reputation of accepting only Oxbridge double blues. In 1907 Winston Churchill wondered if this was really necessary. He sent a telegram to the Colonial Office when he was *en route* from Uganda to the Sudan:

How is this reason (which is their reason) to judge a scholar's worth,

By casting a ball at three straight sticks and defending the same with a fourth?

There was also a fair sprinkling of the small, the tubby and the bespectacled, but with few exceptions they arrived equipped with an independent spirit, courage, ingenuity and unimpeachable integrity. What motivated them to leave their home country and set off to face the perils of Africa?

Some of the young men who went out to Africa were from families with a reasonably solid financial base. However, this does not mean that they did not need to be in paid employment and nor were they fops or layabouts only bent upon the pursuit of pleasure.

Our great uncle, Arthur Collyer, almost certainly went to Kenya in search of a warm climate; perhaps also to do and die because he was mortally ill with tuberculosis. Captain Meinhertzhagen was a fanatical (and blood-thirsty) shot, a well as a naturalist, if that is not a contradiction in terms. Undoubtedly the lure of fantastic quantities of big game motivated some but the reasons were varied. Major Clarence Buxton MC, a descendent of Sir Thomas Fowells Buxton, arrived in Kenya not long after the end of the Great War. Writing to his mother, perhaps pondering on the freedom he had fought for in the trenches, he said *I don't want freedom to do nothing but freedom to do what seems worthwhile.* He had lived a privileged childhood and while much had changed after 1918 in Britain, he could have stayed to enjoy a relatively gracious life but chose Africa.

Hal Williams, whose family did not have money and who had won the Kitchener Scholarship to Cambridge, joined the Kenya Administration in 1931. He wrote later that he had *looked forward to the opportunity of doing some good amongst backward peoples.* He also liked to tease us by saying that his main motive was to get away from his creditors. There may have been some truth in it because, anxious about being pursued by *an august body called the Colonial Service Debt Collecting Agency,* he earnestly hoped, when he arrived in Kenya, that his first posting would be in the *blue, blue, blue* where the cost of living would be cheap and he could repay his university debts.

Whatever the personal reasons for joining the Colonial Service and whatever their triumphs, tragedies or achievements later, they were there to serve and they knew it. Their job was to create an atmosphere where trade and ideas could prosper and where the people could take the necessary steps into the modern world in a benevolent and secure environment.

Lord Lugard, who drew up the tenets for the Service, said that the DC's role was to *maintain and develop all that is best in the indigenous methods and institutions of native rule.* The people of Africa under the British administration were regarded as "wards in trust" which may today appear paternalistic but it was a serious responsibility and part of a governor's oath in the Sudan was to do *right by all manner of men, without fear or favour, affection or ill-will.*

This book is the story of those British men and their wives who many times have been pilloried by the historians and intellectuals who were never there. The worst failing of the men who served in Africa was snobbishness which at that time prevailed the world over.

21

This has now been interpreted as racism which it certainly was not. They simply did their honest best within the understanding of the time; and their achievements are staggering.

Despite two world wars and the worst world depression ever known, they rushed her people through a crash course of living in the twentieth century and then handed them the keys to their bountiful and ravishing land.

In 1880 wrote C.R. Niven in 1946 while serving in Nigeria, *a man or woman would not have dreamed of walking alone, say, the fifty miles between Kabba and Lakoja ...; thirty years later, in a single generation, no one would have thought twice about it ... as the Hausa says, 'a virgin [can now][carry a calabash of eggs from Kano to Sokoto (250 miles) and neither would be spoilt on the way.*

In less than threescore years and ten they lifted broken, dispirited and diseased Africa into a new plane of knowledge, security and prosperity

C.H. Williams (known as Hal or, later in Kenya, Ngombe) Jesus College,
Cambridge circa

Chapter 2

BLUES, NATIVES, HAWKS AND RHADEGUNDS

White settlement in Africa is but a speck in the ocean of time.
Anthropology lecturer at Cambridge, 1930.

During peacetime the men who joined the Colonial Service were required to complete a year's course at Oxford or Cambridge after their degree and before setting out to the colony of their choice; or, as in some cases, the colony which had chosen them. My father tried to enter the Sudan Political Service – the most sought after service – but was turned down. He was accepted by Kenya.

Going to Cambridge on a scholarship from Bedford Modern School, in, we think 1926, Hal Williams, had four glorious years at Jesus College. His full name was Cyril Herbert Williams. I was later told by Victor Mardon who was up at Cambridge at the same time, that one day a few friends were sitting in rooms in Clare and the subject came up of his name. One student said he was reminded of Bluff Prince Hal and thereafter some called him Bluff while others called him Hal which was the name that stuck. Later in Kenya he was also known as "Ngombe" (ox) and sometimes "C.H." He stood six foot four and was built to match with ears that stuck out cheerfully and small eyes that twinkled. When he smiled, his mouth stretched quite straight across his face which endowed him with an endearing innocence. Mardon, told me *He had a charming manner and easy temperament which made him beloved by all who knew him.* Along with almost every other undergraduate, he had the time of his life at University.

Cambridge was not, perhaps for some, the academic pressure cooker that it is today. Competition for places was less intense because many undergraduates paid their own fees. Pat O'Dwyer, who later went to Sierra Leone wrote:

It is time I said something about work for that is really what one went up to Cambridge for. I really did not know what I should read when I first went up but I had made my mind up to go into the Colonial Service if I could. I had decided this when I was at Cheltenham and the Rev. F.W. Gillingham came to preach in chapel. He had played county cricket for Essex and was a famous preacher. He spoke about the British Empire and that there was no greater service one could perform in life than to serve the cause of that Empire as your life's work. After the war (WWII) he was Vicar of St Michaels, Chester Square and I remember going there to a service with Aunt Do and he preached on the International Rugger match, England v Scotland which had taken place the day before at Twickenham and at which he had been a steward. I had just got back from West Africa, blind, and I told him how he had inspired me in my youth.

My tutor [at Cambridge} was Gus Elliot and he advised me to read history. He himself was a history Don and a quite splendid person. His names were Claude Augustus, an Old Etonian himself and the year I went down, 1933, he went on to be Headmaster of Eton where he remained through the War. Finally he became Provost of Eton and got a knighthood. We used to play squash together and afterwards he always asked me back to his house.

I enjoyed reading history but I really did not work hard enough, so much being taken up with games etc ... The most distinguished history lecturer we had was George Trevelyan, who later became Master of Trinity and was knighted. He wrote some marvellous books, of course, but in truth he was not a very inspiring lecturer. However, he was obviously a very nice chap and he offered all in his class to call on him at his house in Grange Road, to have tea with him and discuss any historical questions. What a fool I was never to take up his kind offer, always preferring to be off playing some game.

The post-graduate cadet course was the best year of all. These cadets *were a sporting lot, happy and secure with their degrees and acceptance into the Colonial Service.*

His great friend, Hal Williams, was awarded a rugby blue during this post-graduate year in 1930. The huge importance of such a glory is manifested in two letters from T. Coates, who was probably a master at Bedford Modern School. It seems that in the previous year my father had been in the running for a blue but had not been selected.

Dec. 3. 29. Dear Williams, Rotten luck! I know just how you are feeling and I am more sorry than I know how to tell you.

When my son Dick just missed his Rowing Blue we felt life wasn't worth living. But you will realize, as time goes on, that there are better things worth striving for. Your career and your job is the great thing – and that is where your people will want you to make good.

Please forgive this old man's advice – but you know just what I feel about the whole darned business.

This need make no difference in your chances for the Sudan Political if you are still thinking of going in for that.

What they want is not necessarily a Blue on paper – but a man, a sportsman and a fellow with a clean character – all of which you possess.

Ever yours,

T. Coates

Don't dream of writing. Shall see you at the dinner

The following year Mr Coates wrote with touching delight:

Dec 1. 30

Dear Williams,

The news this morning was tophole and we are all very proud of you. I believe you have beaten all records of past OBM's and that this is the first Rugger Blue.

All this term I have held my peace, and refused to believe this great thing would come to pass until it was known for certain.

There are 6 of us who want to come to see the match. Can you wangle any seats do you think? Of course I know your people must come first.

If it means standing, I am too old & groggy for that game.

Another Old Bedford Modern who had gone up to Oxford was equally generous:

Dear Williams,

Sincere congratulations from the small body of O.B.M.'s at Oxford. In spite of our confidence in the success of our own University, we wish you honour & distinction in the matter of the varsity match.

Yours sincerely,

E.W. Hales

But Hal's glory was short-lived. Towards the end of the varsity match in 1931 Cambridge was a point or two down on Oxford when a penalty kick was awarded to Cambridge. The conversion would have meant triumph. The kicker said to Hal that he had lost his nerve and could not do it. Hal had a go.

At that time the ball was held up by another player and as soon as it touched the ground the opposing side was permitted to charge the ball. However, Oxford charged before the ball was put down and Hal held back, waiting for the referee's whistle. Unfortunately the whistle was not blown and, too late, Hal scrambled to kick the ball but it never left the ground and the match was lost for Cambridge.

Years later not long before he died, Hal had the satisfaction of reading an article in a rugby magazine that said the referee should have blown the whistle that day.

Rugby was not the only game the cadets played of course.

They 'formed a squash Rackets Club (no premises, just played a few matches) and [Ngombe], inspite of his unlikely figure even those days, was a member of it. An extract from 'The Times' records that in a match against Christ's where he played third string out of five for the Colonial Probationers Club, he lost in three straight games 2 – 9, 3 – 9, 6 – 9 to D.F. Kerr who wasn't very good! But the thing is that he played. He entered into everything and was a great-hearted, jolly fellow like so many of his build.

Joining clubs was an important part of university life and Pat O'Dwyer, also a Jesus man, was a member of the Wheatsheafs, the Hawks, the Rhadegunds and the Natives. The Natives, to which my father also belonged, was purely a social club where only kindred spirits were elected. An earlier Jesus man, Ewart Grogan, who later became famous in Africa for his trek from the Cape to Cairo, is still toasted by the Natives: "Grogan!" although present day students have no idea why. It is said that he was sent down after he had put a goat in the Master's study for the weekend but I doubt if that was why he is toasted.

The senior club in the College was the Rhadegunds. Saint Rhadegund was the patron saint of the College. She was a sixth century lady, the wife of a brutal Thuringian king. As she fled from his tyranny, a half-grown field of oats sprang up around her and hid her. As proper sainted ladies of the sixth century sometimes did, she founded a convent in gratitude for her deliverance. In a later century unthinkable goings-on between the convent and a nearby monastery by way of a tunnel forced the disbandment of the convent and there followed the establishment of a seminary for learning, naming it Jesus College.

In order to be a member of the Rhadegunds, a student had to have a double College colour and initiation into the club was to drink port from a half-pint silver bumper. Pat O'Dwyer, who had a university boxing blue and captained Jesus rugger, drank four bumpers.

The Colonial Service Probationers attended lectures on surveying, agriculture and native languages. They built bridges across the Cam with petrol tins which usually culminated in *an adjournment to the nearest pub for necessary discussion. So great was my ignorance of Kenya,* wrote Hal Williams, *that it never occurred to me to ask if petrol tins would always be available.* They were taught the languages used in their destined colonies and they studied anthropology, which subject Pat O'Dwyer

29

found *utterly useless.*

Henry Barnes, who *used very bad language* and had been President of Mexico for a week, taught them law, and health lectures were given by an officer of the Colonial Medical Service who, *from his looks, had suffered from every disease on which he was lecturing.* He advised them *"not to drink alcohol before sundown and to eschew cocktails in any shape or form as they changed the stomach from a membranous bag into a museum exhibit.*

These young men were indeed fortunate. Awarded places at the greatest universities in the Empire, they had exciting jobs assured, provided they got their degrees. But work was only as important as sport and as the Bedford schoolmaster said, they would be judged on both. In 1931 Julian Huxley, who visited East Africa, wondered if this was a good thing.

Our education is inclining us to sport, to a distrust of intelligence when applied to immediate and practical ends."

His concern had been triggered by a delightful evening he had spent at the Residency in Zanzibar when the young officers of a visiting Royal Naval cruiser had been invited to a fancy dress dance.

I have rarely seen young men who still looked such complete schoolboys. ... Immaturity has many charms, as we perceive in puppies, colts or lion-cubs ... [and] looking at these boys, I felt that the British Empire was a very nice Empire. But it is not enough for Empires to be nice; they demand seriousness, free intelligence, and the determination to understand the minds of other nations and of other races.

The extraordinary ingenuity in building railways in East Africa: lowering a steam engine into the Great Rift Valley in British East Africa 1900. With grateful thanks to Nigel Pavitt, author of "Kenya. A Country in the Making 1880-1940"

Chapter 3

"DIPPING THROUGH THE TROPICS"

To view Africa one must get there.

Julian Huxley

Early in July 1931 my father found himself aboard a British India steamship purposefully thrusting through the ultramarine waters off the East African coast, bound for Mombasa and a life in His Majesty's Colonial Service. He caught the first sailing offered to him after coming down from university, his precarious financial position dictating that he left the temptations of Cambridge at the earliest moment. To make matters worse, he had been advised to purchase absurd amounts of kit which he later found were mostly unnecessary but his ever patient bank manager loyally supported him.

The ships taking people to Africa before the days of regular air travel were comfortable, jolly, perhaps even frivolous places, whose passengers were predominantly government officers and where the few women on board were 'goddesses'. Meals were many, delicious and social and elevenses were served on deck: hot Bovril with water biscuits in the northern seas and in the tropics icecream sandwiched between two wafers. Deck quoits, parties, race meetings of little wooden horses and card games wiled away the days at sea as the ships thrummed south. The young men danced with the goddesses until the sun splashed upon the sea and love affairs flared up under the jewelled skies, creating frissons of drama at the canvas pool's edge or the bar.

Julian Huxley who went to Mombasa in 1930 to look at education in East Africa did not enjoy the *organised pleasure of an English boat – secretary of sports, secretary of entertainment, won't you make up a game of shuffleboard, here's Mrs Blank who would like to play deck tennis, of course you play bridge, won't you recite at the performance for the crews of the second class.* His ship – a French line – was still coal fired and in Port Said he wrote: *I could hardly tear myself from the spectacle of the coaling ship. Goodbye to Europe now! What magnificent figures of men, these Arabs – tall, lean, horribly muscular, all dressed in long black shifts, all grimed, all shouting and gesticulating under the flares. A truly hellish scene; but how sadly unpicturesque it will be when all the liners run on oil fuel.*

Pat O'Dwyer recalls that in 1933 on the West African route, a certain snobbery also pervaded on board; only some of which was tongue-in-cheek:

The Army and the Administrative Service considered themselves the tops. In order of precedence were Nigeria, the Gold Coast, Sierra Leone and the Gambia. During the five day voyage to Madeira the men changed into a dinner jacket in the evening. After Madeira the black jacket was replaced with a white bum freezer and with this they always wore a cummerbund. Each country had its own coloured cummerbund. Nigeria wore green, the Gold Coast gold, Sierra Leone blue and the Gambia red. After dinner the grand owners of the green cummerbunds and the gold cummerbunds would gather in two large noisy groups, leaving the few blues and reds on the fringes, uncomfortably aware that they were thought to be rather inferior in the scheme of things.

A couple of years before Pat O'Dwyer travelled to Sierra Leone, John Winders voyaged to Port Sudan:

I doubt if one ever tires of the Suez Canal, he wrote. *The ship's movement is slow and one glides along between the two banks, occasionally passing vessels tied up; at night there is the powerful beam of the searchlight on the bows lighting up the waters* [and] *one has the feeling of passing altogether into other climes and other worlds – as indeed one is, the world of the Orient with heat greater than you have known, with smells other than you have met and people [so] different. For us we were nearing the end of our voyage and the sight of the hills rising in the west, the Red Sea Hills, were like the sight of the promised land. It was moving to think we should probably spend the best days of our lives behind those hills.*

On Sunday morning we sighted Sangareb light and at about midday entered Port Sudan harbour. It was hot and sticky. The hatches were soon off and the [stevedores] swarmed on board. These were red tinted men with curious frizzy hair – the Fuzzie Wuzzies (Beja Tribesmen] of Kipling.

Eventually a British customs official came aboard, very annoyed at having to turn out on a Sunday afternoon, but decent enough to take us poor probationers under his wing and tell us how to carry on. But first we had to pass his customs ... Most of us had, by this time, little enough cash on us and most of us left the quay with hardly anything at all – one man I know had to borrow to clear himself.

As the ships nosed into port the passengers would lean against the salt-rimed rail, watching the small boats bobbing around them and while they waited in the roads little boys would appear like magic and shout up to the white faces peering downwards to throw coins into the water so that they could dive for them. Some children would scramble onto the ship's deck and splash back into the sea glistening and excited, in the hope that a shower of silver would follow. There was always excitement, shouting and laughter as the ship neared the quay. The heat was all embracing and the humid air was heady with salt, seaweed, oil, humanity and rotting vegetation.

In 1931 Kilindini Harbour in Mombasa was *a fine harbour with berthing accommodation for five large ships, as well as anchorage for innumerable others; the dozen or so great electric cranes towered up against the mangroves and palms. The liner* [would glide] *in to her moorings with a score of brown kites about her, wheeling and banking with sharp oblique movements of their forked tails;*

35

and on the primitive native fish-traps by the far shore there [would] sit big-headed kingfishers the size of missel-thrushes.

But before the harbours were built it was a matter of taking passengers off in the roads. Philip Mitchell recalls that when he arrived at Nyasaland before the Great War he could not see the shoreline and the port of Beira. The ship anchored in what looked like mid-ocean and Mitchell, along with a barmaid and a priest, was swung from the ship on to a lighter in a mammy chair dangling at the end of a derrick.

TO KOTON KARIFI, KIAMBU OR OMDURMAN

The railway line to Lake Victoria was not the only one whose cost was carried by the long-suffering British tax payer but it was probably the most expensive (£5,500,000.) The line began in Mombasa and was built over waterless semi-desert, climbed up to 6,000 feet, plunged down the dramatic escarpment of the Great Rift Valley, dragged itself back up to almost 9,000 feet at Mau Summit and crossed innumerable ravines before it coasted down on to the pleasant flat, but hot, Kano plains to reach Kisumu (originally known as Port Florence) five hundred and seventy two miles inland.

When the idea was mooted in Britain to build a railway line from the Coast to Lake Victoria the anti-imperialist Labouchère was waggish in his opposition:

> *What it will cost no words can express;*
> *What is its object no brain can suppose;*
> *Where it will start from no one can guess;*
> *Where it is going to nobody knows.*
> *What is the use of it none can conjecture;*
> *What it will carry there's none can define;*
> *And in spite of George Curzon's superior lecture,*
> *It clearly is naught but a lunatic line.*

It was an immense undertaking of ingenuity, hardship and danger and it brought great benefit to Kenya, not the least of which is the journey from the coast to Nairobi which Miss Lucy Buxton described in her letter home when she and her mother, the Dowager Lady Buxton, visited her brother, Major Clarence Buxton, MC in 1920.

The train left Mombasa at 3 pm yesterday and stopped at Samburu Station at 7pm. The train waits 40 minutes at the different stations where meals are served. ... We had a 2nd class compartment to ourselves so were quite comfortable. Daylight came after 5 am but the moon was quite bright until the sun was well up. We had breakfast at Makindu at 7am and for several hours after that had the most glorious views of Kilimanjaro with its snow-capped cone.

At 11 pm they clambered down to the earth platform at Kiu Station and lunched in the small whitewashed oblong building under the trees while the train filling up with water and fuel, hissed, clanked and screeched like a grumpy dragon. After forty minutes with the blazing sun high overhead, the train continued on its slow climb through the undulating grasslands. *Masses of giraffe, Thomsons and wildebeest and ostriches* wandered amongst the fever trees. In the evening they alighted at Athi River Station from where they were going to Machakos where Clarence was stationed. However, because there had been a mix-up over transport, only a bullock wagon for the luggage had met the train. They, therefore, spent the night in Athi River Station waiting room until 3 am, to leave on foot with the bullock wagon at 4.30.

There was a lovely moon and it was quite cold for the first hour or two's march. We had six bullocks and four men with the wagon and our own boy, Daudi, who carried the lantern till daylight came. We walked until 7 o'clock then had a cup of tea by the road side. It was as well we started so early for it was the open plain with no shade at first. After the first halt, mother and I sat on the luggage on the front limber. The road was just a very rough track, one place where we went down into the bed of a stream [in a later letter she calls it Lukenya Drift], *we were almost upset. ... With the weight behind, the back oxen were pushed on to the middle pair and prodded them with their horns and there was a general confusion of animals. The limber reeled and creaked and the men danced and shouted and cracked whips. The bullocks are the humped cattle and so they have*

37

no traces in harness, just heavy wooden yokes fastened to their necks. Finally, the front yoke broke and the first pair got loose and as there was no wood near to mend it, they were driven in front and we proceeded with four!

We received messages from Clarence on the way. First we passed the Police Officer from Machakos with his safari; he brought a note and a haversack of food for which we were very thankful. Later we passed Mr Johnson, one of the American missionaries, who told us Clarence was sending horses to meet us. At 11 o'clock that morning we halted in a shady place and had a meal and there the messengers met us with two horses and a mule. We rested there for one and a half hours ... and then, having seen the wagon harnessed, we started on our way and reached Machakos at 2.45 pm.

The trains in Africa were for most of us, the height of romance and adventure but in his rather prosaic way, Mr Winders seemed to capture what it must have felt like to be a newly-arrived cadet or probationer fresh from the cool, damp familiarity of Britain. He tells us that in the Sudan:

The coaches were all white, with double roofs to keep them cool, with tinted glass in the windows to prevent glare and shutters to keep [out] the sun. The sleepers were excellent and roomy, and though we were doubled up, we soon made ourselves comfortable. At last the swarm of passengers and those seeing them off separated and the train moved off ...

Very quickly one seemed to leave the heat and the haze of Port Sudan behind and on reaching the first station the air was clear and the sky filled with myriads of stars. The hills looked black and stark in the starlight, the rocks we passed looked as if they had just been molten and had cooled as the night descended. The line was a single one with passing places only at stations. Every now and again the train stopped to take up water and we were able to get down and savour the smell of the cool night desert air. ...

We awoke to a different landscape. The hills had disappeared; we were now on a vast gently sloping plain of sand and gravel, with rocky [outcrops.] We saw our first hill camels, smaller beasts with browner hair than we had seen in Egypt. We passed flocks of sheep and goats and Fuzzie Wuzzie shepherds standing free [with] white 'tob' flung carelessly over shoulders, arms resting characteristically

38

along their curved camel sticks carried across their shoulder blades. Many wore the 'tiffa' from which they got their name with porcupine quill sticking in it.

["We've fought with many men acrost the seas
An' some of 'em was brave and some was not:
The Paythan and the Zulu and Burmese;
But the Fuzzy was the finest o' the lot."]

Kipling]

As the day grew hotter we saw our first mirage: trees looked as if they were standing in water and a train coming in the opposite direction seemed to be crawling through a lake; the sharp outcrops had a shimmering outline. It was a hard dry world.

In time we reached Atbara. This is where the Port Sudan line joins that from Wadi Halfa and where the Nile is first seen. Atbara is the headquarters of the railway system and just as in other parts of the world it seems impossible to pass through a railway headquarters without an interminable wait. The restaurant filled with visitors [and] *the platform swarmed with* [people] *milling around shouting greetings, clasping each other with both arms round the shoulders, slapping noisily.*

In time the whistle goes and we draw slowly out, cross the Atbara Bridge and move away again into the countryside. Much of the time we are now in view of the [Nile], *fringed with date palms. Dhows are tied up by the bank. In the morning they will spread their immense sails to catch the steady north wind which will drive them and their loads of dates up-river to the markets of Khartoum and Omdurman.*

What was awaiting those young men who had left behind them their families and their university salad days to work in Africa? Was it to be success or failure? Loneliness or happiness? Triumph? Disaster? When he had taken all his tropical kit off the train at Nairobi station, Hall Williams had to call on the Chief Native Commissioner. After making his "initial bow" he had a forty-five minute journey to the cool coffee-growing uplands of Kiambu. He was driven in the DC's

39

lorry by a handsome driver dressed in a red blanket and sandals who later became a chief.

Work was about to begin.

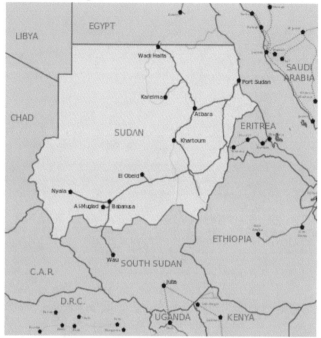

The railway line from Port Sudan to Wadi Halfa and Khartoum

Baraza (village meeting) on the Tana River, c1942. We think the seated man
on the right of the interpreter is probably the chief.

Chapter 4

WHAT DOES A DC DO?

Ship me somewhere East of Suez.'
The man who could write such rot
Should come and live, and the best years give
Of his life in this God-damned spot.
Lines attributed to a DO who died in Tana River District 1915 from *A Nosegay of*
Cacti collected by J.S.S. Rowlands)

Hal Williams was flummoxed when a visitor asked him, "Mr Williams, what does a DC do?" His mind went blank, because he always felt something like A.A. Milne's sailor *his grandfather knew who had so many things which he wanted to do, that whenever he thought it was time to begin, he couldn't because of the state he was in.*
One just buckets along with a mass of things which make the daily round and common tasks and if at the end of the month the cash balances and ones' official work is moderately well up to date one must be content. Major Clarence Buxton MC wrote to his mother, The Dowager Lady Buxton.
Margery Perham, when pondering on the work of a 'political officer' as she called him, concluded that it demanded conscience almost more than brains. The officers themselves would be the first to agree that

they were indeed jacks of all trades but masters of none. In each location to which they were posted, they had to get to know the people, to establish a confident and friendly rapport with them, to ensure that the people could live, farm and trade peacefully, to fight their corner when necessary, to collect their taxes, to stave off famines in the lean years and to improve communications. As magistrates they could not hope to be lawyers, as road makers they were not engineers but they undoubtedly tried their hardest and they did what they considered to be right, with the knowledge and advice available at the time.

A major task of the Government was to try to make the colonies pay; to shift the burden off the British tax payer. The salaries of the Colonial Service were paid for by the British Government, as are, indeed, their pensions today. The fledgling colonial governments in the early years could not hope to cover from taxes the major capital costs of, for example, railways and military expeditions to pacify the recalcitrant or enforce the abolition of slavery. In April 1896 the cost of Government for the East African Protectorate was £91,464 while revenue only came to £32,670. (The value of the pound sterling was fifteen or twenty times what it is today.)

One of the main sources of revenue to the East African governments in the very early days was from the rich hunters which, as W.S. Rainsford described it, were *unable to resist the 'red god's calling.*

Today it may be incomprehensible to many of us that people should wish to shoot African wildlife but it is worth bearing in mind that in a continent as sparsely populated as Africa was before the advent of medicines and peace, the plains and forests teemed with animals, reptiles and birds to an extent that is almost impossible to comprehend today. Indeed, even when we were children in the late nineteen forties it was unremarkable to see, as one drove across the floor of the farmed and populated Rift Valley, herds of impala, zebra, giraffe, wildebeest and Grant and Thomson's gazelles. The less easy to see from a car were there too in numbers: eland, ostrich, warthog, hippo, every possible type of bird and, of course, the predators, lion and cheetah especially.

Africans, and later European farmers, had to compete with them for space. Animals were vital for meat and skins and hunting by wealthy Europeans in Africa's untamed vastness was not only an exhilarating adventure for both African and European alike but it also increased the supply of meat and its bi-products that the African relied upon and had hitherto been able to obtain only with spears, arrows and daring.

Some of the hunters left interesting accounts. In 1908 W.S. Rainsford, an American, wrote of his exploits in "Kenia" in his book "The Land Of The Lion". He included a couple of thoughtful chapters on "A Plea for the Native East African and His Missionary" and "The Country". In this latter chapter he compared the Government to *a strong but ragged eight-oar crew. Individually they are a fair lot, but stroke does not know his own mind and looks a good deal out of the boat, so the men behind him cannot get together. Naturally the boat rolls and has not much pace on and the men growl at each other. Worst of all, the coach is too far away to see properly the crew's work, yet is constantly shouting contradictory orders to stroke, whose one aim seems not to be to win a race so much as to avoid an upset. The crew, too, has a pretty good German boat to race against.*

The 'oarsmen' at work. A meeting to resolve a border dispute between Luo and Nandi tribes was held in February 1909 under the Chairmanship of John

He described the English civil servant in British East Africa, as *a clean, honest, capable gentleman. He is the class of man that England above all the other nations has succeeded in rearing and binding to her service. A man, that under circumstances of loneliness, disheartenment and danger has done more than any other class, I don't even except the soldier, to hold unbroken, in spite of its vast extension, what Kipling in an immortal verse has called her 'far-flung battle line.'*

But Rainsford had criticisms too and these were directed at "coach" in Whitehall and "stroke" sitting in Government House. He pointed out that the six provincial commissioners administering the six British East African districts, who knew the country best, were not given a seat on the Council charged with suggesting local laws and regulations and which was chaired by the Governor.

Rainsford quoted from Professor J.W. Gregory's book called *The Foundation of British East Africa*. After lamenting the *persistent ill luck* which British East Africa has suffered through *pestilence, drought and famine* Gregory opined:

But the blame for the confusion is not all extra human. The clumsiness of men, the conservatism of government systems have been only too powerful for evil. The main cause of disaster in the rule of the Foreign Office (at present the Colonial Office has taken over the Protectorate) has been the lack of a policy

based on a scientific knowledge of the country and its people, framed in accordance with the views of the local authorities as to what is practically and economically possible.

The Professor suggested that the primary need in equatorial Africa was for a special service of men appointed by open competition.

Rainsford generously counters this by declaring:

...the ordinary young Englishman, employed by his country to do one of her difficult nd thankless jobs in a distant land with but little to reward him and much to discourage him, is the most honest, conscientious and successful civil servant in the world. (Rainsford's emphasis.)

He believed that the East African civil servant should be better paid, better pensioned and better supported at his outpost. *'Ah, there is no money,'(they say) 'There are limits to the English taxpayers' capacity to pay up margins of expenditure for unprofitable colonies.' Admitted! But one wrong is done him which might be quickly righted without the cost of an extra sovereign. He should be listened to, and he is not.*

Down the hill from the DC's house in Kakamega, Kenya along a dirt road lined with flame trees was the District Headquarters. The building was long, raised on stilts, and consisted of a line of offices off a verandah which ran the length of the building. The benches along the verandah were always occupied with people waiting to see the DC or DO.

The surrounds also milled with people coming and going.

To a newcomer on the scene it always looks as if something unusual is happening. But it isn't wrote Negley Farson, who visited Kakamega before writing his book *Last Chance In Africa* (pub 1949). He described the scene, first commenting:

This same scene is enacted outside a D.C.'s office everywhere in Kenya, every day. Also, there seems something ominous in those mute, poker-faced creatures who are waiting their turn to go in. But there isn't. The odds are that it will be the most trivial complaint. Or it may be for some advice: a son who ran away, and the D.C.'s advice and help are being asked for (with touching confidence) so that he may be found; a cow has been stolen or a wife has run off; an old man who wants to go "straight to the top" to explain why he should not be asked to pay the 19s poll tax. ... Or it may be just a chief who has known the D.C. for years and has come in for the pleasure and privilege of having a good gab with him. A nun has come in from a nearby Mission, dressed in spotless white and wearing a white solar topi; she leaves a pale-faced young novitiate in the Ford station-wagon while she goes in to see the D.C. An Englishwoman, a settler's wife, comes to the boma to get her mail, and loses her fox-terrier in the D.C's office: he won't come out. ... The happiest figures, one morning when I went over to see "Ngomby" [sic] Williams, were a ring of twenty-two convicts from the big red prison at Kakamega who were sitting on the square of greensward before the D.C.'s office, having a happy little chat.

In Kenya the DC was assisted by his DOs, in this case there were three based at the headquarters. He was also assisted by the clerks who were a hard-working, conscientious, loyal and extremely decent body of men, whose service to the Colonial Administration in Kenya and Uganda has been all but forgotten. They were almost all Goans in 1949 and they formed a service of their own, being posted around the country in the same manner as the administrative officers. They were known as Bwana Karani by the Africans - the writing bwana. With very few office aids and only manual typewriters, they worked hard keeping up with the paperwork and they were in charge of the general administration, the accounts and supervising the African clerks and junior book-keepers.

In addition the District Clerks were in charge of the domestic economy of the station: that is, stores and stores' ledgers and at times they even took *charge of tax collection and pay safaris and supervised stock sales in the absence from the station of the District Commissioner and District Officer.*

In Nigeria it was different. The chief clerks and clerks were drawn from the tribes in the district and the numbers in each district office depended upon the population. For example, some parts of Iboland were populated with around one and a half million people. In such a district there would be up to a dozen clerical staff. But in an area with a scattered population there would be less than half a dozen.

In Sierra Leone the office clerks in the early days were nearly all Creoles: the inhabitants of Freetown and the Peninsular which was Crown land and known as the Colony. In 1827 the slaves were liberated in the West Indies and Wilberforce and his committee had the idea that the liberated slaves should be gathered up and returned to West Africa from whence their forebears had come. On the way 'home' the ships put into English ports and ladies of easy virtue were sent on board to provide company for the freed slaves in their new home, thus killing two birds with one stone, as it were. Freetown was chosen as their haven and the descendents of these people were the Creoles. The up-country people of Sierra Leone did not much like the Creoles who were very correct and God-fearing. They spoke pidgin English and all went to church on Sundays in their best black.

The administrative officers in Sierra Leone were also assisted by Court Messengers. Pat O'Dwyer recalled his first posting when the D.C.,

Humpherson, went out on trek and he was left in charge of the station.

I was quite ignorant of everything of course, but we were very well served with our staff. Each District had a force of Court Messengers, a strength of about 35. There was a Sergeant Major, two Sergeants, four corporals and the rest privates. They were all recruited from the ex-servicemen of the RWAFF (Royal West Africa Frontier Force) all with exemplary characters. When I first went out none of these was literate, but later some literates did join the Court Messengers. They had a distinct blue and red uniform and were very well known everywhere and greatly respected by the people. Being a Court Messenger was a much sought after position, for it commanded prestige and it was a pensionable job. They always knew everything that was going on in the District and we relied on them very much for advice. Also, either one of them, or a clerk, acted as interpreter. It was incumbent on one to learn the local language, which in the Northern Province was Timne. We, appointed as Acting Assistant DCs, were on probation for three years and during that time we had to pass exams in the local language, in English law and in native law before one was confirmed in the appointment. Even though one knew the language however, it was the custom when conducting a case in court, or addressing any assembly, or speaking to the chief officially, to talk through an interpreter. Similarly a chief, even if he could speak the pidgin English which was spoken out there, would always talk in his local language through an interpreter when addressing the DC.

But what did they all do? In Kericho in Kenya an elderly blind man called Arap Aruasa used to spend his days outside the District Commissioner's offices. When a new DO asked him what he was doing there, he answered simply; *"Ninachunga nchi tu."* 'I am just looking after the outdoors.' And looking after was the essence of what a colonial administrator did. Once I rather naively asked a retired DC whether they provided any welfare services for the people and he testily replied that welfare was the primary concern of a DC.

He also acted as a referee. If the District Clerk was known as Bwana Karani, in some places in Kenya the DC was known as Bwana Shauri - the Bwana for problems. Grievances could be aired to the DC and even if the verdict was not what was hoped for, the complainant could go away having got the problems off his chest and a solution reached. The commonest complaints were 'woman palaver' and land disputes. If a wife was proved to have been unfaithful to her husband, then the adulterer had to pay 'woman damage'. However, in Sierra Leone O'Dwyer says that *they would fight and kill each other over land but I don't remember their doing so over a woman.*

Everything landed on the DC's desk. The health of the population; combating the carriers of such diseases as bubonic plague and sleeping sickness and setting up clinics. Law and order matters: personal and intertribal disagreements were constant as many African people were keenly litigious. Simple requests such as one for a sub-post office in a distant location needed to be considered and budgeted for. A chief or headman might come up with a financial or trading idea to be put to the DC and then there were the reports from the higher echelons in the administration to be read and acted upon. And of course, these missives sometimes irked their recipients, as this parody suggests:

SUDAN GOVERNMENT (HOT WEATHER) ORDINANCE, 1936

WHEREAS about the end of May the last official in Grade A
departs for England and remains absent throughout the heat and rains.
WHEREAS the Palace silent stands devoid of all those idle hands
that in the winter give the wives the happiest moments of their lives.
WHEREAS haboubs and drink and heat render all morals obsolete,
I, STEWART SYMES, do now enact under my seal this little Act, with full
dissent of Council and assurances that this command when published in the next
Gazette will cause considerable upset.
(1) Officials shall appear quite bare for duties in the open air; (this section must be
so construed as meaning uniformly nude).
(2) All minutes shall be made to rhyme to while away the summer time.
(3) If any Governor gets annoyed his letters shall all be destroyed; if he demands an
interview give him a rise of pay in lieu. (Letters from the Upper Nile shall stay upon
your desks awhile and never must be shown or lent for purposes of merriment.)
(4) No raspberries shall be despatched to stations which are still unthatched or where

50

the roofs let in the rain for no one in the South is sane.

(5) When telegrams arrive at night be careful not to cause a fright by letting
secretaries see subjects on which they disagree; if they are SECRET you should burn
them quickly in a little urn; if BGC a native clerk should be detailed to keep them
dark.

(6) Despatches must not be mislaid but instantaneously P.A.-ed and if some action
is required and chaps are feeling rather tired an <u>interim</u> reply will keep the High
Commissioner asleep.

(7) If work gets very out of hand a short adjournment to the Grand is indicated and
some Beer will make your worries disappear.

SIGNED by my hand at Erkowit (it is I fear not very neat and just to show you
how I feel I'm going to dance an Eightsome reel)."

ANON

And of course there were the reports to send back to those distant
dignitaries, explaining how things looked from the sharp end. One
Kenya officer who described himself as *the local fuhrer from Il Polei to Tura*
parodied this particular chore in what he entitled his *Monthly Report -*
Mukogodo - July 1959:

There's a forest Mukogodo with dead cedar but no podo
For the rainfall here gives timber little luck.
On the Isiolo border there is sometimes law and order
But on the whole we're living in the Muk.
We see the storm clouds pass to overlook our grass
Which, we admit, is often very shocking.
And confounded geep and shoats that have never tasted oats
Just aggravate a state of overstocking.
We have lions: we have lambs: and we're building several dams
Which elephants are trying to destroy.
Though we sow no seed we scatter alien tribes by the manyatta
But there's lots of pretty views we can enjoy.
We have just begun a school, but we will seem a fool
If there's no Standard I next year to use it.

And though a new health system can treat the sick and list'em
There's very few who care to pay and choose it.
In a slightly backward station of this questionable nation
Democracy is naturally deployed.
Men write to M.P.s letters about tyranny and fetters
And the M.P.s write to Mr. Lennox Boyd.

Some people left the paperwork strictly alone. David Nicol Griffith once discovered some old files in Marsabit dating back to the early years of the Kenya administration. One file, which covered a whole year, had only three letters in it: a request from Nairobi for details of tribal movements, a reminder four months later and the DC's reply - much later still - in which he apologised for not having replied earlier but he had been out a lot on safari.

One of the few suicides that did occur happened in Western Kenya. And it was all the more baffling because he was pleased to have been given the job he had. Although nobody ever knew for certain the reason why he shot himself it appears that a mixture of family problems, an injury to the head and the volume of work may all have contributed to the tragedy. I tell the story not out of intrusiveness but because it is necessary to remember that the men and women who went out to serve Africa did not simply live their lives in a kind of Boys Own Annual pursuit of adventure until the time came for them to retire to the rose covered cottage in Britain, suitably be-medalled by a grateful government. They were doing a difficult job which caused great interest, yes, but also frustration, loneliness and anxiety. Very few, but some, were overwhelmed by it.

We shall call him Archie Snow.

We knew him slightly; he was a friendly smiling man but also because we children were friends with his elder daughter, Tamsin. She had told us of serious difficulties in the family which we had kept to ourselves at her request. One of his colleagues wrote to me: *It would have been nice to find out if Tamsin realised what a delightful, friendly and amusing chap Archie was."* She did. She was devoted to her father.

Snow had also had an accident at a swimming gala which some people - but not all - believed changed his personality and was the underlying cause of the tragedy. The swimming gala was an annual event and much enjoyed by all the participants, especially the children. One of the competitions was known as 'the plunge' and consisted of each competitor plunging into the pool and seeing how far along it he or she could float, head down, without taking a breath.

We can remember the sunshine, the excitement and the triumphs that day which were suddenly darkened as if by an unexpected eclipse. Archie Snow plunged in and floated down the pool for a very long way indeed. Then somebody realised that there was something wrong and he was pulled out. He had lost consciousness. History does not relate what the medical diagnosis was but there was talk of a burst blood vessel in the brain. It was known that he was very short-sighted and some thought he may have cracked his skull when he dived in.

One of his fellow officers wrote:

I knew Archie Snow quite well and liked him a lot. He was a quiet, friendly and gentle person. His wife, Ingrid, was a disagreeable and universally unpopular woman. I was not around at the time of Archie's suicide but always assumed that his marriage had a lot to do with it but I believe he was also going a bit eccentric towards the end. He grew a beard, which was most unusual for a D.C. then.

The Provincial Commissioner at the time was Hal Williams and he had been concerned about Archie Snow. He had had him examined by the local government doctor who had passed him as fit. The officer who told me this suspects that this medical clearance was probably premature.

Snow's senior DO believed that, for whatever reasons, the volume of work running the district overwhelmed him and this was the catalyst for his tragic decision. Certainly, his widow put it about that the Provincial Commissioner had put too much pressure on Archie but his senior DO was of the opinion that there was good reason for concern about the lack of output while another colleague told me that the PC *certainly did not contribute to Archie's state of mind.*

I was the senior DO during the whole time Archie Snow was DC." he wrote. *"I had been posted there in 1952 under the previous DC, and took over temporarily as DC myself after Archie's death.*

My office door faced his, so I was in close contact with Archie whenever I was in the boma. All the same, my job was somewhat independent as I looked after the network of African Courts, did most of the magistrate's work and made up my own programme of safaris. I was not therefore part of the day-to-day administration of the location on the ground. This was the job of the other DOs and agricultural officers. However, Archie used to have a basket of 'elevenses' sent to his office each morning and regularly invited me in for a coffee and a chat. I thought at the time that I was fairly close to him but on reflection, after his death, I realised how little I knew of his inner feelings... Archie himself never let on to me [about personal tensions] *though we did of course discuss everyone else's problems!*

At first meeting, and for most of the time, Archie was a friendly and gregarious person with a ready laugh, but I learnt from one or two small incidents that he was extremely sensitive underneath, as I shall explain.

Before coming to the district Archie had had a mainly desk job in Nairobi. On arrival at the district it was clear that he relished the idea of being DC of such a large district in Kenya (in terms of population). He seemed to be full of energy. Within a couple of months he had organised a weekend social safari to Mt. Elgon for an assortment of officers and wives. I did not go as we had a young family.

Occasionally Archie would come up with some 'unusual' scheme, such as cutting down some of the tall, dark trees near the DC's house (abandoned after a couple of days); constructing a complicated set of traffic islands at the T-junction by his house (not that there was all that amount of traffic in the boma); and damming up the water furrow to make a swimming bath (stopped by the Divisional Engineer).

If I remember correctly he gave up going on safari fairly soon after he arrived, on the pretext that there was far too much office work to do. He gave up writing monthly reports. After I took over I naturally wrote the annual report for that year and, finding the departmental contributions for the previous year, I wrote that one too. I believe that no annual report had been written for the year before that either.

In fact when Archie died, we found a number of metal safari boxes full of papers which had not been dealt with and the African District Council estimates for two

54

years in his safe. These should have been submitted to the PC's office - one lot well over a year before. The PC and I spent a couple of days sorting out the papers.

The picture I have of Archie in the office was of a man who had let the job get on top of him. He shuffled paper about, welcomed any interruption and achieved very little. I know from personal experience in my later career that once you let yourself get overloaded, your output decreases.

My recollection is that the situation I have described had set in well before his swimming accident and this seems to be confirmed by his failure to submit reports and deal with the estimates etc. over a long period of time.

His extreme sensitivity did escape control on one or two occasions. A particular incident was when we put on a concert to raise funds for the church building. It was called "Much felling in the Trees" and based on the BBC series "Much Binding in the Marsh". The Education Officer who wrote most of it was posted away and I got left to compére it, including taking part in the final theme song in which we poked fun at all and sundry, including Archie's aborted swimming pool project. At the end I happened to pass Archie who said tensely 'Not a performance to enhance one's promotion prospects.'

Another instance related to the complicated traffic islands he laid out near his house. One morning we found that someone had driven straight across them. Archie was furious, quite out of proportion to the offence, and seemed to take it as a personal affront. He did not manage to identify the offender - though I think quite a lot of people knew who it was.

I had no idea that Archie was contemplating suicide. We knew later, from a paper Ingrid found after his death, that he had contemplated such an act years before when DC Maralal.

So it was, one sunny morning before breakfast in Kakamega, Archie Snow left his house and went down to the river, taking with him a gun which one of the DOs had left in the DC's safe for safe-keeping. He walked some way up the river filled his pockets with stones and shot himself in the head.

To our great sadness, my sister and I never saw his daughter, Tamsin, again.

****

55

Major Buxton described much of the work of a DC as "pettifogging trivialities" and some of it was but as it has always been and always will be, those trivialities could be blown up a bit and tempers frayed. In Kericho, there landed on David Nicol Griffith's desk an order from Nyanza Provincial Headquarters in Kisumu to *transfer a truckload of prisoners to Kisumu. This I arranged. However, the day before the transfer was to take place, a signal arrived on my desk cancelling it; I read it but forgot to do anything about it. When the prisoners arrived in Kisumu - a journey of about 60 miles - they were sent straight back again, and a stiff reprimand came later in the mail. The District Commissioner, Kericho minuted me with the words, 'I hope the prisoners enjoyed their tour of Nyanza. You may have to pay.' [Then] the Provincial Commissioner (Ngombe Williams) wrote and asked me to show cause why I should not be liable for the loss. I was astounded and sent him a letter explaining how I could not possibly be criminally liable! He replied that he had not asked for an exposition of the law from me, but to justify the procedures by which such losses should be prevented.*

Budgets were prepared and money was tight. Each DC was required to know what the people in his district required and to transpose those needs into requests for financing from Provincial Headquarters.

Unexpected balances of annual grants lapsed at the end of the year, and a prudent DC took care to draw the remaining money as advance payments to the contractors for the next years work....Wedderburn Maxwell (1921) DC Western Nuer, once contrived in this fashion to finance the building of a much needed road for which he had applied in vain year after year. Hardly had it been completed when approval at last arrived, setting him a pretty problem in accounting.

Budgets could also be used as an excuse too of course. In the early 1950s Princess Margaret was due to visit Kisumu and some of the local missionaries petitioned Hal Williams, PC Kisumu, on the unsuitability of the Princess being made to watch bare breasted tribal dancers. He replied by stating that there was no vote in his budget for hundreds of pink brassieres.

In the office there might be an unexpected visit from someone who had suffered a reverse of fortune or simply the dotty. One morning a

European woman walked into Rex Niven's office in Nigeria and, without a word, peeled off her shirt, stood for a moment in front of his desk, then put it back on again and walked out.

The DC's office was not a terribly pressurised place by modern standards although the job weighed heavily on many and it took its toll as can be seen by the verse in the poem at the beginning of this chapter. One of the most important tasks for an administrative officer was to communicate with the people for whom he was responsible. Much of this was done through public meetings. In Kenya they were known as barazas and officers would attend them frequently to announce, discuss and listen. They generally lasted two or three hours. Sometimes they became heated but in the main they were a useful forum for the exchange of information, opinions and ideas. In the Sudan they were known as tribal gatherings and they took place over several days. Brian Carlisle describes one thus:

As D.C. one met the tribal authorities a great deal and where there was dissent against a ruler one met the dissenters, whom in some cases forced changes on the Authorities. Opportunities for policies to be discussed and grievances aired existed particularly at tribal gatherings, a sequence of which were held in the Winter months at pre-determined places. Grass "rabukas" were erected for the D.C.s and for visitors from Province Headquarters or Khartoum, and here we camped for a week or so discussing not only tribal matters but education, health, veterinary and agricultural matters. We maintained that for the Beja's of the 1940's this was a more satisfactory sort of local Government than to assemble some councillors, elected under some suffrage system in a red brick building in Aroma or Sinket. In a district with so sparse and scattered a population we foresaw real practical difficulties in introducing universal suffrage and whilst I was in the district it was not attempted.

It must have been early in 1947, wrote Frank Loyd, later Sir Frank *and I think the place was Malakisi, on the western side of the huge district which was perhaps still called North Kavirondo, later to be renamed North Nyanza, Kenya. Hal Williams and I (his senior DO) went there to arrange the appointment of the local Headman, whose predecessor had just died (a natural death of drink, probably.) I think we had with us a driver and 1 or perhaps 2 tribal policemen.*

We were very democratic even in those early days and the custom was for anyone who fancied the job as Headman (low pay but no doubt good perks) to appear on the appointed day, and for his supporters to line up behind him. Unless there was some unusual degree of skulduggery we would normally count heads and choose the chap who had the most supporters.

On this occasion competition between the two leading candidates was intense, and when the DC announced his decision, the defeated one became really abusive and obstreperous and did all he could to rouse his supporters to violent opposition. He came up shouting at the DC while continuing to stir his supporters to such a pitch that a riot was obviously going to develop. The DC then told him to shut up and push off to which our chum made an offensive reply. The DC then slapped him across the cheek with his open hand, which had an instantaneous effect on the (very large) crowd and the riot was stopped dead in its tracks.

Unfortunately the DC's finger had caught the edge of the culprit's eye in the course of the slap and it became quite bloodshot. He did his best to cash in on this being clear proof of the assault and the whole situation was a bit awkward. But there was no doubt in my mind that the DC's prompt, if strictly improper, action stopped dead what would otherwise have been a serious riot and a very dangerous situation for him and me.

The incident was, of course, reported to the Provincial Commissioner and to Nairobi but nothing further transpired and peace returned to the turbulent district of North Kavirondo.

****

The ceremonial visits provoked W.G.R. Bond to write "one of the best known satirical poems in the Sudan corpus" on the opening of Kosti Bridge by Sir Reginald Wingate in 1910.

OPENING OF KOSTI BRIDGE

By W.G.R. Bond

Stand still, police; for God's sake people cheer,
And do look pleased, that's why I brought you here....

58

See that sufficient people stand about
To hide the corner where the flags ran out....
Is anyone with any just complaint
Out of the way and under safe restraint?
Where is the plaintiff as to whom I say
'I settled in his favour yesterday'?
General Salute; now all that man can do
Is done, and only luck can pull us through.

His Excellency. Loquitur: 'Sheikhs, omdas, notables, officials both
Civil and military, I am nothing loath
To say that I am very pleased to see
So many flags, such signs of loyalty,
Such progress, such advancement, such content,
So few who languish in imprisonment,
So marked an increase in the public pelf.
Chiefly I'm Mabsut khalas with MYSELF'

The book "*Set Under Authority*" about describes very well the daily round
thought out British administered Africa, which put into practice the
herculean expectations of the Governor: the killing of hopper locusts in
their breeding grounds, prison inspection, police drill and musketry,
inspection of Government animals, presiding over the annual board for
the assessment of business profits (a particularly exasperating task), the
estimating of the total sugar requirement, allocation between
merchants, arrangements for delivery, storage, distribution and
payments of duties. Then there was town planning and siting of
factories, tanneries etc away from residential district: *The normal*
instruments of building control was a weekly town ride. The DC, the medical officer
of health, a surveyor, a building foreman, a public security officer, the town mayor
(omdu) and the sheikhs.
The variety of tasks and immense amount expected of them should
have been daunting but on the whole, they accepted it all with

equanimity. In Nigeria Rex Niven was appointed to take charge of an Audit. *This special posting, like all my other ones, was apparently based on my total ignorance of the subject....when we checked the cash balance they were 2 shillings short. There was a fearful hullabaloo: the ancient chief, fierce-eyed and vigilant, was furious, and everyone scurried round. The mats were taken up off the floor of the mud-built Treasury and shaken outside in clouds of dust and, behold, in a dark corner .*

shillings were discovered. Whether they were the ones we were looking for or not, I accepted the omen and called off the search. All sank back with cries of relief.

Accounting for the cash was of course the responsibility of every administrative officer as this unhappy story from the Sudan demonstrates.

The safe at District Headquarters was in the daily charge of the Cashier but it was laid down by the Condominium Government that it was to be checked once a month by the Mamur and once a month by the District Commissioner or one of the Assistant District Commissioners. In the Beja District there were three of the latter but one of these would often be on leave and none of us would actually spend many days in each month at District Headquarters in Sizhat.

The Cashier at Sizhat was called Taj es Sirr, a humble man in his 40's, very polite and seemingly conscientious. Now we should have done surprise checks but in this particular year both the Sudanese ADC and myself had been unknowingly deceived by the Cashier because when either one of us said that we were coming to check the safe he had said that the cash needed tidying up and to save our time he would do this first. He must have treated the Mamur the same way.

I don't recall who it was first became suspicious but when a spot check was carried out, instead of £2,000 there was hardly anything there at all. An enquiry discovered that he had been advancing the money to the staff of a religious teacher in the town and when a check of the safe had been ordered he had been slipping down to the market to borrow the money from some of his merchant friends. I don't know how he ever thought he could get away with it at the end of the day, but the poor chap went to prison for several years and all the District authorities including myself quite justly got a severe reprimand. I have never again allowed any Cashier to adjust his cash before I count it.

Perhaps one of the most difficult of tasks was to dismiss someone from their post and Bryan Sharwood Smith found the dismissal of Emir Yakubu of Bauchi for malpractices one of his saddest duties.

Yakubu of Bauchi, [was] descendent of one of Shehu dan Fodio's flagbearers... and four places only below the Sultan in chiefly precedence. If ability and charm were all that were required in a chief, Yakubu's position would have been assured, but personal rule was all he understood and all that he was prepared to understand.

The final act took place in the drawing room of Government House. The Emir, his turban more loosely wound than usual, his gown crumpled from his long journey, sat hunched in an armchair. Grouped around him, a little unhappily, were his Waziri and ruling members of the council. The next few minutes would give scant pleasure to any of us.

'Sarkin Bauchi' I began, 'I greatly fear that we have come to the end of the road. You have lost the confidence of both your council and your people, and nothing that your council and I have been able to do has persuaded you to change your ways. It is no longer possible for you to remain in office. You must now make your choice. Either you must go into retirememt or face formal deposition. You should let me have your decision by this evening. There is no more to be said.' I rose and the Emir rose with me. We shook hands, and he left. A few hours later, his answer came. He would go into retirement.

So it was that Rainsford's 'ordinary young Englishmen' tried their best to be honest, conscientious and successful. This advice was given to John Longe by Douglas Newbold, Governor of Kordofan in the 1930's.

I only ask you to work hard, appreciate other view-points (ie Departments, province HQ, central government), keep calm and unruffled in face of difficulties and set-backs, have a broad plan for your district, respect continuity, and identify yourself with this province.

Visit neighbouring districts and make friends with your D.C.s, Nazirs and Mamurs.

Don't be precipitate or iconoclastic, but go about with reasonable reform. Consult everyone before change. Give your subordinates plenty of rope, but make them tell you what they are doing. Keep an eye on local administration, trade and markets.

Be compassionate, considerate, discriminate, impartial, and philosophic. These are virtues of action, not necessarily of inaction. ...

This is all rather grandmotherly, but I am responsible for justice, happiness and prosperity to a million Sudanese, and I have to take it seriously. So do you.

The Indian community in Kakamega hosting a tea party c 1950.
(Hal Williams, then DC, third from the right)

To,

C. H. Williams Esq., O.B.E.

District Commissioner, North Nyanza.

KAKAMEGA,

Dear Sir,

We, the members of the North Nyanza Indian Association, have assembled here this afternoon to present an address and express our heartiest gratification on your achieving the honourable post of the Provincial Commissioner, Nyanza Province, and also to demonstrate, in our own humble way, our deep and sincere sense of appreciation and gratitude for the real services you have rendered to each and every, whether poor or rich, in North Nyanza.

We have not the slightest hesitation in saying that elements are so combined in you as to make you a person most eminently fitted for the office you have been holding.

This Indian School, in particular, has been the recepient of much encouragement and help from you. Despite difficult conditions obtaining during the War, you helped in each and every possible means, and still due to your honest endeavour this institution will get a bright shape and furnish higher education to the Indian children of North Nyanza.

We have found you at all times to show all the qualities necessary in a good Administrative Officer, and can truthfully say that if the whole of the Administration contained men of your type, the Colony would be the better and the way of the wrong doer would be thorny.

In asking you to accept this Address and Casket we would wish that your tenure of Office be a period of prosperity and relations with this Province of lasting memory. We wish you, Mrs. Williams and family a happy long life, while in this country memories to cherish for years in future.

We are,
Yours Sincerely,
The President, Managing Committee and
Members of N. N. Indian Association, Kakamega.

KAKAMEGA.

9th Sept. 1950.

Printed by:- National Printing Press, Kisumu.

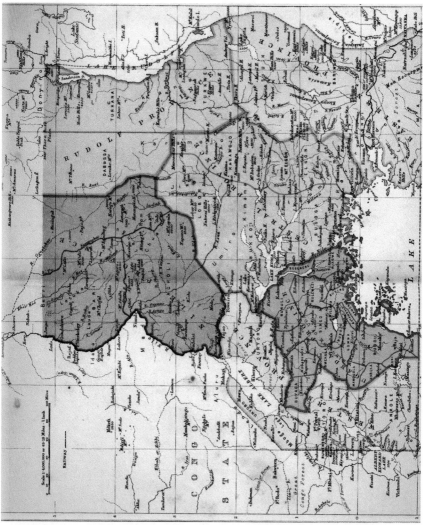

Compiled by Sir H.H. Johnston GCMG, KCB for his book "The Uganda Protectorate" marking the Administrative Divisions. First Published in 1902, it shows that what became Central Province in the Colony of Kenya was, at the beginning of the 20th Century, part of the Uganda Protectorate. NB The Lake is Lake Victoria.

Chapter 5

THE KEDONG MASSACRE
And the death of Mr Andrew Dick

At the end of the nineteenth century, the administrative officers and the local people were struggling to make sense of the new and alien world they all found themselves participating in. Sir Frederick Jackson was an outstanding early administrator. His interest in and his compassion for the Africans he encountered meant that the early faltering steps of the British administration were guided by decent, kindly and impartial men such as Jackson. His account of the Kedong massacre demonstrates the honest and respectful effort by Kenya Africans and British administrators to adapt

The Kedong massacre on November 26, 1895, was a very terrible affair, and several versions of it have been published from time to time, but real facts are as follows:

A large caravan of eleven hundred men, of whom one hundred and five were Swahilis, the rest Akikuyu, carrying food supplies for the Eldoma Ravine Station, was despatched from Fort Smith by Mr Gildisson, the officer in charge. Such a caravan ought to have been under an European official, and one was actually available at the time, but for some reason or another it was most unfortunately sent off under a Swahili headman, a man I knew well, who was too young for the job.

All, however, went well until Naivasha was reached on the return journey, when a considerable number of both Swahilis and Akikuyu began to get out of hand, and by the time they reached Kijabi the headman had lost control of them. From Naivasha to Kijabi they were accompanied by several Masai elmoru (elders), who

Sir Frederick Jackson KCMG, CB

He was a diligent naturalist and was a supremely happy man. *If you could be an enemy of Bwana Jackson who would want you for a friend?* Lord Cransworth's forward to *Early Days in East Africa* by Jackson.

did their utmost, not only to urge the headman and askaris to persuade their men to behave themselves and do nothing likely to disturb and excite the Masai, but warned them that there was a very large morans' manyatta (warriors' settlement or village) *close by and just ahead.*

66

The Masai elders then hurried on to this manyatta and urged the moran to remain quiet. Next morning the first half of the caravan passed without a disturbance, but the rest deliberately went out of their way to create one by entering the manyatta and molesting the morans' ditos (young women and girls.) *One Swahili even attempted to drive away a cow. This was too much for the moran and one of them, 'seeing red', speared the Swahili and was himself promptly shot dead by another; in a very few minutes the manyatta and its near vicinity was a shambles.*

It was there that the majority of the 98 Swahilis out of the 105 were killed. Then followed a merciless butchery all the way from that point to an open space at the foot of Mount Margaret, on which was a small [Masai] *manyatta of elmoru and kokos (old women) and it was there that some seventy odd panic-stricken and exhausted Akikuyu stopped, and pleaded for protection from the* [Masai warriors] *now mad with blood-lust and coming up behind.*

To the credit of the old people, men and women, they did all they could to intercede but they were pushed on one side and in a minute or two the massacre was over, for the Akikuyu who had gone ahead of the spot were not followed up.

When I passed along the road about five weeks later there were skeletons everywhere, and the road itself was strewn with basket-work hamper lids (used in their donkey transport when moving to fresh grazing-grounds,) stools, dressed leather garments – all loot – and small loads of white china clay which were being brought down by the Akikuyu for ornamenting their shields, or their persons during a dance.

Altogether four hundred and fifty-six Akikuyu were killed, and it was interesting to note that the majority of the skeletons seen by myself were quite perfect, even to the first joints of their fingers and toes. This showed very clearly that while the vultures and ravens were able to deal with them, Hyaenas and jackals had not been numerous enough to do so, and had not touched a single one of the seventy or more that lay within an area twenty yards square at the foot of Mount Margaret.

It was certainly the most gruesome and horrible march of four miles or so I ever experienced, and if ever a spot in East Africa could claim to be a 'Valley of Death', the Kedong Valley could do so early in December, 1895.

At the moment when information of the massacre was brought in by survivors to

Fort Smith, Lenana, the Masai Lybon (leader or head witch-doctor) was actually on a ceremonial visit, and that in itself was convincing proof that he had nothing to do with it; but he must necessarily have experienced many anxious hours (I believe he subsequently admitted it) until he found himself quite free to return to his people when he liked. [The statement of the Masai Lybon's treatment by the administration] *on that occasion very greatly impressed him, and he frequently referred to it as an example of the white man's justice.*

There were at the time at Fort Smith, three Frenchmen, Monsieur Versepuit, Baron de Roman, and a man named Spork, who had worked their way from Kilimanjaro on a shooting expedition. There was also a man named Andrew Dick, late Chief Accountant of the Imperial British East Africa Company, but at the time 'on his own.' He had been doing transport work for the Uganda Government, and had fitted out his safari for a trading venture towards Rudolf, when he realized that here was a favourable opportunity for annexing, as a reprisal on the Masai, a quantity of the best of all trade goods, viz, cattle.

The upshot was that he defied Gilkisson and bullied and taunted the Frenchmen into joining him, and off they started with a considerable armed force. They found the Masai had already moved away from the valley, but succeeded in rounding up a lot of cattle near the foothills of Longonot. The moran made no attempt to recapture their stock in the valley; but, adopting the old and well-known native tactics, they got well ahead of the raiding party, under cover of the bush and stunted acacias, took up a position in a small ravine flanking the road on the first terrace and there waited. For some reason of their own, instead of dashing forward and driving off the cattle when they had reached the terrace, while the Europeans and the strong rear-guard were still struggling up the steep path below, they waited until the latter arrived and then attacked.

The Frenchmen told me that at one time the situation was far from pleasant, and for some little time they themselves were kept very busy with their sporting rifles, until the moran were driven back to the shelter of the ravine.

It was then that Dick committed an act of folly that led to his death. He shortly before, close to the edge of the ravine, killed a moran who had a particularly long-bladed spear, and went forward to secure it, but while stooping to pick it up another moran dashed out towards him. Dick was prepared, but his Colt's repeating rifle failed him. Directly he threw it up the moran crouched and ducked behind his shield, and when Dick realized the rifle was jammed, he turned and ran. Then, according to the Frenchmen, there followed a series of bluffs by Dick and ducks by the moran, the former running and then whipping round and aiming at the latter, who continued to duck until he realized that the rifle was either empty or useless. Then instead of ducking, he came on and just as Dick turned to run, drove his spear through him and nearly a foot of it beyond his chest. The moran was himself shot immediately afterwards. So died Andrew Dick, a very brave man.

The gist of the above was the first bit of news I received at the Eldoma Ravine

Masai Moran c 1895

Station on arrival there from Uganda on December 22nd 1895, to take over charge of the Eastern Province, which at that time embraced the Rift Valley up to and including the Kedong, Nandi, Lumbwa, Elgeyu, Kamassia and Baringo.

Two days later the three Frenchmen arrived, and it was from them that I heard the details of Dick's death.

It was, of course, my duty to proceed as soon as possible to investigate and report on the matter, and little Martin, who had built the station and was going on leave, accompanied me to Fort Smith. On the way down, close to the Gilgil River, we came across two Masai moran sitting under a leleshwa bush, who, when we were about seventy yards apart, stood up and came forward holding in one hand a wisp of grass as a peace offering and in the other a spear.

69

The Masai, then more or less concentrated round about Naivasha and the Kinangop Plateau, had, through their scouts, heard of our approach, and these two moran had come out alone to meet us. It at least showed that they were not wanting in courage. One of them was Laigulishu the Laigunan (captain or leader) or Tereri's moran, a man who has figured so prominently in all negotiations ever since. (See Chapter 7)*

On reaching Naivasha we found Tereri and a host of Elmoru assembled, and the whole afternoon was spent in taking down the evidence of both elders and moran who were present on the occasion. During my two and a half years' residence at the Ravine I held many scores of shauris (conferences) with the Masai and their neighbours, but none of them impressed me so much as that one. The calm dignity of both old and young men, as they stood slowly wielding a light rungu (knobkerrie) to emphasize their words, passing it on from one speaker to the other, giving their version fluently, without hesitation, sign of fear, or bombast, was a very remarkable display of oratory.

The statements by the Elmoru who accompanied the caravan from Naivasha to Kijabi were particularly fine efforts, and showed very clearly that they had done everything possible in order to avoid a clash. I came to the conclusion that unless the evidence of the survivors to the contrary was equally weighty, there could be no possible doubt that the behaviour of the caravan as a whole was abominable, and that the Masai received the greatest provocation.

On reaching Fort Smith, I was told that Mr John Ainsworth had arrived there from Machakos some time previously, on the same inquiry as myself, so at once walked over to his tent, where I found him, very busy as usual, writing. After greetings he said, "Well, what do you think about it?" to which I replied, "My dear John, I have only heard one side of it, but I am, so far, of opinion that your people started it and had only themselves to blame," to which he replied, "I am glad to hear you say that, as I have come to the same conclusion." We then gave each other the gist of our respective inquiries. We were also agreed on the unwarranted action of Dick. It was decided that the cattle taken should not be returned but be regarded as a fine, and the proceeds distributed amongst the relatives of the Akikuyu who had been killed."

John Ainsworth, Provincial Commissioner, Machakos.
(With thanks to The Maclellan Wilson Collection)

Arthur Collyer, DC Rumuruti with Masai elders, c 1906

Chapter 6

LOOKING EACH OTHER IN THE EYE

Nobody knows about the Africans, however long you live there. I mean when people ask me about them I just say that I lived forty-five years in Kenya and it was long enough to teach me how little I know. If you did know anything it was about only one tribe.

These words were spoken to me in 1990 by Kit Taylor, who, having been born in the same year as the new century, arrived in Kenya in 1904. Although there is undoubtedly a common thread of characteristics that run through the disparate African peoples, some of which are secret and incomprehensible to outsiders (as with all races), each tribe - and even sub-tribe - has its own unique traits and customs.

In Nigeria alone *there are four hundred and more tribal languages and dialects in daily use, but there are more tribes than languages,* while in Uganda, a much smaller country, there are thirty three tribal languages. It would therefore have been almost impossible to have adjusted the laws of the land entirely to accommodate these disparities. But when Lugard had conquered northern Nigeria he *publicly declared that there would be no interference with the religion of the people, or with their customs, or with the established courts of law. The old ways would continue uninterrupted insofar as they did not conflict with natural justice.*

Although the administrators had much to learn about the intricacies of the African people, particularly in the early days, and some Africans were vexed that power did not lie with them, they had the security of

73

knowing which tribe was in power and the certainty that those administrators were above reproach. For *without integrity we had no right to be there*"as Eric Loveluck said. Justice was untainted by tribal or marital loyalites and law-making was unmuddied by politics. Life under the British was the most uncomplicated and unstressful time most African people had ever known.

Our own childhood attitude to the Africans we came in contact with was equally uncomplicated. When Hal Williams was the DC in Kakamega , he was, of course, the senior person in the station, the King's representative no less; the biggest fish in the small Kakamega pond: the Bwana Mkubwa. (the Big Man)

With complacent certainty we were convinced that we three children were top of the social tree. This, however, was not because our father was the Bwana Mkubwa, but because our ayah (nanny) was the only woman we knew who had a set of false teeth. We called them a 'duka set' (bought from a shop); and, what is more, she always wore shoes. It is not very laudable when we look back on five year old snobbery, but under the cool gum trees where we played we felt a certain lofty pity for the other children whose ayahs could not rise to a duka set and a pair of shoes.

We did, however, find her black legs stretched out before her as she sat on the ground gossiping with other ayahs, awfully useful for drawing on. With a stick we would draw a picture. If we were not pleased with it, we would lick our fingers, rub it out and start again.

The relationship that existed between us children and the servants was, certainly from our point of view, an easy unquestioning acceptance of each other. They were kind to us but never made a fuss of us. We were left to weave our schemes around the Boma, dig a hole to Australia, pedal around the leafy dirt roads or attempt to sell mud bars of 'chocolate' to passers-by. If we were sinful the Africans usually left us to be found out by our parents, rather than to interfere. They were never busy bodies.

Sometimes, as a rare treat, we were allowed to join them at their mid-day meal. Shamelessly we would loiter around them hoping for an invitation, while the men squatted, heels flat, beside the brazier. Maize cobs roasted in the embers, their singed seeds almost unbearably delicious, and a vegetable and meat stew simmered on the top of the brazier beside which sat a cake of warm posho (maize meal cake) on an

74

enamel plate. If our luck was in, the men - sometimes with understandable irritation would call us to join the circle and we would squat down, respectfully quiet, break off a piece of posho, dip it in the stew, catching some vegetable and juice on it, and reverently eat it.

Throughout British Africa there are more stories of the warm and the witty, the funny and the tender incidents which occurred between the British officials and the people they served than there were stories of resentment, hatred and violence. In the Sudan a condemned man fanned the face of the DC who was stricken with malaria, as they both travelled to the nearest town. There were the families who named their babies after their employers, and the servants who took great risks in order to protect the Europeans they worked for.

However, the perception of what it was like seems to have changed. Thirty years after Nigeria had become independent I asked three young Nigerians what they thought about the days when Nigeria was a British Colony. They were slightly startled, almost as if it was a taboo question, but one of the three waxed eloquent about how awful it had been. He particularly liked the term *raped and looted our land*. After a few minutes his tirade ran out of steam and he looked at me, half defiant, half shame-faced and said, *Well that is what I think ... But my mother wouldn't agree!*

That was one view formed by somebody who was only a baby when Nigeria became independent and those young men were not alone in believing this line of thought but my own steward, an elderly man who believed that under Colonial rule, unlike the present day, had allowed his 'labours and strugglies' to reap rewards, had contempt for the young who had come to believe that those days were bad for Nigerians. Current Nigerian education of history appears at least to encourage those young men's very negative views. I heard a well-known Nigerian author in a speech alluding to the idyllic village life that had existed before the white man arrived and had turned it all upside-down.

But in East Africa at least, the explorer, J.H. Speke, saw a very different picture. In his *Journal of the Discovery of the Source of Nile* written in 1863, he wrote:

At present the African can neither help himself nor will he be helped by others, because his country is in such a state of turmoil he has too much anxiety on hand looking out for his food to think of anything else. As his fathers ever did, so does he. He works his wife, sells his children, enslaves all he can lay hands on...

But clearly there was tension and doubt as these extraordinary looking pale people appeared, dressed in ridiculous clothes and having a confident swagger about them, as if they had some unimagined knowledge.

David Nicoll Griffiths, a DO in Kenya, provides an inkling of how some Africans felt about it when he met a very old man in the Kitui area in the mid 'fifties:

[He] was reputed to be 110 years of age and with a remarkable memory. Others before me had spent time with him and (so I believe) made detailed notes of what amounted to a history of the Kitui Akamba, and I felt that I should pay my respects to so venerable a person. I was told by Chief Kasina that he would agree to answer a question if I put it to him, so I asked him what his earliest memory was. He replied that he could remember the consternation caused to the tribes by the penetration inland of the first European explorers (Ludwig Krapf and Johannes Rebmann had reached Mount Kenya by 1849); consternation caused primarily by the fact that the full powers of the witchdoctors were having no effect on them, nor subsequently on any Europeans.

Similarly Joy Williams told us that she asked a chief in c 1948 what he thought was the white man's greatest invention. She had thought he would say the train, the car or the aeroplane but after thinking about it he told her "The match."

For some, of course, the arrival of Europeans offered opportunity but first they had to overcome the natural human resistance to change. One of the problems of life in Africa before the arrival of other cultures was that the customs and superstitions of village life suffocated innovation. Charles New was a missionary in 1863 and in his *Life, Wanderings and Labours in Eastern Africa* he describes the customs which suppressed progress:

The laws of the country are those of 'ada' (custom). The question with the Wanika is not 'what is right?' but 'what is the custom?' And before this they bow with the utmost servility. ... Reform they abominate; improvement upon the old state of things is not allowed. The son must not aspire to anything better than his father has had before him. If a man dares to improve the style of his hut, to make a larger doorway than is customary; if he should wear a finer or different style of dress to that of his fellows, he is instantly fined; and he becomes, too, the object of such scathing ridicule, that he were a bold man indeed who would venture to excite it against himself."

"The whole social life of the native is permeated by the rules of conduct summed up in the word thahu (ceremonial uncleanness). This may arise from a variety of causes,

76

some of them of a serious nature, as homicide, others being, apparently, purely accidental, such as the collapsing of a house. A man who becomes for any of these many reasons thahu (unclean) must go through a more or less elaborate ceremony with a doctor, according to the degree of his uncleanness, to the more serious cases involving the killing of a goat. Until this has been done he is unfit for general society and cannot associate with his fellows.

As recently as 1945 some tribes were finding it difficult to grasp new concepts. Discussing the largely unsuccessful results of a pilot project with the Zande people to pave the way for the social and economic development of the south of Sudan, the then Director of Agriculture, A.G. McCall, excused the failure of the scheme by pointing out how the tribe was when the agricultural officers began their project to encourage the Zande to grow some cash crops. He considered them to be:

A very primitive people, still dependent upon and content with subsistence agriculture, subservient to a feudal hierarchy of autocratic chiefs and their every activity ordered by superstition, fear of magic and witchcraft, oracles or tribal custom.

And in East Africa it was little different as Nicoll Griffiths notes:

It was indeed from the coming of the Europeans that witchcraft began to lose its ascendancy, and this loss was accelerated by the fact of its inclusion in the Laws of Kenya as a criminal offence. Nevertheless, there were still witchdoctors and they did still practice. A man came one day to the hospital at Kitui complaining of feeling unwell, but the Medical Officer could find nothing wrong with him so he was admitted for observation. His condition slowly deteriorated without the medical staff being any nearer to a diagnosis, and we decided to make enquiries in the Reserve. It became clear that he had fallen foul of a witchdoctor who had assured him that he would die before the next harvest. This harvest was not far off, a campaign was launched to identify the culprit; it succeeded, and I was somewhat embarrassed to learn that he was the President of one of the African Courts in my Division, paid by the Government and appointed to administer tribal law without fear or favour! With the prospect of durance vile staring him in the face he reluctantly came to Kitui and lifted the spell. The victim recovered rapidly. Later investigation uncovered a second recent case, in which he had told a victim that he would break his leg before the new moon was seen. Sure enough, a week or so later the man got off a bus before it had come to a complete stop, fell - and broke his leg. The African Court came under new presidency.

There was, therefore, for the most part, a yawning gap of culture and education. Unsurprisingly, the British officials, settlers and traders were at times paternalistic and snobbish. We can remember times when, if we had been African, we would have writhed in frustration at the actions and attitudes of some Europeans. Kennedy Trevaskis, (later Sir Kennedy Trevaskis KCMG OBE) returned to Northern Rhodesia after the war, some of which he had spent in the Administration in Eritrea, and he also was most unhappy about the bland arrogance that he had encountered.

I left for Northern Rhodesia under protest and I continued to protest having arrived there, and yet it was no bad thing that I should have had a chance to sit back in a state of detachment after so long a spell on the whirligig of Eritrean politics. In that sense I could not have gone to a better place. Northern Rhodesia and Eritrea were different worlds and they were moons apart....

Who, for example, would seriously have believed that here, in a British colony in the year 1950, a full blown colour bar would be flourishing? But it was. Segregation was total. Africans were not even allowed to enter white-owned shops. Wasn't this pretty shame-making? I put it to the local Provincial Commissioner, James Murray, for whom I was working as an Assistant. He looked surprised and said that he supposed it was a matter of what you were used to. I found it shocking, no doubt because I was not used to it. He, on the other hand, did not even notice and he could assure me that the Africans did not resent it in the least. Since every one was content with things as they were, why upset them?

Reprehensible as this was, and Trevaskis believed that it was more down to indolence than malice, it was not just the Europeans who felt that the lines of propriety were crossed if the races fraternised too closely. Joy Williams was surprised by the indignation of our houseboy, Salambo, when a leading politician, Tom Mboya, was invited to lunch. He was the guest of honour but Joy was embarrassed that Salambo refused to serve him first.

The question of club membership is one which is often pointed at as demonstrating a racial colour bar and to some extent this is true. However, one lady told me that when one is far away from home and living under the pressures of life it is understandable that one should be able to relax with one's own kind.

That being said, in 1951 a Nigerian Judge was blackballed from the Benin Club. The Resident in Benin was angry enough to withdraw the membership of himself and all his staff.

But it was easy to slip into the easy way of socialising with the people with whom officials had plenty in common and in the Sudan in 1946 Sir James Robertson was moved to remind his subordinates of the importance of social contacts with the local people. He wrote:

I feel very strongly that members of the British populations, are far from living up to the policy of the Government, ie to further the interests of the Sudanese. This is a major cause of suspicion and dislike of the British by the Sudanese. Many British seldom make any attempt to get into contact with their Sudanese staff or to meet them socially and influence them in a friendly way. It is little use planning for the political, economic, and educational future of the Sudan if we fail over the personal affect ... I should be grateful if you would personally encourage British officials to get to know and make friends with Sudanese officials. It is not always easy, but a real effort on these lines would pay handsome dividends alike to the Sudanese and to ourselves.

Reginald Davies went out to the Sudan in 1911 and he describes in his book *'The Camel's Back'* general mutual admiration and camaraderie. On one occasion, he and his "remote chief", the Inspector of Northern Kordofan, met to hunt down highwaymen who were robbing merchants on the Duem road. They called together the senior chiefs of the Kababish and Hawawir to meet the two officials at Jebel Haraza (which was quite some days' ride from the scene of the crimes.) The Sheikhs who foregathered there were told the story and asked to arrest any Tabrians who might try to take refuge with their people. The Sheikhs assured the officials that if the highwaymen took refuge with their tribes they would not remain undetected for long, 'except if they hide themselves under the ground'.

When official conversation was over, the Sheikhs looked around the straw rest house and asked what the "coloured paper" was for. They were playing cards with which the two men had played piquet on the moonlight halts and they set about teaching the Sheikhs poker which they played with enthusiasm.

Soon we were seated round a table and dramatic challenges were being exchanged in Arabic. Bluffing seemed to come to the Sheikhs quite naturally and the calling of a bluff, too.

'You increase me three sheep, you say? Good and I increase you a she-camel also!'

The bets were only imaginary and there was much laughter.

And much later Brian Carlisle also remarked upon this mutual regard that existed between Europeans and the Sudanese. In a letter to his fiancée, Hazel, in 1953 (a time when agitations for independence were gaining momentum) he described for her what he had been doing that day.

Ted Bickerstith came up in the morning for a meeting and came to lunch bringing an old Sudanese DC with him from Medani, who doesn't know English so our conversation throughout was all in Arabic...This afternoon I had a pleasant ride round the town on my horse chatting with many people. The Sudanese are so polite and charming and you can always get a laugh out of them.

The bond that existed between the Africans and the British was not considered remarkable; simply pleasant. Each cared for the other in their own fashion. Before she was married, and long before the Mau Mau of course, Joy Williams found herself alone on a remote farm. She never felt any fear because she knew that 'the chaps were nearby'. And so long as each individual behaved within the acceptable codes, there was no question of the boundaries of decent behaviour being crossed.

But some people did break the acceptable mores of behaviour. In the late 1920's Margaret Collyer, a formidable spinster pioneer, felt strongly about this.

Now that I have the opportunity I shall voice a matter that has often been uppermost in my thoughts which others perhaps have not sufficiently taken into consideration. In the days when ex-soldiers and closer settlement became the cry, amongst others a class of people came out to East Africa quite unused to having servants wait on them. Since black labour was very cheap these people were able to provide themselves with cooks, houseboys, and personal servants, a luxury they had never before known, and still less did they know how to treat their employees...[They] could be hit, knocked about by the men, and nagged at by the women, most of whom were afraid to be left alone with native servants at night. Cases of outrage and insolence by natives invariably occur to white women of this type. ... The outrages that have from time to time occurred when women have been left alone on farms are, nine times out of ten, entirely their own fault. I have myself seen women treat their personal servants, who have access to their bedrooms, in a most unbecoming and familiar fashion, allowing them in their rooms when they themselves have been less than half clothed, and, because the servant happens to have a black skin, ignoring before him all the niceties of decent behaviour.

This brings us to the question of sex. This is not so easy to assess because the subject was simply not discussed and certainly not in front of us children. But we can be sure that the thoughts strayed often enough among the unmarried officers, especially on lonely nights in distant places.

> *The maids of Merimandi*
> *Have breasts like moulded bronze*
> *And lips like sugar candy*

And eyes like muddy ponds.
The boys of Merimandi
Are a straight and comely breed
Their legs are never bandy
They smile like Ganymede.
And when a full moon's handy
Both girls and boys steal down
To Rigl Merimandi
To win lov's golden crown.
And little hares all sandy
And friendly frogs and bees
Creep down to Merimandi
To peer behind the trees.
No Dink nor naked Zande
Can taste such subtle joys
As the moon of Merimandi
Gives Arab girls and boys.

A Nosegay of Cacti" collected by J.S.S. Rowlands

Intermarriage was occasional and became almost unheard of and, as the Colonial Service became more regulated, it was increasingly frowned upon by the Colonial Service. The reason was unequivocal: it was necessary to maintain an easy and clear-cut authority without having to revert to hard disciplinarian methods because of murky social loyalties. More importantly, it was also necessary for officials to be able to move to different tribal areas without accusations of bias.

But in the early days in the Sudan in 1924 the intake of cadets were surprised to be informed that the Government had no objection to them 'marrying' Sudanese girls when serving in the out-districts.

'You cannot expect to find a sweet young virgin', they were told, 'so make sure she is healthy, and don't pick one from your own district or you are bound to be accused of partiality.'

Word of this announcement must have gone abroad and caused adverse comment, for no such official advice was given to later intakes.

It was this potential charge of partiality that provided officers with a sound reason as well as an excuse for rejecting tempting offers of this kind. Celibacy worried the Sudanese, who could not understand it, and darkly suspected homosexuality. As one grew older one was continually urged to do something about it.

81

'We understand,' said the President of a Baggara Court on one such occasion, during an interval between cases, 'that you Christians marry for life, and it is natural that you should think twice before committing yourself, but why not marry one of our girls in the meantime? You can take your pick, and when the time comes to divorce her, recover your cattle, and any of us will be happy to take her on.'

A handsome offer, and an intriguing prospect of having the candidates lined up for selection. But, as I pointed out, I was due to settle a boundary dispute with their neighbours and could get no credit for impartiality if I were united with them by ties of matrimony.

Outside the Service and particularly in Nigeria, European women met Nigerians at university in Britain and then came to Nigeria to live. One of these women who, when I met her, was an elderly and greatly respected widow, told me that although she had attended functions with her husband she always felt very looked down upon.

In Nigeria there was a distinguished circle of rich and sophisticated captains of commerce, together with Chiefs and potentates, often many times richer and certainly much more ostentatious than the British, who mixed socially with the Colonial Service and other Europeans. Official functions were graced with tall, richly dressed men and women with elaborate headdresses embroidered in gold and silver thread.

A love of sartorial elegance was an African trait and Henry Rangeley was able to admire a similar taste to his own when he had just arrived in Northern Rhodesia in 1902. He was introduced to Chief Lewanika, who was on his way to England to visit the King.

The chief was accompanied by his Prime Minister and a very fine pair of native gentlemen they were. I was introduced to the Chief as 'Mr Rangeley, who is going up to make laws for your people' and the old gentleman bowed from the waist and raised his hat, at the same time extending his hand, just as a polished Frenchman would do. We then gazed at each other in admiration. Both the Chief and myself fancied large shepherd's plaids, and his trousers and my coat would have made a suit. He did not speak any English and had perfect manners - for they were perfect under all circumstances.

Family relationships aroused great interest in the Africans and Johnny McCall, in Eastern Nigeria who was visited by his brother, Alan, *always told the Native chiefs that Alan was my brother. Comments varied from "What a fine boy your brother!" (joy of Alan) to 'Oh, sorry sir.' (joy of me)*

Africans are great laughers and we remember the weak jokes Hal Williams was fond of making sent them into paroxysms of mirth. On the whole their humour was strictly of the banana skin variety and nothing made them laugh as much as the discomfort of others.

In some areas of British administered Africa a great deal of diplomacy was required to maintain a constructive balance between the Government and the Chiefs. This happened where indirect rule was the name of the game. Sir Bryan Sharwood Smith who served most of his time in Northern Nigeria wrote:

We were taught at all times the prestige and authority of the chief and his administration must be upheld and that, should need arise to lodge a protest or to administer a reproof, care must be taken that neither he nor any of his subordinates or officials should be humiliated in the presence of subordinates or of the public. We were taught, too, that a government officer must on no account issue a direct order. Orders must always come from the chief or his representative. Only a grave emergency would justify deviation from this rule....

From the political point of view we were trying to train the natural leaders of the people to manage their own affairs to the point where we would be able to hand over complete control. From the practical point of view there was only one administrative officer to perhaps one hundred thousand northern Nigerians.

In most cases it seemed to work well and, in the main, with affection. When Sharwood Smith left Gwandu in the thirties he had to take his leave of Usumanu, the 16th Emir of Gwandu who *was one of the most dynamic and, at the same time, most lovable personalities with whom I ever worked. Erect and broad shouldered, the very personification of a warrior prince...I felt as though I were being parted from a family into which I had been accepted. For all of [the council] I had conceived a deep affection, above all, for the old man himself....My leave-taking with Emir Usumanu and his council took place in the engineer's house, where I had moved when my successor came to take over the division. The bond between us had grown strong and enduring, and as he drove away, he threw the folds of his cloak across his face.*

Bryan Sharwood Smith, in his book which is sub-titled "But always as Friends", found himself having to counsel the Chiroma, the heir apparent to the ageing Emir of Kano. Chiroma was arrogant and *autocratic in his manner and methods.*

'Chiroma, your father is an old man and I pray that he may be spared to us for many years yet.' Sharwood Smith told him, *'But these things are in the hands of Allah and the time could come, quite soon, when a new Emir will be appointed. The choice, as you know, does not lie with me but with the Traditional Selectors. They may well choose you; I think they will. But of this I am sure. You have many*

83

enemies in this city. Therefore, unless you begin now to make yourself more acceptable to the common people who live within its walls, and unless you begin now to show sympathy for their grievances, on the day that you are chosen as Emir there will be rioting in the streets, stones will fly and blood will flow and things could happen that could make it impossible for your appointment to be approved.'

Sharwood Smith continued:

As I spoke a stony expression came over the Chiroma's face and his brows knit. For a while there was silence. Then his face cleared and he turned to me with a smile and said "You are quite right. I will remember what you have said ... always."

It is perhaps hard for some to believe that the atmosphere in British Africa during those few short years was so uncomplicated. Of course it was not the garden of Eden and apart from such rebellious outbreaks such as the Mau Mau and the Dini ya Msambwa there were resentful young people about such as there always have been in any country and ever will it be so.

It was not only the British who were sometimes baffled by the gulf which divided the African races from the British. The subtitle of Sir Bryan Sharwood Smith's book comes from a speech of one of Nigeria's finest sons, Sir Abubaka Tafawa Balewa, who said on Independence Day, 1 October 1960, *"We are grateful for the British officers whom we have known, first as masters and then as leaders and, finally, as partners but always as friends."*

Despite his deep knowledge and regard for the British Sir Abubaka could still be surprised by them. When he was Minister of Works and Transport in 1951 he was taken by his Private Secretary, R.L. Armstrong, to see the replacement of a junction in the 36 inch water-main to the Lagos water supply.

The operation had to be done when demand for water was at its lowest, in fact between 1 a.m. and 3 a.m. When we arrived, the excavation and timbering had already been completed, the water had been shut off and the faulty section removed. The work of connecting the new section was in progress and the Minister saw it being lowered into the trench and correctly aligned. In the trench under the brilliant arc-lights the operation was being directed by a British senior Inspector of Works helped by another British Inspector and his African staff and workforce.

The whole operation, well planned in advance, was completed within the time-limit and the flow of potable water to Lagos resumed. The Minister appeared to be intensely interested in every detail as the Water Engineer explained each process as it occurred.

84

On the way back to Lagos in the car, he was for the most part silent. Suddenly he turned [to] me, 'There were Europeans down that hole with the Africans' he said. 'It happens all the time Minister.' I replied.
'Do you know,' he said, 'I never thought it happened like that.'

The D.C.

Arthur Collyer poses in his unsuitable suit with his white pith helmet at Rumuruti, Kenya. His sister, Olive, is clearly teasing him with this caption.

Chapter 7

NOT FAIR DEALINGS

The Saxon is not like us Normans. His manners are not so polite.
But he never means anything serious till he talks about justice and right.
When he stands like an ox in the furrow with his sullen set eyes on your own,
And grumbles, "This isn't fair dealings," my son, leave the Saxon alone.

Rudyard Kipling

One forgets the endless scroll of past failures on which the names of men of every race are written and the miseries they have inflicted on this continent of suffering, and remembers only those who with patient fidelity gave their lives to bring nearer in Africa the long-delayed victory of justice.

Dr Norman Leys, who wrote those words in his book "Kenya", said that Arthur Collyer was one of the people he had had in mind when paying tribute to those who had tried to bring the victory of justice to Africa. He was an admirer and friend of Collyer's, whose service in the early Kenya Administration was both brief and melancholy. Nonetheless, during the short time that he was an administrative officer in the Colony, Collyer displayed a stolid stout-heartedness as he faced his own inevitable early death while at the same time risking the opprobrium of his superiors by defending the rights of the Masai. He arrived in Kenya from Oxford in c1900 but it may have been a year or two earlier. Both his family and he himself probably hoped that the warmth of the tropics would help him recover from the tuberculosis from which he suffered. Of course, this was simply not going to happen in those days. A medical friend of his wrote after his death. *Only doctors know how inefficient they can be.*

As he was our great uncle, we have been able to study the photographs which he and his sister, Olive, took during the time that they lived in the DC's house in Rumuruti from 1905 until 1911. They made a beautiful garden in the semi-desert around the house which gave pleasure to DCs and their wives throughout the colonial period. They were able to do so by storing water in a dam or pond. Most of the tribes of Africa moved to new water sources when necessary and the Europeans brought the ancient skill of water storage to that part of the world. Who knows, that garden and pond may be there still.

Arthur was a tall and rather heavily built man in his late twenties or early thirties and although he does not smile in any of the photographs, there is the ghost of a twinkle in a couple of them; but there is also a sadness about him which is rather heart-breaking.

From the few papers that survive, it seems that he coped with his illness by ignoring it. A friend of the family wrote that *His was a fine character and he faced his broken life with the utmost courage and patience.* These do not seem to have been merely kind words they are borne out by records. From 12th December to the 29th of December, 1910, for example, he went on safari, walking every day: ten miles, fifteen miles, twelve miles. He only remained in camp on the 19th *waiting for the Masai to come back with with H[ut] T[ax] money.* On the 25th of December he only walked six miles, but he made no mention that it was Christmas Day. Never once does he allude to tiredness or ill health. We quote from his entry in notes made on a tax collecting safari north of Rumuruti on 17 December 1910 which is written in pencil on a large lined pad. It is typical of his plain, utterly practical style: *Up the hill, through some olive wood. Trees rather stunted and then a descent to Lorogli District. Camped on* [illegible] *Narok* [river] *close to the east end of it; water was not flowing – march about 4 ½ hrs. Before descending all the Lorogli country was visible and Kisunia[?} to the East. 13 or 14 miles. The country is very dry but there's still plenty of grazing. Here there are signs of not being so fed down as the country near the boma. Collected taxes from plain"*

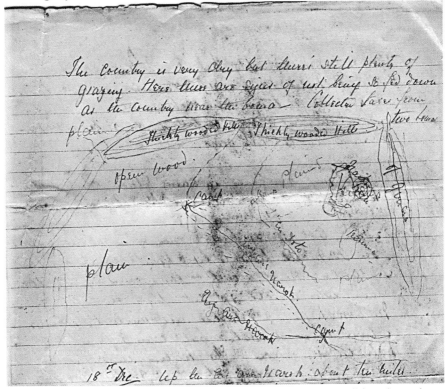

An extract from Collyer's notes appears to show that he was walking through largely uncharted country.

The notes of this safari ended with:

28 Dec: Long march across dry plains which appeared as though they would never end. A little rain on the road. No water passed. Early in the march it took us about an hour to shake off an unfortunate rhino who would not go away.

He was in the [illegible] and finally after running parallel with us and then crossing us in front he made off; latter part of the march over very bad going on account of [illegible] valley of the Narok. Camped on a small ravine at a good waterhole called the Saneburuburu. The afternoon lion scare which turned out to be hyenas. Distance 15 to 16 miles.

29th Dec: Along the valley of the Narok to where the Aiyan comes in about 14 miles – country very dry indeed. One boma of Masai on the Aiyan – every appearance that the light rains have failed over most of the district.

Physical courage he certainly seems to have had in some measure but it was the sorry business of the moving of the Masai tribe where Arthur showed moral bravery.

Many Europeans, settlers and officials alike, liked and admired the Masai tribe. They must be one of the most beautiful people in Africa and they are considered to be brave and gentle, with independent and warrior-like characteristics. They did have their detractors, though, who considered them to be dirty, hubristic, and indolent with distasteful, even cruel, sexual practices involving children.

They raided also so that their warriors might blood their spears, usually by falling suddenly, in organized armed parties, on virtually defenceless hamlets or single individuals. And they raided to provide themselves with human breeding stock, women capable of bearing children.

Their own women, while still 'Nditu', that is, little girls of from nine or ten to fifteen or so, were assigned as concubines to the 'manyattas', the camps of warriors or 'Moruak' (sing. 'Moran'). After a childhood as a promiscuous barrack prostitute these unhappy creatures were of course little use as the mothers of the next generation, so these were acquired by spears in an earlier day, and since by purchase for cattle, usually from the Kikuyu, Chagga and Arusha.

Arthur Collyer was devoted to the Masai and he spoke their language. From around 1905 until early 1911 he was District Commissioner at Rumuruti which was the area in which the Northern Masai lived, known as Laikipia. He had their interests very much at heart and at one time he asked for *permission to import Merino rams to cross with the woolless Masai sheep* [but he] *was forbidden to do so, on the grounds that if the*

Masai began to breed for wool they would begin to steal sheep from their European neighbours.

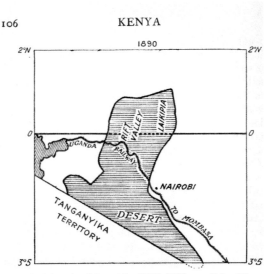

The area occupied by the Masai in 1890 ("*Kenya*" by Norman Leys)

In 1906 the tribe had become split into two sections when Lord Delamere and a London syndicate were granted permission to buy land on the floor of the great Rift Valley: that gargantuan fault running north/south with its golden grasses, lakes and volcanoes. Before the advent of the colonial administration, the Masai grazing areas extended from the Uaso Nyiro River in the North East of Kenya, right across the Rift Valley to the Tanganyika border to the south west of the Rift, and beyond. They were lords of an immense area of wonderful land and they were fiercely protective of it, demanding money off strangers who wished to pass through it – or face their spears.

From 1890 the tribe's fortunes changed for the worse. Disease and famine swept across the land, killing stock and decreasing the tribal numbers dramatically. The Rift Valley looked, for all the world, virtually unoccupied. Nevertheless, in order to accommodate Delamere and his friends, a treaty was drawn up in 1904 on the

91

instructions of the Foreign Office. Lenana, the chief Masai Laibon spoke for the tribe. This treaty proposed to move the Masai out of the Rift Valley, leaving them with a split territory north and south of it with a half-mile-wide corridor across the valley floor in order that the two sections could remain in close contact. The Foreign Office would not allow the Masai to be moved out of the Rift without the tribe's consent by treaty, but nonetheless: *The Rift Valley was most unwillingly evacuated.*

The half-mile-wide corridor across the Rift was never honoured. Some say that the reason for this was fear of spreading tick-borne diseases which is probably partly true. But the fact remains that the redesignation of the Rift Valley separated the two sections of the tribe by many miles and this created a great problem for them and for Lenana, who lived in the southern section. The northern section, led by Legalishu, was allocated the land north of the Rift, to the Samburu lands north of Rumuruti. By not honouring the clause in the treaty allocating a half-mile-wide corridor across the Rift, Lenana – who was the senior of all the Laibon – found it difficult to exert his influence. The plan had been that the two sections would meet regularly at a religious site at the Kinangop. Norman Leys says that the splitting of the tribe caused *great unrest and mistrust ... and these were increased by the rumour, then freely talked of in the country, that the northern reserve was to be given to Europeans.*

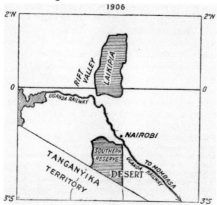

Showing the split Masai reserve in 1906.

92

Poor young Arthur. Liked and trusted by the tribe, he *made a special tour round the reserve to give assurances that the Government would keep its solemn pledge;* that what had been agreed by treaty would not be changed. For someone who was described as a man *with absolute straightness and conscientiousness* and *a very warm and loyal person,* what a blow he must have had when began to dawn on him that the new Governor, Sir Percy Girouard, was plotting to persuade the tribe to move out of Laikipia altogether.

Arthur Collyer's safari porters and askaris.

At the end of 1909 or early 1910 he was sent on a six week reconnaissance of the additional land south of the Rift Valley which, it was proposed, would be given to the entire Masai tribe. From his notes, the fear of shortage of water was a very real one. (see Chapter 10)

A pencil-written, and rather difficult to decipher, report covers a discussion between Arthur and thirteen elders, (all named) including Legalishu. Legalishu was an interesting character. Rather odd-looking, he was nonetheless described by Sir Frederick Jackson as a spare and wiry little man who excelled as a *patriot, delegate, obstructionist, call him what you like.* At this discussion Mr Collyer asked the elders' opinion on the proposal being discussed between Lenana and the Governor of the Colony *to move the Masai, as the N. Masai reserve is not sufficient for Masai stock. The Masai will get a part of Ologorot – there are two rivers Mangori and Oigani. H.E. told me to tell [the] Masai that they will get Ologoroki and not to be afraid [about lack] of water as it will be irrigated. Will send a man to see about it ... H.E. wishes to tell the Masai that the boundary of Laikipia cannot be extended.*

Another influential figure, Loyele, who had inspected the southern area commented: *We gave all the information of the country that we travelled and all Masai say it is insufficient but if Govt wants to move the Masai – can do so – we have no strength to fight with Govt.*

All the elders felt the same and Legalishu summed up the rather sad theme of this meeting: *We are willing to obey the Govt order as it is not our order. Formerly you said that we will get this country and road to go to Laibon S. Masai Reserve – we know that all our stock will die if we are moved the other side.*

A Masai family in the Rumuruti or Laikipia area c 1908 (family archive)

A series of negotiations took place, one of which was in May 1909 when Arthur went down to Nairobi and accompanied the Governor at a meeting with some of the tribe. Considering that there were no cars or roads, this seriously ill young man did not spare himself. In February 1910 the Governor had a meeting with the Masai elders *at the camp known as Kiserian, close to the kraal of Lenana.* Reading the

94

report, written in Mr Collyer's hand and then typed up, presumably for the benefit of His Excellency, everything looks logical, constructive and friendly:

After greeting Lenana, His Excellency reminded him that he had previously expressed a wish to see Lenana and the Chiefs of the Northern Masai.

He wished to discuss the question of the position of the lands now occupied by the Masai. The government had formerly made an arrangement that some of the Masai went to Laikipia while the others remained in what is known as the Southern Masai reserve, and had promised at the same time to send an officer to Laikipia whom the Masai knew. This had been done. [ie Collyer had been sent to Rumuruti.]

Since this arrangement had been made, circumstances had altered, and now the Government feared that unless all the Masai were located in one locality they would be split into sections, and the Northern section would be pushed farther north. His Excellency pointed out that this would not happen today but that he could foresee that it would happen in the future.

There then followed discussion about which land in the south would be allotted to them.

Masikonde and his children. c. 1910. Taken by Arthur Collyer

Masikondi was now asked what he had to say, and he expressed his opinion in

95

favour of moving with the other Purko [N. Masai] from Laikipia so that the
Masai should all be together.
Legalishu also expressed his opinion in favor [sic] *of the move. ...*
At his Excellency's request Mr Collyer addressed the Laikipia chiefs, telling
them that as a friend of the Masai he was satisfied that the proposed move was to
the interest of the Masai themselves.

This appears to be disingenuous of His Excellency and it put Collyer
in an impossible position. Just how unhappy he felt about it is
encapsulated in a letter which Leys says was sent to the Governor
"by a subordinate official." These phrases demonstrate the flavour
of the letter:

...the Masai left the Rift Valley five years ago in obedience to the wish of the
Government and ... in return for that surrender of their best land they were given
by the Government a promise never again to be disturbed; ... most of the Masai
now in the northern reserve prefer to stay where they are; ... they are to go from
country ardently desired by Europeans ...

The great bulk of the natives who have experience of the nature and working of
our occupation of the country believe that it is designed for the advantage and
profit of officials and their fellow-countrymen. If one tries to explain the contrary
one is met with almost universal incredulity, ...

The careful deliberation of the Government, its conferences and consultations, the
very kindliness of its representatives, will by many natives be put down as
hypocrisy and guile of those who prefer to take without the trouble of using force.
In the view of some men this attitude is more serious than sedition.

Leys is coy about who wrote this passionate letter to the Governor.
He says it was a "subordinate official" but then a paragraph later
refers to the views expressed in the letter as "Mr Collyer's frankness"
and it is known in our family that Arthur wrote a "Minority Report"
which leads us to conclude that he might have be the author of the
letter and sent a copy to Dr. Leys who was also incensed over the
affair.

A year later the rug was well and truly pulled out from under the
Northern Masai case when Lenana died and, according to Leys

96

expressing with his last breath the wish that his people should always obey the Government, especially by leaving Laikipia. And leave they did, in 1911. Some of the elderly and many thousands of cattle died because of the cold on the high Mau range which they had to cross.

Once his usefulness was finished, Arthur Collyer was posted to Nyeri under something of a cloud. He wrote to Dr Leys to say that *the manoeuvres etc., that have been employed with regard to the Masai have sickened and embittered me. I have always said that the policy of putting the Masai into one area was right, but I cannot uphold the methods that have been employed to bring this about.*

His physical condition deteriorated rapidly in Nyeri and his sister, Olive, who had been such a staunch companion to him, increasingly did his work for him. He was said to worship the ground Olive trod on but he died without her beside him because she was on a tax collecting safari.

Amongst his papers I found a letter from a Mr McClellan to my great aunt, Olive, about Arthur's death. Looking up McLellan in "Tribute to Pioneers", it seems that McClellan was senior to Collyer and based at Naivasha: he was *responsible for the movement of Masai from the Rift Valley.* Are his condolences tempered with a wisp of guilt?

Naivasha Oct. 26. 12
Dear Miss Collyer,
I was very grieved to hear of the sudden death of your brother with whom I had been associated at one time and another for several years and had always considered one of my friends in the country.
When you and he left for Nyeri it was hoped that the fact of a healthy station and reasonably good house accommodation would have a beneficial effect on his health ... [illegible] I well knew that Mr Collyer had a great admiration for the Masai, as had most officers with whom they came in contact, especially in the earlier days of our administration, but he expressed to me pleasure in leaving ... the Masai under existing conditions. I can only hope that the change of work and climate was not detrimental.

Yours sincerely,
Sgd: J.W.T.   McClellan

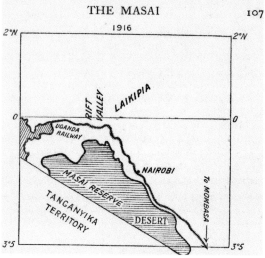

Post Scripts

Arthur Collyer was not the only person to lose his job over the Masai moves. Sir Percy Girouard resigned. Dr. Norman Leys died six years after Arthur – also of tuberculosis.

Many years passed and Arthur Collyer's niece, Joy Williams, found herself in 1945 living in Narok, District Headquarters of the Masai area where the whole Masai tribe had lived since 1911. One day a very old man arrived in the boma looking for "Collyon's" relative whom he wished to salute in Arthur's memory.

One of the problems was that the Masai tended greatly to overgraze land. Joy Williams told us that when he was in Rumuruti, Arthur Collyer would show visitors, including Masai elders, to the line between the European managed land and the Masai grazing areas. The comparison between waving grasses on the European land and the dusty sparse Masai grazing was stark.

It was not just the European farmers who gained from the Masai move from Laikipia. The Samburu tribe, long harassed by the Masai, had found themselves steadily being pushed northwards by their hubristic neighbours. There are many scenes of bloody battles still named and remembered. Since the Masai moved south the Samburu and the ranchers have coexisted in relative harmony.

Arthur Collyer and Freize

Hal Williams (and Pansy) with his Italian counterparts from Somaliland c
1933

Chapter 8

NEW BOY AT THE OFFICE

The first six months as a supernumary DO in Kiambu, fifteen miles outside Nairobi, gave Hal Williams cause *to wonder if I had chosen the right career.* He was allotted a gloomy vicarage some distance from the Boma (administrative station) in which to live. He could not, of course, afford a car and living away from the other houses as well as being the new boy, it was a lonely start.

He had also been somewhat daunted to learn that the decision to post him to Kiambu was made because of his reputation as a cricketer. He was a keen cricketer and he had captained his school side but he was not sure he was up to being the lynch pin for the officials against the settlers in a match which loomed shortly after his arrival. Fortunately he did not disgrace himself and he was relieved *to get a quick thirty odd* as his contribution to an overwhelming victory for the officals.

Six months later he was posted to Meru where a chance meeting gave him the opportunity he sought to work in the "blue, blue, blue" and he found himself, in 1932, appointed District Officer, Mandera.

Mandera is to be found in the northern Kenya desert at the junction of the borders of Somalia, Ethiopia and Kenya. At that time the

Boma consisted of *a piece of sandy desert, surrounded by barbed wire in which were to be found numerous temporary buildings and the DO's house.* To the north was Ethiopia – Abyssinia as it was then known - and to the east was Italian Somaliland whose boundary was marked by a few broken beacons.

The DO's house was a flat-roofed stone dwelling which was said to have been erected by a previous DO named Pease who let it be known that anyone wishing to see him would only be attended to if he had brought a stone.

There was a tree opposite the house which was riddled with bullet holes, inflicted, it was said, by Hugh Grant who would fire at the tree whenever he left the house, using two duelling pistols he kept on his belt. There lived Hal, 23 years old, with memories of England still fresh in his mind and accompanied by a terrier-type called Pansy.

A mile from Mandera ran the River Dawa which supplied the station with water. A string of camels loaded with barrels would make their daily trek to and from the river. Hal began a vegetable garden on the banks of the Dawa. He grew tomatoes, French beans, beetroot and carrots but baboon ate most of the produce. They also had a go at Pansy.

When he arrived in Mandera a rebuilding programme was initiated. He was given six hundred shillings for station buildings such as the tribal police lines, a customs shed and a new roof for the office *using a few main poles for support, wire netting and makuti* [dried dom palm leaves.]

Besides the DO and the tribal police, the station was inhabited by a British Policeman called Horley, soon to be replaced by Bertie Instone, a Goan cashier called D'Costa and an interpreter, Ahamed Abdi. The Policeman and the DO took turns to stay in the Boma while the other went on safari.

There were also four or five tribal policemen. These were men of good character who came from the local tribes. Discipline was strict with a high standard of conduct expected and *regular shooting training was de riguer at Mandera.*

Amongst his other duties, the DO was the Customs Officer, required to collect duty for goods brought into Kenya for the purpose of trade. He also had to patrol the border against illicit activities from Italian Somaliland. One of these was leopard trapping. In 1933 leopard had been added to the schedules of animals for which a licence was necessary and trapping became an offence under the Game Ordinance. However, the Italians had no such ordinance and there was a great demand from them for skins.

Although the population in the Northern Frontier Province was sparse, it consisted of small tribes and sub-tribes scattered over the desert, and peace had to be maintained between them. This was further complicated by the nomads constantly shifting back and forth across frontiers which made tax collecting and law enforcement haphazard. In the Mandera area alone Hal's parishioners, as he called them, consisted of Gurreh, Regodia, Murille, Marehan, Leisan, Gurre Murre, Shabelle, Ashraf and Warabeh. It must have been rather confusing to a young man from the home counties.

Some of the tribes were agricultural people but the majority were nomads. To complicate matters still further the Gurreh were not only sub-divided into three but they all had a long-standing feud with the Regodia.

The Gurreh liked to embroider their stories and were prone to exaggeration. One night during the *Jilal* (dry season) two exhausted Gurreh came into Hal's camp at Kilitcha and told him of five Gurreh dead during a raid. *They told me how they had personally buried two of the dead and they had seen the other three stretched out by the river.* When he hurried to the scene of such slaughter, he found only one man had been killed.

The Government employed headmen to act as the link between each tribe and the administration. Each headman was well-known to the DO, in whose gift the appointment was and a mutually respectful relationship existed. The Headmen were helped by two sub-Headmen, or "sagale" recognisable by wearing turbans. As there was

103

money in these appointments, DO's were cautioned to watch for turbaned pseudo-sagale after backsheesh.

Although there were one or two lorries in the District, the main form of transport at that time was camels, hire of which cost 50 cents per day. If, however, a camel died while on Government duty the owner was reimbursed thirty shillings with no hire paid.

Luxuries were few and it was a solitary existence for a young man but it was here that Hal was introduced to *that heavenly nectar of whisky in water cooled in a 'chargul' swinging from the side of a lorry or camel* after a hot and tiring day.

District Headquarters was at Moyale, about one hundred and sixty miles to the west. There resided the District Commissioner, Major "Mug" Mullins. Letters were exchanged between them, taken by lorry or camel.

Unfortunately Hal's letters to his District Commissioner no longer exist but correspondence from Mullins to Williams give an interesting picture of the subjects which preoccupied a colonial servant in a distant, sparsely populated African outpost.

They are often long, detailed and domestic:

Please send the lerios and kibets as soon as you can as mine are very old now. Kibet is the more important mat on a camel. It is put on first furry side downwards and the lerio on top, furry side upwards. Kibets are made from the bark of various trees.

They also showed a cadet that if a man stayed in those desert wastes too long he could veer between being crankily anti-humanity to touchingly eager for genial company in the space of a few days.

2 October 1932 Moyale

Dear Williams,

... I am glad to hear that things are OK in Mandera because I'm damned if they are here. The Boran and the Wagaleh have got stuck into each other again and there are now seven less Wagaleh and thirteen less Boran in the Moyale district. ..

6th November 1932 Moyale

... I'm glad you are enjoying Mandera: I wish I were there instead of here! Let me know how long you are going to be on safari roughly. I arranged with Beetham to send his draft intelligence reports here for typing – it saves contradictions. I seldom alter anything, but we don't want to send two reports to the P.C. [Provincial Commissioner] from one district which don't agree.

Cheerio,

Yrs

A.C. Mullins

PS I shouldn't worry about the 'Mr'.

12 December 1932   Moyale

I'm glad you enjoyed the safari even if you didn't meet many people. I think one is frequently disappointed up here in the number of people one meets on safari – or rather doesn't. ...

I don't know where Abdulla Alio and Aden Heist want to make shambas [fields/gardens]. They usually have them on the Ramu – El Wak road and do quite well so there is no earthly reason for them to come to the river. ...

Thank you for the lerios and kibets and for the gum [gum Arabic] ...

I am sorry to hear that tax is coming in so slowly but we must just go on nagging at them and being hopeful with the rotten markets we have. ...

I'm afraid I can't find you another cent for the office roof as the vote is already overspent. We will see what can be done when I come across. ...

Sorry to hear you have been finding Weir queer. He is I know a bit strange at times. ...

Norman arrived yesterday so my peaceful existence is disturbed. I'm afraid that having spent a certain time in Turkana and the north I like to live my own solitary life and don't like having anyone with me and having to entertain them.

27 December 1932 [my father's 24th birthday] Moyale

Just a brief scrawl as I am absolutely snowed under, and with these blasted Xmas holidays no one will do anything.

Chiefly to thank you for an extremely pleasant stay in Mandera which I enjoyed immensely. *I only wish that I could have managed to stay longer and see more of you.*

I know of no definite results but we beat you [probably the varsity rugby match] *and England defeated Australia by 10 wickets.*

I will write a decent (I mean longer) letter.

29 December 1932 Moyale
Dear Williams,
This too I am afraid will be a somewhat brief letter. There seems to be such a lot

to do and the P.C. has asked all sorts of questions in the last post - not to mention the fact that there are five headmen here and I am feeling perfectly foul.

We had a fair journey back. Birchaka was a running river and we had to go round on the old road where we got stuck and had to unload. We had a fairly sticky time and met several more running rivers before the Ali Wando which was too deep to cross in the dark. After that matters improved.

Yours,

A.C. Mullins

Early in 1933 Gerald Reece took over from Major Mullins as DC Moyale. From his letters he gives the impression of being a martinet whose irascible tone at times must have been rather trying to a young DO stuck in Mandera often on his own for long periods. However, Joy Williams told us that the general attitude towards Reece – who rose far in the Colonial Service and was made a knight of the Realm – was one of affectionate tolerance.

Although he did not appear to be blessed with a cheery, calm nature, he was hard working, he travelled his district constantly and his heart was in the right place.

The Moyale people are not very mindful or considerate. He complained from safari near Malka Re. *I have had no mail for three months. ...*

I am writing again because I did wrong to worry you about the likelihood of a raid. Do not let it worry you. I have no definite information. ... One can do no more than send out a patrol or two and keep one's eyes and ears skinned. One must maintain a fair sized garrison in the boma. ...

Very many thanks for sending off the wireless messages and for dealing with the sick man and for borrowing the posho [maize meal] *and for sending the meat camels. ...*

Please tell Muhammed Aden that I will buy his goats unless they are very big ones. 4/- and 5/- [shillings] is too much now-a-days, but I like to help the old man when I can.

I heard no firing in the direction of Dolo yesterday.

G. Reece

Letter from Gerald Reece – 20th March, 1933.

When I was at Dolo recently Basha Minda, who is in charge of the soldiers on the Oddo side, asked that a rifle which belonged to him and which had been stolen by Bou Marehan last year, should be returned.

2. It appears that one of his men, Maio Abdi by name, was assaulted by a Bou Marehan who then fled to British territory with his rifle. The rifle was taken from him and given to the District Officer at Mandera.

3. Would you kindly investigate the matter.   *G. Reece*

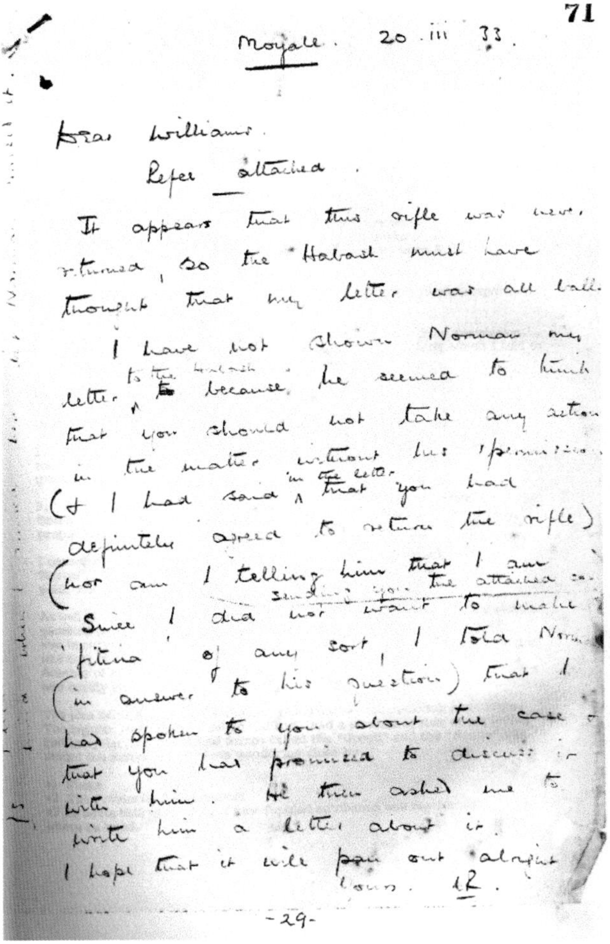

71

Moyale. 20.iii.33.

Dear Williams.

Refer attached.

It appears that this rifle was never returned, so the Habash must have thought that my letter was all balls.

I have not shown Norman my letter to the Habash because he seemed to think that you should not take any action in the matter without his permission. (& I had said in the letter that you had definitely agreed to return the rifle) (nor am I telling him that I am sending you the attached since I did not want to make 'fitina' of any sort, I told Norman (in answer to his question) that I had spoken to you about the case & that you had promised to discuss it with him. He then asked me to write him a letter about it.

I hope that it will pan out alright

Yours. GR.

-29-

Letter from Gerald Reece – 20th March 1933.

Dear Williams, Refer Attached.

It appears that this rifle was never returned, so the Habash must have thought that my letter was all balls.

I have not shown Norman my letter to the Habash because he seemed to think that you should not take any action in the matter without his permission. (and I had said in the letter that you had definitely agreed to return the rifle). (nor am I telling him that I am sending you the attached since I did not want to make a 'fitina' (quarrel*) of any sort, I told Norman (in answer to his question) that I had spoken to you about the case and you had promised to discuss it with him.*

He then asked me to write him a letter about it. I hope that it will pan out alright. Yours GR.

24 May 1933   Moyale
I hope that you are getting me 12 – 20 recruits for tribal police from Regodia and Murille etc. I don't want Gurreh (but the KAR [Kings African Rifles] do.) Every effort must be made to get Somali T.P.s [tribal police]. ... It is no good recruiting one man at a time. We must take on about 20, and amongst them there may be perhaps one or two who are suitable. I like to try them out here with boxing, riding, gymnastics, running etc & shooting. What I most care about is that they should be able to tell the truth, shoot and ride a horse. ...

They should not be allowed to get swollen heads but they must not be required (as used to happen) to do all the dirty work for the Police when on safari. They are a separate unit with definite duties of their own; not a gang of shenzi askaris [shabby soldiers] to be used for herding Police mules and fetching their water etc. ...with the result that only boys or shenzi town sods will agree to enlist as tribal police. ...

But don't worry about anything. I think you are doing a very good job of work, and any time I may criticise at Mandera is not due to your fault. I am looking forward to seeing you again.
G. Reece

20 August 1939   Moyale
Dear Williams,
Will you please note

  1. *That Tribal Police should never be allowed to wear anything when on duty except regulation clothing. When off duty they may wear uniform if clean and complete, or their own clothes, but not half and half. I write this because I find that here they have acquired a habit of going on safari with shirts, police puttees, shorts, etc etc., worn together with their official dress, which looks too awful. When wearing uniform, even if they are merely visiting the dukas (shops), of course belts must be worn & the clothing must be clean.*

110

2. *That Glenday (the Provincial Commissioner) worries me persistently if monthly intelligence reports are unduly delayed. He minds about this very much.*

3. *That camel safaris from Moyale should not be diverted without permission. ... Infinite bother has been caused by your sending my last safari, which I told to go to Mandera, to el Wak.*

   GR

9 Sept 1933   *Dedatcha Korma Adow*
Dear Williams,

1. *Will you please come on here in the lorry at once. I have with me some 60 female camels that I have collected for tax and hear there is no grazing for them around Muddi. ...*

2. *I am considerably exercised in my mind over the state of affairs I find here. ... I am now awaiting you to come with me into the Degodia area proper, for which you are primarily responsible.*

   I cannot believe that you are deliberately disobeying my orders about tickets to be given to heads of villages for any & every portion of tax paid. And I must conclude that all these people are telling me lies.

   GR

As well as the duties of tax collector and customs officer, the DO Mandera was also gazetted as Assistant Immigration Officer while yet another of his duties was to survey the border with Italian Somaliland and mend the beacons. He was not, of course, a surveyor but *that did not matter in the least.* Another of his tasks was to construct a road alongside that boundary. *This was hardly an autobahn as it was only four yards wide.*

The idea behind the new road was to help control Italian-Somali marauders. The regular Italian army, called Centuri, had a strange system of employing two irregular, undisciplined forces called the "Googly" and the "Banda" who raided the Kenya nomad clans wandering close by.

The Italians took a great interest in the goings on at Mandera and sent innumerable spies to report. My father found the Italian Officials very obliging over small matters, but a general air of suspicion and distrust seemed to prevail with regard to British subjects, especially government servants, who visited Italian territory. They were invariably followed about, watched closely and, no doubt, reported upon.

The River Dawa not only supplied Mandera with water but it demarcated part of the boundary with Ethiopia. When the meagre rains fell, the tribesmen would move away from the river to graze, returning during the *Jilal*. In the Ethiopian province of Oddo on the Kenya border, Hal Williams wrote that *the Abyssinians were wild and lawless and it was hard to tell who were soldiers and who were bandits. They used to levy a fine on all stock grazing on the Abyssinian side of the Dawa during the Jilal. This was encouraged by the Ethiopian officials although I made an agreement with them that they should not levy a fine on stock which had accidentally strayed across the dry river.*

On the Ethiopian boundary the Policeman, Weir's replacement, Bertie Instone, said that the senior Ethiopian official was a tall one-eyed man called Birara who could not speak Kiswahili but, having been educated in Cairo, spoke French. He would arrive accompanied by two or three officers *festooned with cartridge belts, armed with rifles, plus an escort of a dozen or so riff-raffish lads armed with rifles. A youth walked behind Birara holding a parasol over [his] head.* Instone added that Hal Williams entertained Birara with his 'heavenly nectar' which *he reckoned was well worth it, for we certainly got most of our stolen stock back, minus, of course a few as commission.*

The scarcity of water was a constant source of friction. *We have been having a good deal of trouble over the Boran"* wrote Reece from Moyale in August 1933, *"murders & quarrelling with the Habash at the wells.*

During the *Jilal* water could only be found in the river by digging and life was particularly perilous for the nomads who were constantly harassed, not only by Ethiopian officials but also by rustlers from the Ethiopian side of the border who would swoop upon the cattle

112

which congregated in their numbers by the side of the Dawa. Consequently, the DO at Mandera was obliged to spend much of the *Jilal* on the banks of the Dawa. *The result of this," said Hal, "was that the DO could see many of his 'parishioners' without having to travel too far.*

Grazing principles had to be strictly observed in order that there should be sufficient for everyone; *First, the grazing away from the river should be finished before the river grazing was touched, and second that cattle should take precedence over camels in the use of river grazing.* He pointed an accusing finger at the Regodia tribe who he said were the chief culprits in breaking the latter rule.

Grazing rules, leopard licences, tax collecting, picking out twenty Somali with a potential for boxing and telling the truth (but not having swollen heads) sharing his whisky with bandoliered Ethiopians to ensure the return of his parishioners' stock, and responding to cranky letters from his superior. These were not by any means a light responsibility or a life of ease but it certainly beat into a cocked hat most other forms of employment for a twenty-three year old from Bedford.

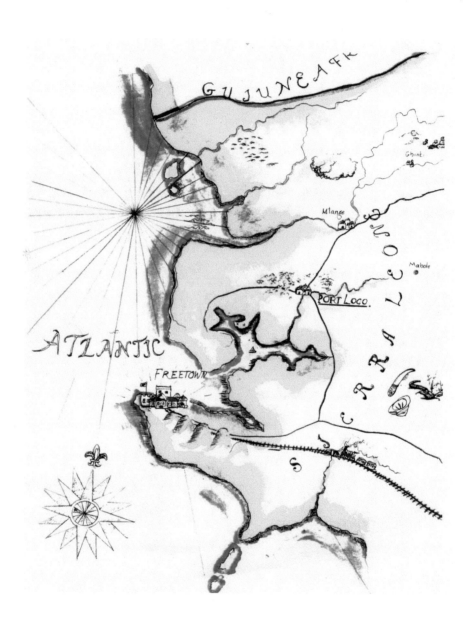

With grateful thanks to Angus Forbes for drawing this map.

Chapter 9

BABY TAYLOR'S MOSQUITO

In the early nineteen thirties a magnanimous Government of Sierra Leone decided that the Assistant District Commissioner at Port Loko could have a house. Until then he had lived in a mud hut with a grass roof.

£60 (there were twenty shillings to one pound) was allocated, but even this munificence was barely sufficient, despite the fact that a labourer's daily wage was only one shilling. The Assistant District Commissioner at Port Loko at the time was Pat O'Dwyer. He decided to cut costs by clearing the area himself. Because it was evening when he started work, he discarded his khaki topi, or helmet. He set about chopping at a large bush when he suddenly felt a terrific pain in the top of his head as though a nail had been driven into it, and a two foot, stumpy green mamba fell onto his shoulder and slithered to the ground.

Unsure about the type of snake which had bitten him, O'Dwyer went to the house of his superior, the District Commissioner, 'Baby' Taylor. Now, Baby was busy. He was writing a report and clearly his mind was not on his subordinate's predicament because he asked "Are you sure it was not a mosquito?"

The young ADC returned to his hut to consider his options. His servant, Brimah, immediately knew it was "a very bad snake" and wanted to call upon the services of the local witch doctor. Official British advice was to cut the wound open, apply permanganate of potash and tie a tourniquet round a point nearer the heart.

Strangulation seemed to defeat the object and other options appearing to be limited, Pat asked Brimah for a brandy. By this time his head had swelled to an enormous size and when he pushed his finger into it, it left a great indentation. He was not in pain but he was distressed. Feeling thirsty, he tried to swallow some water which simply sloshed down his nose. His head and throat had become paralysed. *I could not even get rid of my own saliva.* he recalled.

The Court Messenger visited him and reassured him that he would not die but when Baby Taylor strolled along in the evening to see how the 'mosquito bite' was faring, he saw the ghastly sight of a watermelon sized head.H*e fair got the wind up* and sent for a doctor. *The doctor arrived the following evening and gave me an anti-venom injection, for what it was worth at that stage, but the system had been dealing with the poison and I was getting better. The doctor observed that if I had been bitten on any fleshy part where the vessels are bigger I would have been a gonna.*

As it was, his thick thatch of hair also provided some protection and the small blood vessels filtered the poison through slowly enough to allow the body to rally its defences. In three days he was back at work but thereafter he was constantly prone to malaria and his tour was cut short. He was admitted to the Tropical Diseases Hospital in London under the care of its head, Sir Philip Bahr, who found that this young man in his early twenties had a very much enlarged spleen. This was owing to the organ having to produce white corpuscles in huge quantities in defence against the snake's venom.

Thanks to his youth and a strong constitution, therefore, and plenty of hair, Pat O'Dwyer's service to Sierra Leone did not end in disaster. At least, not then.

He served for another twelve years but he often fell prey to malaria. On Trafalgar Day 1945 he met with a catastrophe, or, as he put it, he met his Waterloo. [See Chapter 13.] and it can be speculated that although clearing the ground for the ADC's house may not have been entirely where the first seeds of calamity were sown, there is no doubt that the dramatic turn that took place in Mr O'Dwyer's life some ten years later was probably aided by disturbing that green mamba quietly minding its own business in a bush in Port Loko and which Baby Taylor thought might have been a mosquito.

Clarence Buxton MC. c. 1925

118

Chapter 10

"THE POSITION ISN'T EASY OR COMFORTABLE"

Comfort and ease were not the style of Major Clarence Buxton MC, nor were they what he sought. During much of his service in Kenya he tirelessly represented the interests of the tribe he was administering at the time. His efforts did not always win him popularity with either his colleagues or with the settlers.

Major Buxton was a tall, rangy man with a strong jaw, bright blue eyes and a powerful intellect. We knew him when we were adolescents in the late nineteen fifties. His daughter, Carissa, used to invite us to their farm in Limuru. Of course, to us he seemed pretty ancient, and it was hard to believe then that once he had been young, optimistic and valiant.

He was born on the 14th of January 1892 into a world which was spinning towards the inconceivable nightmare of the First World War. In 1914/18 his carefree youth was lost forever on the battle fields of France though his determination and courage remained intact and all his life he was unafraid of disapproval or unpopularity.

In the light of today's general views on the colonial period some of his opinions were ahead of their time. His skirmish on the drawing of the boundary between Kenya and Tanganyika is a good example.[see also Chapter 7] He wrote to his mother in January 1923:

I want to try to get the boundary between this country and Tanganyika altered. It is an absurd arrangement which follows no reasonable alignment except so far as an atlas is concerned. Obviously, from the point of view of convenience, we want a boundary which follows clearly defined features such as rivers and ridges and which places each tribe under the same administration. At present the Masai and Watende are divided by a boundary which exists only on a map and cannot be observed in reality.

He then wrote an official letter to his District Commissioner explaining the practical difficulties of policing such an artificial line. This would involve *constant patrols, if not the establishment of police posts in order to prevent transgressions of the boundary by those Masai who have been returned to this district.*
He offered his superior a history lesson:

Just a century ago the New World was closed by President Munro's famous warning 'that the American Continents are henceforth not to be considered as subjects for future colonization by any European Powers.' Consequently the full force of Europe's colonizing enterprise turned to a fresh field for expansion which was opened by the exploration of Africa and the advance of science in its application to tropical hygiene, modern weapons and tinned food.

The Dual Alliance of France and Russia and the Triple Alliance of the Central Powers and England's isolated independent position provided that 'precarious equipoise' which a clash of competing ambitions in Africa might easily upset. With this background, Englishmen and Germans appeared in East and Central Africa and met as rival claimants for the control or exploitation of vast almost unknown regions ... The treaties were not the fruits of a blood-stained field in Europe or Africa but a wine laden board at Hatfield and Potsdam. ...

A bargain was struck between European bidders who could exchange Zanzibar for Heligoland without recourse to plebiscite or thought as to the effect that such an exchange might have on the indigenous population.

It is true that slavery and the slave trade had been abolished and the appellation "Protectorate" was meant to be more than a euphemism but there is no indication that African territories were regarded by European powers as other than profitable possessions. Indeed when it was found that Uganda did not pay and was difficult to manage, the British Government decided to withdraw. In resisting this proposal and advocating another aspect of the case, Bishop Tucker, through his appeal at Exeter Hall did much to arouse that sense of responsibility. ... as well as securing Uganda for the British Crown.

Quoting from R. Coupland's 'The Slave Trade and The Scramble' Major Buxton reminds the DC of Article 22 of the League of Nations Covenant: *The Mandate for East Africa Council of the League of Nations on July 22 1922 declared that governments should promote to the utmost the material and moral wellbeing and the social progress of its inhabitants and to help them as the covenant implies, in the course of time to stand up for themselves.*

120

Buxton observed that:

To those colonies and territories which, as a consequence of the late war, have ceased to be under sovereignty of the States which formerly governed them, and which are inhabited by peoples not yet able to stand by themselves under the strenuous conditions of the modern world, there should be applied the principle of well- being and development of such peoples from a sacred trust of civilisation.

He therefore asked his superior to give consideration to the boundary question *in the interests of those living in Africa instead of in the light of European jealousies.*

Although the facts today demonstrate that his idea did not find favour, Major Buxton was right but putting one's head over the parapet is rarely a comfortable experience. There are the risks of vilification and disfavour from those in whose gift is continued employment, transfers or promotion and perhaps even the loss of valued friendships. It is perhaps possible to speculate that Major Buxton's ruthless honesty did exact a price for he never reached the highest echelons of the Colonial Service when his ability, his integrity and his defence of the rights of Africans required that he should have been recognised and the Colony would have profited from giving him greater responsibility to put into effect the principles he espoused.

His position became even less comfortable some six years later when he took on his Provincial Commissioner, the Governor and some powerful and determined settlers over the demarcation of the Simba water holes.

When, in 1906, Arthur Collyer inspected the southern Masai grazing areas with some representatives from the Laikipia section of the tribe with a view to relocation, [see Chapter 7], he could see that water, or rather the lack of it, was going to be a major problem to the tribe. It would have been no surprise to him, therefore, had he lived to 1929, to have seen emotions running high over the Simba water holes.

These watering places were situated in the land alongside the railway line, south of Nairobi which had been allocated to the Masai. The railway also served as the boundary between the Wakamba tribe and the Masai; and they were not friendly neighbours. To try to ease the tensions between the tribes and to keep the Masai away from the railway where they were inclined to make off with wire and other things, the Government decided to create a mile wide buffer zone along the line. The problem was that included in this buffer zone - which was being given to European settlers - were the Simba water holes.

At that time (1928) Major Buxton was stationed at Kajiado as District Commissioner. As any DC worth his salt would, Buxton took the part of the Masai and he was incensed by the arbitrary decision to cut the mile wide zone and remove from the tribe their valuable waterholes. But he did not relish his position and despondently he wrote to his mother, the Dowager Lady Buxton, on 27 April 1929:

My career in the service is not favoured by circumstances. I am meeting much opposition again over the mile zone and Simba water holes which I maintain should be in the Masai reserve by prescriptive right and because they require the water and grazing.

Affairs have reached the state where I have drafted a letter to the Secretary of State and I have told my Provincial Commissioner that I shall send it off if any attempt is made to move the Masai out of the area....The hard fight has been in getting this Government, including my PC, to take the matter up when the boundary was supposed to be finally fixed in 1926.

But tactics were important and he later became concerned that if a memo he had written for his mother to show her political contacts should become known, this would be counterproductive to the cause. He therefore wrote to her on 8th August 1929:

Will you be very careful of that memo on the Masai boundary as I think Moore, the Chief Secretary would be less sympathetic if any agitation started in England before Sir Edward [Grigg the Governor] has had a chance of considering this matter. From the enclosed you will see that I have asked for an interview. The Chief Native Commissioner and Deputy Native Commissioner both told me that Sir E.G. was the only real difficulty so I wish to meet the real difficulty as soon as possible. He arrives next week.

Describing the settlers as 'the opposition', he added that they were getting very indignant and were putting up a strong counter-attack anticipating Sir Edward Grigg's support.

The following month he reported:

The settlers have now got a section of the Mombasa road made south of the line, penetrating in places into the Masai reserve. It is probable that they intend to press for it to be the boundary. Deck, my PC, is just a fool and a funk and but for him the matter would have been decided long ago in favour of the Masai. The Masai will certainly bring up the matter again at the CNC meeting at Ngong on the 24th and I am quite determined to see HE about it.

Matters came to a head when the Executive Committee decided against the Masai claim. It is not difficult to imagine the sensation the news made in Buxton's District Headquarters for he rushed to intercept the boat train to Mombasa at Voi and dashed off a letter to his mother while the train waited:

I have now addressed the Governor personally, showing up their [the Executive Committee] report in no uncertain manner. It will put HE in a difficult position. He has never given me an interview yet but can hardly refuse it or ignore the letter which I have sent accusing of bias, injustice and stupidity.

Governors were appointed from London and during the first thirty or so years of Kenya Colony's existence, many of them appeared only to give lip service to that 'sacred trust of civilisation' or of Lord Lugard's dictum that the Africans' rights were paramount.

More often than not in Kenya they sided with the settlers, either because they were enormously attracted to the swashbuckling likes of Lord Delamere and his forceful friends, or because they wished to relieve the financial burden being shouldered by the British tax payer, or simply because they dreamed of Kenya becoming a second Canada populated by sturdy, loyal British stock.

Favouring the interests of the settler over the African made life for the officials extremely irksome and awkward. They were the Governor's civil servants and their principle aim was to protect the interests of the African tribes they served and yet they and the Governor were often not singing from the same hymn sheet.

Sir Edward Grigg believed that the central aim of a colony should be settlement and still more settlement and that *settlement will be rapid, efficient, and successful in proportion as it concentrates upon those industries which are least affected by the vagaries of the native labour supply...Along the right lines the labour supply is sufficient for great development ...There are forms of primary industry in some ways the surest and most profitable, and which native labour is not an important factor at all.*

It is not surprising, therefore, that although His Excellency Sir Edward Grigg wilted in the face of Buxton's determination to see him, he was less than happy to face him.

The interview came off at last in Grigg's bedroom. he wrote to his mother in July 1930. *"It lasted over an hour and was distinctly trying. Within minutes HE was livid with me and only allowed me to see his neck which grew crimson with rage. However, I kept my temper and head and [made] my four points:*

(a) No Akamba ever south of the line.

(b) Reconsideration of the whole case by Executive Committee on legal and moral grounds.

(c) No demarcation of boundary until areas used by Masai have been marked on a map and considered.

(d) Legal claim under Crown Lands Ordnance prevents any eviction.

History does not relate what the Governor said to his DC but by this time feelings between the settlers and Buxton were also running high. This battle over the Simba water holes exemplifes the tremendous tussle that went on between the settlers and the officials, exacerbated by a vacillating Government. It was at this time that some hot-headed settlers were hatching a plan to declare independence from Britain. The idea was to kidnap the Governor and to take over government of the country by the Europeans, for the Europeans. It was a wild and daft idea which foundered at the last moment because Lord Delamere withdrew his support. Nevertheless resentment was rife. Buxton wrote to his mother in November 1930:

FOB [Wilson - settler at Ulu] Frank Joyce's partner started a violent attack on me for allowing some cattle from the Masai reserve to enter his farm north of the line. The incident occurred in May with Frank Joyce's knowledge and approval. ... FOB thinks he can get me moved and the Masai claim turned out by representing that I have deliberately infected the farm [with pleuro-pneumonia] from the Masai Reserve. Lord Francis Scott is supporting him in Legislative Council attacking me, and the dear old Kenya Government as usual sits on the fence uncertain in this case which is the tougher nut to crack. I have asked that Ld F.S. and FOB and the Chief Vet Officer, who is their puppet, may meet me before the Executive Committee and substantiate or withdraw the charges. It will be interesting to see how they take this challenge and how they stand up to the bowling. ... I feel as Admiral Harper did about Jutland; 'the British Government and people have a right to know the truth.'

One of the leaders of the settlers told Buxton that he was in a minority of one and that even Deck, his Provincial Commissioner, only lent him half-hearted support *because he daren't do otherwise.*

But it was becoming clear that Major Buxton's battling style did not much suit the officials either, one of which visited him and read him a lecture on respect for his seniors:

I asked if he was quoting from St Paul or someone else or referring particularly to some senior and if so who but he only replied that it saddened him to think I had no confidence in my colleagues. He then showed me something he had written about 'paramountcy'. It expressed exactly what I have thought and said for at any rate the last five years since I was in charge at Meru. 'Good' I said, 'Who are you going to show this to?' to which he replied, 'No one. I should get the sack if the Executive Committee saw it.' That admission is most illuminating, for it shows the attitude of the Kenya Government to those who think like that and very few dare to stand up to the Kenya Government. Hence the distrust of my colleagues - all but a few.

Furthermore he believed that *whatever may be said about the way I put the matter, every honest man who knows this situation would admit that the whole question would have been settled against the Masai irrevocably, boundary dug etc, if I had not taken up an uncompromising attitude.*

In the meantime letters from the settlers were becoming so emotive that they *nearly burst into flames* and Lord Delamere was in Britain putting a wholly inaccurate picture of the Masai land claim before the British public. Delamere was declaring that the Masai now owned the finest grazing land in the world. To which Buxton countered that if Delamere's premise was correct why did he and others get the Masai moved from the land they preferred in the Rift Valley and Laikipia, if the best land in the world was at that time already vacant? The plain truth was that the Masai were pushed out of the good land into inferior land and that they could only use about half their reserve, the rest being unfit for animal and human life. He then instructed his mother to *tell Charlie* who must have been a prominent person on the London political scene, suggesting that Charlie heckled Delamere after his talk *'Native problems in Africa.'*

For his part, Clarence assured his mother, he would continue to fight against the injustice and stupidities of the Kenya Government *But the position isn't easy or comfortable.*

Post Script: The mile wide zone of "the finest grazing land in the world" and which included all the Simba water holes was offered to a Mr Thomson by the Land Department for one shilling an acre. Thomson protested vigorously and the Land Department caved in and sold it to him for fifty cents an acre.

Birthday party for Sylvia given by her mother, Agnes Budge. With thanks to
Sylvia Honeyman who is holding her mother's hand.

Chapter 11

THE DOMESTIC ROUND, THE COMMON TASK

In 1949 we were a family of five. There was our father, Hal Williams, District Commissioner, Kakamega District who Negley Farson in his book "Last chance in Africa", described as "a quiet and unruffled man ... who firmly believes and lives up to the precept that a District Commissioner must be the very father and mother of the people entrusted to his care." Our mother, Joy, was diminutive, practical, shrewd, and busy trying conscientiously to support Hal whom she adored. Our brother, Richard, was ten, hero-worshipped by us, his twin sisters, but was often away at boarding school. We were five years old and busy with such important matters as keeping the white rats away from the terriers or devising ways to evade Mum's lessons which she received from a postal correspondence course.

The day began with morning tea at 6.30 and Hal's's first duty was to drive round the boma to check that all was well. (The word "Boma" has many meanings. It can be a corral for stock; a compound, an administration centre or even a village such as Kakamega was in 1949.) We would scramble into the back of the box-body with the dogs as the early sunlight flung golden rods over the African morning. The first stop was the brick works. Lines and lines of terracotta bricks lay outside a long thatched shed. Later the prisoners would be puddling the mud and turning out the bricks. The next port of call was the prison. Dad would park the box-body under a tree and he would disappear inside to check that all had been well overnight. We visited other places such as the sewage works but finally he would drive us to the grass airstrip at the other end of the boma and he would yell out of the window to us sitting in the back on the wooden benches to buckle our seat belts. He would then, amid much shouting and excitement, "take off" along the strip at the exhilarating pace of forty miles an hour and cheerfully we would all go back to the house where a delicious hot breakfast would be waiting for us.

L to R: Veronica, Cissalia, Sue (with Quiver) and Meshak

Sue, Veronica and friend

The house was set in wide spacious gardens surrounded by eucalyptus trees. There was a guest house to one side, about thirty yards away, behind which was an outside "long-drop" lavatory. I was certain that a hooved devil dwelt at the bottom of the pit. Between the guest house and the main house was our own children's garden where I do not think we grew anything successfully other than barberton daisies.

Hal enjoyed his few years as DC Kakamega and for us children it was a halcyon time of freedom such as is unimaginable today and where the atmosphere was pleasant and constructive amongst all the people, of every race, in the boma.

In Chapter 14, Colin Campbell, alludes to unexpected visitors landing on our parents when they lived in Kakamega, one of which was his future wife, Jackie. From our point of view as children, all visitors added greatly to the gaiety of life. Joy Adamson, who later became famous by rearing the lioness, Elsa, came the day before we were off to boarding school for the first time at the age of six. To my astonishment and fascination she thrust her hand into her blouse and withdrew a bush-baby which she wanted to give us. Joy was deaf to our entreaties to accept it.

The Governor, Sir Philip Mitchell, would occasionally sweep into the boma with his retinue all decked out in khaki and scarlet. He would set up camp in a eucalyptus grove nearby.

Hal Williams with the Governor, Sir Philip Mitchell, in Kakamega.

Another visitor, this time to Kisumu when Hal was Provincial

Commissioner, Nyanza, in the early 1950s, held me spell-bound as he bent over to tie his shoe-lace within reach of Sandy, the rather bad-tempered ram who was tethered in the garden and had been presented to Hal by a visiting chief. Sandy headed for the visitor's tempting bent-over behind, administered the inevitable and sent the poor man toppling over.

Many visitors were on fact-finding missions for some government department or learned body. Many of them considered themselves to be "experts" of course. One DO in Nigeria developed the theory that the expert of this happy band simply needed to fly over the country and look down upon it to reach the right conclusions. "It was admitted that they had to come down to earth at night, of course, but this enabled them to meet Africans and make mental reservations about the Europeans they found there, who gave them hospitality."

A.F.B. Bridges, whose book **"So We Used to Do"** in an excellent account of the everyday life of a District Officer in Nigeria, mildly recounts:

One day after lunch I noticed a tall figure in a ten-gallon hat walking up the drive and went out to meet him. He said, "Say, can you tell me if there is a ho-tel here?" I found afterwards he had been three months in West Africa and must have been well aware that there wasn't. So I suggested he come and stay. He said his wife was at the "deepoh" so I went in the Austen 7 and collected one large American female and a very large wardrobe trunk from the railway station. He was a talented artist and a quiet friendly man of whom I saw little as he was always out sketching. She was a holy terror ... She was collecting information for a book, her husband doing the illustrations. ... A friend later gave us the book, from which one gathered that they had lived rough in native houses and market places — there was no acknowledgement whatever of the hospitality they had received, but the illustrations were beautiful.

One or two of the more eccentric DC's in the more distant outposts went to some lengths to avoid visitors. One 'bog baron' (as the southern administrative officers were sometimes known) in southern Sudan posted people on the road leading to his headquarters to warn him of any unwanted arrivals. The Governor of the Province arrived one day to see the tailgate of his subordinate disappearing in a cloud of dust.

The living conditions could be primitive. In many areas of Nigeria even as late as 1960 there were few modern conveniences. No electricity, no radio and no electric lights. In a country where darkness falls throughout the year by 7pm, lighting clearly required attention and light was either the candle-lamp which burned an ordinary candle supported from wilting by a metal jacket and spring. There was also the carbide lamp, or the clockwork lamp both of which could easily go wrong. There was often no running water and some were lucky to have as much as a bath while in 1941 the toilet was of the bucket and sand-scoop variety.

The DC's House, Rumbeck, Southern Sudan. With thanks to Hazel Carlisle who painted this in the late fifties.

It was a lonely life for bachelors and if a man was lucky enough to have met and become engaged to a lady in England, the waiting for her to join him was almost unbearable. Brian Carlisle was in just such a position in 1953. His frustration was exacerbated by the fact that Hazel's family were unhappy about her going to live in the Sudan once the couple were married.

My darling, he wrote in March of that year, *sometimes all this wrangling about when you are going to come out makes me feel an awful cad and beastly selfish. But seeing other people bring their brides out ... I just thought it was the natural thing to do but this criticism does give me qualms. But when a man really loves a girl like I love you, this separation really is absolute hell and I don't want to prolong it. I think in a way it is worse for me than an engaged man in England because I live alone and after 5 years out of 6 in outstations in the Sudan I am fed up with being alone.*

Once the officials were married and had families, more often than not there were pleasant activities in which the families could take part for a DC's duties were many and various. The DC Tabora, Tanganyika in the forties was James Budge. One of his responsibilities was to make sure that Dr David Livingstone's memorial house south of Tabora was being kept in good order. His small daughter, Sylvia, sometimes accompanied him on these inspections. The house was – and still is – long and low, built of mud and wattle. It had been used as a rest house for Livingstone and other explorers.

Sylvia was always impressed by the neatness of a vegetable garden owned by an old Arab who grew aubergines and peppers in neat straight lines alongside the memorial house. There is an equally neat line, a chronological one this time, because this old chap remembered Dr Livingstone visiting in the 1870s. Sylvia told us this in 2014.

Joy Williams wrote an account of her least favourite station. Kwale was in the hills above the coast south of Mombasa. She wrote:

We were only stationed here for a short time – I think about a year.(1944/45) It was a one-man station; all other staff such as medical and PWD (Public Works Department) being in Mombasa. As there were no other children in the boma we decided that Richard, then six, must go off to boarding school and [he] was duly despatched to Turi, though not before he had a mild go of malaria. The house was a three roomed building consisting of a long living room – dining at one end and sitting room the other, where there was a fireplace which on chilly evenings was very welcome, for although at the coast, Kwale was up in the hills several hundred feet up. There was a bedroom opening off either end of this room and a large verandah in front. Behind and separate from the main building was the kitchen and also an outside guest room and, of course, outside pit loos.

In a way it was a lovely boma, tropical yet cool and with a beautiful view out to the sea, and yet from the very start I didn't really like it. I always had a sense of fear when Hal went on safari, which wasn't like me, who used to rather enjoy being on my own. There was no doubt that the whole area was haunted as was really much of the coast, though why this was so, or by what I simply have no ideas. Even Hal remarked on it when he had been on safari down to an area on the Tanganyika border. He said, when he came back that it was a horrible place and quite unnerved him. The bungalow too had an unpleasant feeling especially the bedroom where the children slept and in fact my toddler twin daughters would never go into that room by themselves.

I remember I had a man there one day, I suppose an official visitor, and he was washing his hands in the bathroom when he asked if I had noticed anything strange about the house. As I had to be there a good deal on my own, I firmly said 'no' but in truth it really confirmed that I wasn't just imagining things. On another occasion I walked down to a spring below the boma but left again very quickly and never visited it again although it was a very pretty place: a spring down in a hollow surrounded by palm trees and grass. However the really worst occasion was when Richard and I were out for a walk and came to a path that led out across a grassy field towards the edge of the hill looking across to the sea. We started off down this path thinking we would come to the edge of the hill and have a lovely view both below us and out to the sea. About half way across we came to some burnt out huts but before we even got near them I felt that I couldn't take another step, and so turned back. I don't think that Richard noticed anything, and I couldn't define the feeling although it was fear, but of what?

Finally a nice little story of how legends are made – I was going into Mombasa on the local lorry and we came to a plantation of coconut palms, and the driver said that when that plantation had just come into bearing a traveller had asked the owner for a drink of coconut milk which the owner refused to give him so the traveller cursed the plantation and said it would never have any more coconuts. It never had borne any fruit since. There were certainly no nuts there when I saw it, but I'm afraid it had a more prosaic reason as the local agricultural officer told me. It had been planted where there was solid coral close to the surface of the soil and once the trees got to that layer they had insufficient soil to nourish the fruit, though sufficient to keep them alive. Why do people spoil a good story?

When Joy talked of Kwale and Lamu and other places at the coast later on, she felt that her sense of fear stemmed from the centuries-old Arab slave trade. The caravans would head for Gedi, Mombasa, Lamu etc, and despatch the slaves to the market in Zanzibar. The Arabs had developed settlements and farms to supply the caravans as they came through. Perhaps one was at that cool spring just outside Kwale.

Joy Williams in conversation at the Coast in Kenya.

One day when she was on her own in Kwale and Hal was away, she was feeding her hens when a very bedraggled man arrived in the garden. He was an American airman and his 'plane had crashed and caught fire higher up the hill. There were several crew, of which only one had been killed getting out of the burning wreckage. Joy helped them all to the house and somehow found bedding for them and the verandah became the hospital ward where they remained for a few days to recover while she tended their injuries. All in a day's work.

Tanganyika was a German colony until the close of the First World War when it was held in trust by the League of Nations. The British administered Tanganyika but German planters and businessmen remained there. James Budge was stationed in Tanga at the outbreak of the Second World War when the German civil population whipped up an anti-British riot which made itself felt outside the DC's house. His wife, Agnes, armed herself with a kettle, with which lethal weapon she told her daughter that she hoped the rioters would be sufficiently impressed to "buzz off."

At the outbreak of World War II the German population had been given the option of either going south to Southern Rhodesia to incarceration in a camp or of going back to Germany. Four year old Sylvia Budge had a much loved German friend with whom she played. Her parents chose to go back to Germany: one moment she was there playing happily with Sylvia, the next she was gone never to be seen again. One cannot help thinking in hindsight that the little girl's parents may have made an unwise decision.

By the time Hal Williams, became DC Kakamega in 1948 we three young children largely ran barefoot and wild. There were servants in the house and garden with permission and responsibility to keep us in order while Joy set about doing what she could in the district. She joined the East African Women's League (EAWL) who were pushing forward a programme at that time to encourage the teaching of useful household skills such as spinning, weaving, dying, sewing, hygiene and child care. Spinning wheels and wool were acquired and off this energetic and diminutive DC's wife would go in a small lorry to some outlying district. We were often put in the open back of the lorry where, oblivious to the bumpiness, noise and dust, we looked forward to the picnic.

At a distant little village, not more than a hamlet, there would often be an airy mud and wattle building. There the women and their infants, with a trained African teacher, would be learning to comb and spin the wool. There may have been a loom too. The dying of the cloth that was woven caused my mother many a headache because the fashion for colours changed from year to year, so she would be told that the 'in' colour was green and would order lots of green Drummer dyes, and then the next year no one would look at her proffered greens, and all wanted yellow! Many of the young women could not use scissors or a needle and thread and Joy would sit among them teaching them.

Child rearing and hygiene was also talked about while sewing progressed. Some of the children running around their plump mothers had the protruding bellies of malnutrition. Mum would tick the offending mother off and give them guidance about feeding small children. All this was taken with gales of giggles as the other women enjoyed the discomfiture of their friend. Laughter was much in evidence at these gatherings.

Joy also made it her business to support the small cottage hospital in Kakamega. It was a cool, spotlessly clean place exclusively for the native population. The wards were separate houses joined by stone paths through the lawns and each had its own verandah. Who paid for this medical care, its buildings and its staff, we do not know. I remember seeing a child with dreadful burns round the head, having fallen in the open fire in his parents' hut but even he seemed peaceful and comfortable with his mother who stayed with him.

Many of the European women saw it as their duty and probably pleasure to help the people amongst whom they now lived and many of their efforts, though rarely rewarded, were without doubt of value. The EAWL was founded in 1917 and made a wonderful network that helped many of these redoubtable women to work within a framework to contribute to the good of the people of the young colony. It is still going to this day.

Veronica and Sue with our brother Richard with the matron, and possibly the doctor's daughter, and some of the patients at Kakamega hospital 1949

An afternoon tea party in Olive Collyer's lovely garden on her coffee farm, Ndumbwini, Kabete, Kenya.

Chapter 12

"A VERY GAY, A VERY GALLANT, AND A VERY MUCH MISUNDERSTOOD COMMUNITY"

Sir Edward Grigg. 1930

If we are to improve the position of the native races generally and permanently, our own people must be freed from fear for their own future as far as humanly possible. Fear is the curse of so many policies and the father of so many narrow and selfish councils. ... Get rid of fear for our own future and the whole outlook changes. Natives would then no longer look as something alien-protected, right or wrong, by Downing Street, often owing to incorrect information or inaccurate data. They at once become part of our people whom it is our duty to protect and encourage.

Hugh Cholmondeley, Third Baron Delamere, August 1927 (The Dual Policy in Kenya by M.F. Hill 1943/44)

Richard Cox, in "*Kenyatta's Country*", wrote in 1963 that the Kenya settler was slipping into history: *and when, like the Dodo, he is extinct, the memory of all that he was and tried to be, all that he did to make Kenya a country, not just a colony but a real country, will be forgotten.*

There are tales about the Kenya settler which make one's hair stand on end. Steamy stories of drugs, drink and wife-swapping create

139

frissons of fascination and the antics of the notorious "Happy Valley Set" make good, but highly inaccurate film material. If one believes it all, it is easy to reach a conclusion that Kenya settlers were unpleasant, over-indulgent and arrogant sex fiends. Many people who were not there at the time do not like to know that, in fact, most Kenya settlers were decent people who worked hard and cared for their employees.

Cox believed that most settlers were also unusually eccentric and he commented that there is something about them *of Lawrence Durrell's renegade diplomat who put on a dinner-jacket to eat hippo steak in the jungle. Except that Kenyans [did] the reverse. They invariably put on pyjamas and dressing-gowns for dinner. Indeed one Governor so disliked this practice that he would stay up-country only on the understanding that his hosts dressed normally in the evening.* Cox added that after a few months in Kenya one began to look out for idiosyncrasies as instinctively as if one were gathering the evidence needed to certify a relative.

Farming in Kenya in the early part of the twentieth century was risky, perilous even. Before the Great War transport was entirely dependent upon horses, mules and oxen. Ox tongas were quite a popular mode of transport for people living some distance out of Nairobi. One of the reasons for this was that horse sickness was a scourge. The longest guarantee that could be given for a horse at a sale was five days. The ubiquitous tick and tsetse fly spread diseases which killed horses and British breeds of cattle and sheep with impunity and crop diseases were also endemic; many of which were unknown to science. Droughts and floods which are still the way of things in Africa, caused heartbreak and bankruptcy. One day a farmer could be desperately searching for 'a cloud the size of a man's hand' as plants withered under a pitiless African sun, and the next the heavens could open, raising water levels in the rivers three feet or more in an hour, sweeping away seedlings and dam walls.

Many, if not most, settlers had bank loans and most of the time, their endeavours constantly teetered. When disaster struck, a glum ride into town to visit the bank manager was a necessity to try to avert the loss of the farm. After World War II Arthur and Patsy Horner in Kitale lost their farm and sold Patsy's wedding ring in order to pay off their labour. He later became a Colonial official. (see Chapter 21: "Independence")

After the Great War the Government changed the currency from rupees to shillings. The rupee had been valued at 1s 4d but after the change it was valued at 2s. Almost overnight overdrafts were increased by two thirds. One of those to suffer badly from this change was Colonel Ewart Grogan and he never was able to forgive the British Government. Many soldier settlers who had put their gratuities into farming and borrowed heavily on them were also ruined.

Under these conditions, it is scarcely surprising that there was a certain amount of eccentricity about.

The people who farmed outside Nairobi in the area known as Kabete were some of the earliest settlers in Kenya. Theirs was a cordial and largely undivided community who, despite some opposing interests, enjoyed friendly relations.

Mr Charles Taylor went to Kabete in 1909 and in 1927 he married Kit, a serene, beautiful and wise person who herself had arrived in Kenya as a little girl in 1904. Their daughter, Kathini, was brought up in Kabete and we are indebted to her and Kit for many of the vignettes they have given me about Kabete and its settler community. Charles Taylor was an energetic coffee farmer who also involved himself in many other areas of Kenya's development and business including the formation of the East African Power & Lighting Company. Kathini remembers the senior chief in the area, Chief Njonjo (father of a later distinguished Attorney General) sitting on the verandah discussing matters of common interest such as rain, or the lack of it, locusts, crops and earthquakes while they drank tea and the old Chief sniffed very strong snuff.

Miss Olive Collyer went out to Kenya in 1908 and, after her brother,

Arthur, had died in 1912 while he was serving as DC Nyeri (See Chapter 7: Not Fair Dealings) she settled in Kabete where she bred horses, grew flowers and vegetables for the Nairobi market and later grew coffee. She was an active member of the embryo Jockey Club and, together with Lady Muriel Jex Blake, she was a founder of the Kenya Horticultural Society. Kathini said that Miss Collyer, who was our great-aunt, was a good-looking woman who wore long divided skirts and long-sleeved coats made in a faded khaki. Her only concession to femininity was a pretty scarf. She was unconventional and Kathini remembers the parson announcing one Sunday, "Now let us pray for rain". "Hear, hear" boomed the response from Olive. She never missed Christmas dinner with the Taylors and every year she was seated on Charles's right until Kit decided to rearrange the seating plan because, she said, she wanted to stop Charles and Olive spending the whole evening discussing manure. The servants, firmly ignoring the convention, which they knew perfectly well, that the lady on the right of the host should be served first, blandly continued to accord Olive the privilege of being served first. She was much admired by the Kikuyu who lived in Kabete and was known as "Nya Weru" – the woman who works.

She was outspoken and strong-willed but she also had a tender streak. Kit told me of how, when bread was rationed during the Second World War, she gave all her bread to the African children and consequently became worryingly thin. Once, when she visited Olive, Kit remarked how tired she looked. Olive said it was only because one of the labour had a sick child and she had sat up all night caring for him.

Another lady I interviewed was Mrs Victoria Kabetu. Her father-in-law, Stephano, had been the first African train driver in Kenya, thanks to Olive Collyer who persuaded him to try for it and pushed for him to get a place at the training school. Victoria also told me how she remembered Olive occasionally picking her up with all the other African children in the area and taking them to her house for a children's party.

A settler group: L to R: Olive Collyer, Nancy Southern (?) and Margaret Collyer

The church at Kabete was built after the Great War. A lady from Gilgil, Mrs Grist, had extended a kindness to one of the first builders in Nairobi. He told her that if ever he could do anything to repay her she only had to ask. She never had any intention of taking him up on his offer until she moved to Kabete when she asked him to build the church.   The people who attended the church were farmers, missionaries, officials and professionals, the latter of whom were mainly from Kabete Veterinary Laboratory.

As the fabric of a new English society was being woven in Kikuyuland, there were no parishes in Kenya, but Kabete church was linked to Kiambu – perhaps ten miles away as the crow flew. One day it was mooted that this arrangement should change and Kabete church should join the church of St Marks, Parklands which was about five miles away. This would have been a more logical arrangement and the vicar of St Marks, Mr Carlisle, had set his heart on Kabete joining up with St Marks. However, at a very heated meeting the Kabete congregation   unceremoniously threw the suggestion out.

As the meeting broke up, the desolate vicar of St Marks walked away,

143

shoulders bowed. Olive ran after him, put her arm around his shoulder and said, "Mr Carlisle, Mr Carlisle we do like you most awfully. It is just that we have always belonged to Kiambu."

Canon Harry Leakey and his wife, Mary, were early missionaries, settling at Kabete in the 1890s. His descendants have since distinguished themselves in different walks of life in Africa, not least in the field of archaeological discovery. Sometimes Mary and the children would return to England for longish periods and Leakey's letters to her have drawn an interesting picture of life in Kabete with its frustrations and periods of loneliness.

One afternoon in the very early days of the Kabete community, Canon Leakey found himself having to entertain to tea some visitors from Britain. He decided to invite the settlers. He described to Mary how he had rushed about preparing the party seemingly for days and how nerve-wracking it had been. Finally, all was ready and, to his relief, the party started to get into its swing; until he saw Olive Collyer galloping down the drive with a bundle of sticks under her arm. He had forgotten to boil the water for the tea.

Dr Jex Blake was a brilliant internationally renowned physician who specialised in hearts and lungs, while his wife, Lady Muriel, created a wonderful botanical garden on their coffee estate, Kyuna. She had lustrous brown eyes and she wore dresses made of chintz or floral furnishing linen as she found they did not show the dirt when she was gardening.

Kit Taylor rode over to visit the Jex Blakes one day. She and Dr Jex strolled along the shady paths through the riot of plants (planted, not for show but where the plants would thrive.) 'Haemanthus' he said, pointing, 'The flower of blood.'

'Oh how I wish I had learned Latin at school rather than German!' lamented Kit.

'Maybe so, my dear Kit, maybe so; but in this case it would have availed you nothing. The word happens to be Greek!'

Given such commonplace pleasantness, which is what we ourselves

144

remember in Kenya after World War II, the skewed reputation of the Kenya settlers has been a source of wry amusement and sometimes even sorrow to many of us. However, there was indeed an arrogant element that discomfited our young and naive selves and still does when we recall it, but we did not often come across it.

Just after the 1914-18 war Lord Delamere bought a 20 acre plot from Douglas Cooper's farm on which he built Loresho House not far from the Jex Blakes. Soon after it was completed he decided he wanted to buy a further 200 or 300 acres on which to plant coffee. He wrote to Douglas Cooper to explain that he would not argue about price but he did not propose to pay: it would be on mortgage.

Douglas Cooper's son, Jim, was a small child then and he accompanied his father to Loresho House, riding a Somali pony while his father walked, using, as he always did, an ebony stick with a spear at one end. At the house the small boy sat on the lawn with his grazing pony while his father and Delamere discussed business sitting on deck chairs on the shallow verandah.

A Masai approached with a chit on a split stick and offered it to Delamere who took no notice. The Masai tried again with a grunt. I watched entranced as Delamere without apparently interrupting his conversation hurled my father's stick at the Masai who ducked and stood away while Delamere remarked to my father, 'I hate being interrupted, don't you Cooper?'

The odd thing was that it was known by settlers and Masai alike that Delamere had a special relationship with the Masai.

Colonel Ewart Grogan could be described as an arrogant man but he was also brilliant with a defiant and rebellious streak and a caustic wit. He once said, *East Africa is the home of the leopard, the tick, the baboon and the amateur official.* His early claim to fame was an epic walk from the Cape to Cairo all, they said, for the love of a lady. But the ever generous spirited Kit Taylor reminded us that far more important than that – and all but forgotten now – was that he donated his house and garden at Muthaiga to build a children's hospital for all races. It was, and still is, known as Gertrude's Garden, after his wife.

145

Jim Cooper described to me a rather harsher picture of the early days when Kabete was little more than a buffer zone between the Masai and the Kikuyu.

He recalled how when he was about six years old he had been watching oxen ploughing part of his father's property. At the end of each headland, as a guide to the ploughman, a stake was planted and on this stake was a human skull. There were several ox teams and several stakes with skulls. When he was older his father told him that their property was described as a 'frontier farm' to keep the peace between the raiding Masai and the Kikuyu.

In about 1947 the adult Jim was working on the coffee farm, paying the pickers and, while they were waiting for the cart to return with more berries, an old Kikuyu, Waweru, was holding the company enthralled by a story he was telling.

I had been counting the money Jim wrote, *and had not been listening so I asked him to start again. He recounted the story of how in the year of the great famine, the year the Government came — miaka ya serkali — which I took to be 1897, the Masai came raiding from Dagoretti. He, with other members of the Kikuyu warrior age group retreated and came along the ridge where we were then sitting. After the raid, when the Masai returned along the ridge the Kikuyu attacked them. 'The men were killed and the women, as was the custom then, had their right hands cut off. Ai! Ai! ... That is where it happened.' He pointed to the ridge on Kirime Kinwe where I had seen the skulls as a small boy. Perhaps that was the last Masai raid.* [See Chapter 5]

Before, during and after World War Two, Muthaiga Club had a reputation amongst outsiders of a prurient bent, for being the hub, the veritable hotbed of what some described as the "Tatler Group": those aristocratic bad apples hell-bent upon the high life of sex, drugs and champagne. The club had originally been set up to provide settlers living on farms outside Nairobi with a place to eat, stay and socialise. We remember it in the fifties as a charming, spacious place with a quiet air of relaxed courtliness and effortless efficiency.

At the end of the fifties or the beginning of the sixties, Kit and

Charles Taylor were having lunch at the club one day.

While we were lunching, Ewart [Grogan] *came in. He was by then very blind and deaf. He walked into the dining room rather like an old lion and we called him over. 'Ewart come and lunch with us.' We were half way through our lunch when an extraordinary procession passed us. It was General Wainwright, who lived up Rumuruti way, looking very dignified, walking with a stick. His sister came after him with two sticks, very, very dignified and a young man – the ADC as it were – followed them. Ewart Grogan turned to Charles and said, 'You know, Charles, this place is supposed to be some sort of Moulin Rouge!'*

Perhaps, after all, the Kenya settlers' club with a reputation for high living was not very different from a London Club.

Let us end this attempt to capture something of the flavour of the Kenya settler community with a funeral. We hope our great Aunt Olive Collyer would not mind; perhaps she would smile. When she died in 1949 she was buried at Kabete church. At her funeral which we believe was the first to be attended by African and European alike (Africans were fearful of death and shied away from it) the church and churchyard were overflowing. Jim Cooper told us that Denis Burke and a friend had been deputed to tamp down her grave after the service. As he was stamping on the soil, Burke remarked, *'This must be the first time that anyone has stamped on Olive!'*

"Write her as one who loved her fellow men."

147

Pat O'Dwyer standing second from the left. Hal Williams is also standing
fourth from the left.
Jesus College Natives. 1930

Chapter 13

A STORY OF COURAGE

He dressed the line, he led the charge,
They swept the wall like a stream in spate,
And roaring over the roar they heard
The galloper guns that burst the gate.

Sir Henry Newbolt tells the stirring story of Sir Robert Rollo Gillespie, serving in India, who, on hearing that *The Devil's abroad in false Vellore*, rode out at dawn, *riding alone* to rout *The Devil that stabs by night* who had attacked the barracks at Vellore.

Rollo Gillespie, described as "the bravest soldier" and who was killed in action in India in 1814, would have been proud of his descendent, Francis Denis Gillespie O'Dwyer who was also one of Britain's bravest sons. But his courage was more of the quiet kind.

O'Dwyer was born in 1910 and he was brought up in the ranching country of Entre Rios; an especially enchanting area of the Argentine where rivers and marshes appear as if by magic as one rides over the grassy plains and where the population of wading and water birds was almost as great as that of the cattle and sheep that so enriched that country. In those days *the English literally ran the Argentine*. There on the family estancia of La Honoria, young O'Dwyer lived a *marvellous open, carefree life*.

He was educated at Cheltenham (Cheltondale House) where he was Captain of rugby, Captain of boxing and Captain of the College fives.

149

At Jesus College Cambridge, he read history. He was Captain of Jesus rugby and he won a university boxing blue as a heavyweight.

Even the Great Slump could not have dampened the optimism of this handsome and gifted young man as he went for interview into the Colonial Service. He had been taught that there was *no greater service one could perform in life than to serve the cause of the Empire.* Only twenty-five men passed into the Service that year, out of three hundred hopefuls, and as he stepped aboard the SS Adda in June 1933, bound for Sierra Leone, his spirits were high. *Here at last I felt I was launched on the ship of life*, he wrote.

For thirteen years O'Dwyer served Africa in the kettledrum humidity of West Africa not far from the notorious Bight of Benin *(There's few come out, Tho' many go in.)* He spent those years tramping through the swamps (shooting the odd duck on the way) and along the tie-tie bridges swaying precariously over the crocodile-infested rivers, sitting in village courts as a Magistrate, collecting taxes and listening to the worries of the chiefs, headmen, farmers, miners and fishermen who lived in that isolated and often inhospitable region.

Pat O'Dwyer was deprecating about the life he led in Sierra Leone: its dangers and the loneliness; the ticklish diplomacy required to overrule a chief who had decreed that a debtor should be pledged as a slave to his creditor; the courage to settle a strike of iron ore miners who were too angry to parley - an action for which Pat was described as a "staunch fellow". And he underplayed the intelligence and humanity required to try defendants for murder who believed they had the power to transfer their spirits into wild animals.

As we have recounted earlier, it was a snake which delivered the first blow to his promising career. [Chapter 9] It was little short of a miracle that the snake bite did not kill him but during the remainder of his service O'Dwyer constantly was prey to malaria and other tropical diseases. In January 1945 he was posted to Moyamba district:

(where the language was Mende and of course I spoke Timne which was the language of the Northern Province.) But I had been DC of every district of the North except Koinadugu and I was very glad to go to Moyamba, mainly because of the excellent tarpon fishing at Shenge.

The doctor in Moyamba was Tweedy, an Irishman whom I was very fond of. His wife was also there, at that time quite deaf.

Moyamba was a very busy district which should have had an Assistant, but while I was there I did not have one. So I had to work pretty hard getting round the District in the rainy season and looking after Moyamba itself.

One day in the office a woman came in and said that her daughter had been killed by the head of a secret society whose object was to murder a girl, to cut the heart out, eat it and then to smear their bodies with the fat around the heart. By doing this they thought they became impregnable to man. The murder was alleged to have taken place in Shenge. I sent a Court Messenger out to get some evidence but he came back without any. I shortly went out on trek planning to end up at Shenge where I would do some fishing and, among other things, enquire into this alleged murder. After visiting the other chiefdoms I got to Shenge one Saturday evening, October 20th 1945. I arrived there by launch and ordered it to return to Bonthe, as I would not want it any more on this trek because I would return to Moyamba on foot - a two day march.

In the ordinary way, on trek, I would go into court and deal with complaints brought by the people as one would on any week day. However, I thought that I would take the next day, Sunday, off and go fishing. There was excellent tarpon fishing off the coast here but I had never landed one.

There was an old fisherman at Shenge whom I called Captain Huff. I sent for him on the Saturday evening and asked him if he would take me out in his dug-out canoe the next day and provide two more boys to paddle.

Sunday was a glorious sunny morning and soon it got very hot out at sea. I caught a barracuda and then a king fish, but what I really wanted was a tarpon. These fish have very hard and impenetrable mouths. It is just impossible to get a hook to pierce either the top or the bottom of their mouths and only along the sides, where the mouth opens, is it soft enough for the hook to penetrate. When the tarpon first takes the bait, which in my case was a spoon, it takes it very gently and so you have no idea what kind of fish you may have on the end of your line. Then, as soon as he feels the hook he takes an almighty leap into the air. So often in the past and I had seen the hook come out of his mouth while he was in the air and that meant another tarpon lost.

Suddenly I felt a slight tug on my line so I struck, not too hard to pull the bait out of the mouth of whatever might be nibbling when I saw a lovely great tarpon leap into the air. A tarpon has very tough scales and nothing will penetrate them; as he jumps these scales shine like a bright light in the sun. He is a beautifully proportioned fish, so to see him jump is some sight.

I did not see the hook fly out of his mouth but I could not be sure that I had not lost him until I reeled in fast and found him still on the line. He would then make a terrific dash and my reel went singing out with that thrilling sound. Up he jumped

151

again. When he landed the line went limp and I thought I had lost him. I reeled in quickly and he was still there and off he would rush again and the reel would sing. Six times he jumped like this; each time he landed and the line went limp I thought I had lost him, but each time he was there still. After that the poor old tarpon had no more strength to jump. Think of the energy to hurl yourself out of the water. He still had lots in him though and he rushed about in the sea with my line coming in and out in time with him. After half an hour he was getting tired, I could tell but, damn it, I was getting much more so.

For some unaccountable reason I quite suddenly felt all in. I had a leather butt holder round my waist into which I put the butt of my rod which I held with both hands. But by then I just had no power in my arms and hands and was quite unable to hold the rod. I could only put it under my right armpit, rest the length of the rod on my knee and feebly work the handle of the reel with my right hand. My left hand was limp by my side.

Gradually the poor old fish came alongside the canoe. I then saw him open his mouth, so I said to Captain Huff, "Shove the gaff down its mouth". He did this and pulled the fish into the canoe. We were dead beat as we both lay down at the bottom of this canoe. I told Captain Huff and his two men to go for the shore. The fish and I were about the same size, both lying prostrate as the boys paddled.

As we went towards the shore I could not bear the hot sun beating down on me and as we passed one of the two Gilmorris Islands I asked the paddlers to stop; I had to get into the shade. These two little islands off the coast of Shenge are covered with huge trees and with no habitation, human that is, but an absolute haven for bird life; every kind of sea bird. On each island there is a baracoon: a huge pit, lined with stones which are now all covered over with moss. This was where the slaves were pitched which had come from up-country and were sold by the chiefs to the slave traders before being trans-shipped across the Atlantic to the West Indies and the Americas. It must have been dreadful in those baracoons but at least they had the sky above them. Once they were put into ships they were chained down in the holds of the ships and of course many perished before they ever reached their destined shores.

I lay down by the side of one of these moss-covered baracoons and felt dreadfully ill. I wanted to relieve myself and stood up to do so. I was horrified to see that what came out was thick and quite black, just like Guinness, but no froth. I realised that something was wrong, so I thought that I had better get ashore. I got back into the canoe and the men paddled for land.

When I arrived the news went round the village that the D.C. had caught a tarpon. In those days no African could land one for none of them had the tackle. The Paramount Chief came down with all his Tribal Authority and the band played.

The Chief was called Caulkner. He had got his name from the olden days when the slave dealers used to call into this coast. They were English and they gave their English names to the natives or some of them would have children by the native women and the issue would take on the names of their father.

The fish was weighed and it came to 96 lbs. It then had to be cut up and distributed around all the necessary people from the Chief himself downwards. I felt dreadful but had to play the game and pretend to be all right. Finally when all was cut up and the people had gone I was able to lie down on my camp bed in the Rest House.

The house was a round mud building with a grass roof, situated on the edge of a cliff, looking out to sea. The Chief had ordered that the mud walls should be covered with country cloths to decorate the place a bit for the D.C. When I lay down on the bed I felt dreadfully cold - it was boiling outside. I asked my boys to pull all the country cloths off the walls and put them over me. These cloths, made by the natives from the local cotton are thick anyway and I had a mountain on top of me, but I still felt cold. I managed to take my temperature and it was 104.

I had six Court Messengers with me on this patrol and the one in charge was Sgt Bindi Bekadu. He had been a Regimental Sergeant Major in the Royal West Africa Frontier Force and an excellent chap. He immediately despatched one Court Messenger to Moyamba to call the doctor. It was about 30 miles away and it had to be walked, so it was a couple of days before he arrived. Whilst waiting, very feverish in my camp bed, I had a deputation from the Court Messengers, led by Bindi Bekadu whom I can remember standing at the door saying to me, 'Sir, we all know from what you are suffering. You are the victim of a swear. The head of that Secret Society which murdered the girl, whose mother came in to you in Moyamba, has put a swear on you to let you expose him and so he makes you ill. There are only two ways open; either you give us enough money with which we shall bribe him and then he will pull the swear, or you give us permission to cut off his head and with his death the swear will also die and you will recover.' I answered that I was afraid I could not accede to either of these.

Two days later Harold Tweedy and his wife, Dorothy, arrived. The Court Messengers had got the people of the village to make a good sized shimbeck for them alongside the rest house. Hal Tweedy took a sample of my blood and apart from the black water fever which accounted for the colour of that pee on Gilmorris Island, he found that I had the bugs for Triponomosiasis, or sleeping sickness, as well as malaria.

Nobody really knew how one got black water fever except that it has an affinity to malaria and also that it may be a form of quinine poisoning. It was usually fatal. The pathology of the condition was that the red corpuscles flowed out of the blood and clogged into the kidneys. Thus when one passed water this was mixed up with these red corpuscles which made it very thick and black. One therefore died either through anaemia through having no red blood cells or through the kidneys not functioning at all.

The sleeping sickness is caused by the bite of a tsetse fly which had bitten either an animal or a person with the disease. Malaria had been a constant complaint of mine out there, the cure for which, in my day, was quinine. As advised by the doctors, I took quinine every day prophilactically as well as increased doses when I had the fever on me.

Hal Tweedy thought that he must have some help so he sent off to Freetown for a European nursing sister to be sent out. In the event they sent another doctor, Dr John Busby and a sweet girl, whose name I cannot remember. The Tweedy's therefore returned to Moyamba. Hal had reckoned that it was best to do nothing but made me drink in order to obviate the black water fever.

When the nursing sister saw me she thought that I was going to die. John Busby, who thought the same, then gave me a massive dose of a drug called triparcimide. This drug was specifically for the triponosomiasis. It was only in vogue for a short time. There was no known drug that could deal with blackwater fever but triparcimide had a miraculous effect on me. From being practically at death's door, within a few hours I was quite a new man, though dreadfully weak.

The HQ of the Army in Freetown got to hear of my plight and they knew that Jack Wanklyn was my brother-in-law. They sent him a signal that he could use any form of army transport he liked to get down to see me at Shenge. Imagine my delight therefore when I saw old Jack walk into that rest house.

I was in bed in Shenge for ten days and there was nothing much for Jack, John Busby and the girl to do. Both Jack and John Busby fell in love with the girl. She used to wash me and massage my back in the most marvellous manner and I too, though utterly impotent, fell in love with her.

I always had a dog with me called Hank. He used to lie under my bed and suddenly he developed symptoms of rabies. Jack took him out and shot him. Jack always believed in juju and when he heard the story of the head of the secret society who had put a swear on me he reckoned he would go out and shoot him. But he did have the sense to ask my permission first which of course I refused.

John Busby thought that it was time I was transferred to Freetown so he sent off there for a launch to transport us. We were all on the cliff where the Rest House stood, looking out to sea, when one of the others called out, "Oh look, there comes the launch." I was in bed but could see out perfectly well, but as I looked out to sea I could detect no launch. I just thought it odd, but not important.

154

I was carried down to the seashore in a hammock. The launch could not come right alongside so the Chief and his Tribal Authority were all drawn up in the water ready to say goodbye to me. I shook his hand from my hammock and told him that I would soon be back and I would take that case about the missing girl and other matters.

I remember that trip back to Freetown very well and was joking away with Jack, John Busby and the girl. An ambulance drove me to the European Nursing Home in Hill Station. It was evening and the sun was going down over the sea. We were looking out westward, of course, and as the sun went down, I saw that green flash on the sea that one gets in this part of Africa; a mysterious optical illusion.

In the morning, it was still dark when an orderly came and shaved me. Later one of the nurses brought me some breakfast. It was still dark; I just thought that they started very early in this place, so I asked the time. She said it was 8 a.m. when the sun would be quite high in the sky.

I suddenly realised that I was blind. The triparcimide had paralysed my optic nerve. That green flash was the last thing I ever saw.

My first reaction was one of anger. I was absolutely livid and swore like a trooper, so much so that the Matron came and ticked me off. I felt angry for about a limit of two hours and then a strange metamorphosis came over me. I suddenly had a feeling of utter relief. I felt that all the weight had been taken off my shoulders and felt light and happy. I felt perfectly well, I just could not see. In a sort of a way this feeling has never left me although I do remember hanging over the rails of the ship which took me back to England, thinking how easy it would be to jump overboard in the night. I could not be found and that would put an end to it, for I saw no future in life.

There was a future for Pat. He married Bay and had a family. He became a successful physiotherapist in Eastbourne. When we knew him, he always blithely ignored his blindness as though it was but a minor impediment to living. He played golf and chess and always had a gentle disposition and an enquiring mind. The only thing he did not like was his friends coming to see him and watching the television with half an eye during the conversation. When Hal did this Pat detected it and gave him a ticking off. My father, of course, humbly apologised.

155

J.A.G. McCall arriving at Otako village, Nigeria, to settle a land dispute in 1947

Chapter 14

SERVICE IN THE OUTPOSTS

Whosoever will be chief among you let him be your servant.
Memorial to the Colonial Service, Westminster Abbey

..the evil that men do lives after them; the good is oft interred with their bones."
Mark Anthony in Julius Caesar by William Shakespeare

Trying to do the fair thing

In 1917 in the Sudan Reginald Davies records that slavery was a constant problem for the Government:

" The nomadic Arabs needed manpower to water their flocks and herds. This involved drawing the water from the wells and pouring it into troughs whose walls had to be kept in good repair. The flocks and herds were kept at a distance until the troughs were ready. The animals were often thirsty and it required several stout men to hold them back and to protect the trough walls.

Young men and boys would fetch a tempting price for this work and the unwary would sometimes find themselves being carried away into the desert.

The Sudan was jointly administered by Egyptian and British officers. The system was described as a condominium. An Egyptian officer was at a well-field in search of tax evaders.

As usual [there were] no animals, but a number of Arabs and Negroids were busy drawing water into troughs. At sight of the officer's military helmet-badge one of the latter dropped his dilwa (bucket) and rope. Clicking his bare heels and saluting smartly, he said, 'I am No. 2639 Private Mohammed Kuli of the Military Works Department in Omdurman.' The officer kept his head and told the young man quietly to go on drawing water until his master appeared to superintend the watering of his camels. In an hour or so the Arab arrived and was promptly arrested.

The boy's story was remarkable ... he was from the Nuba Mountains and had been recruited after a military patrol against his hill. In Omdurman he had been enlisted as a boy trainee in the Military Works Department and had become a stone-dresser by the time he was old enough to be promoted to full private. Soon after this event, in the afternoon of the Friday holiday, he was invited by two old sweats from the same company, also Nuba but from another hill, to go into the town and drink millet-beer. Towards evening the three of them, with Mohammed Kuli no doubt as drunk as his companions could make him, went into the deserted quarter of the town. There, among the broken-down buildings ... two Arabs were awaiting them, evidently by prior arrangement, with two camels. To them the boy was sold, like Joseph by his brethren, having first been stripped of his military clothes and given a suitably dirty cotton wrap.

Mr. Davies made the punishment on the Arab master fit the crime while his case was pending. The newly freed slave was employed as a stonemason and his ex-owner, in irons, carried the bricks and mortar for him.

Davies also told the touching story of two Nigerian brothers who were on a pilgrimage to Mecca when the younger boy, who was about ten, was kidnapped whilst his older brother was out cutting and selling grass and wood. The child was passed from hand to hand until he was sold to a Sheikh and his son who shut him up in a hut far away. His older brother travelled from village to village, posing as a religious mendicant, singing Hausa songs, in the hope that the child would hear him. His devoted persistence was rewarded when the little boy heard the singing and cried out for help. The case came before Davies who was at that time Chief Inspector, Northern Kordofan and the Sheikh and his son who had bought the child were sent to prison for five years.

When it came to do the fair thing, in Kenya in about 1896 Frederick Jackson found himself on the horns of a dilemma but in the event, the people resolved themselves. Jackson went to Ravine to take over from "little Martin" (who was said to be one of the very earliest, if not the earliest, district officer in British East Africa). A one-eyed man, apparently from southern Kamassia, who Jackson described as a "Lybon" or witchdoctor, came to see him and was introduced as a very useful man. Jackson explained that:

For a few months he proved himself to be so. But he was not a Kamassia at all; he was a Uasingishu Masai, and, true to type, he soon began to stir up trouble. It first started through his followers, one small lot after another, leaving him, and joining Mirumbi [a neighbouring Kamassia chief]. I confess to being prejudiced against the man from the first, as even when pleased, or when his face was in repose, there was always an evil look in that one eye of his.

However, I gave him every chance, until he proved himself to be a real disturbing element, when I first cautioned him, and then warned the Kamassia themselves against him. But it was no use, he had more power and authority over them than I had, and to show it, he one night sent a raiding party to attack Mirumbi's one 'manyatta' [homestead] at the foot of the hill just below the station.

It occurred about 2 a.m. in bright moonlight, and was so well and expeditiously carried out that, in a matter of a few minutes, they had killed two moran of Mirumbi's cattle guard, lost two of their own, set fire to all the huts, except Mirumbi's which was enclosed in a small stockade, and got away with all his cattle, some forty odd head. In one of the huts a poor old crippled woman was burned to death.

I had heard the 'kalele' (noise) but took no notice until the bugler sounded the 'alarm' and 'fall in', when I was out in a jiffy in gum-boots and a dressing-gown; but the raiders had too long a start and got clean away.

Such a direct challenge was impossible to ignore, and as I was a firm believer in the principle that it was better and more merciful to hit hard and get it over, when it was deemed necessary to hit at all, a strong punitive force was raised and commanded by

Colonel Ternan, at that time Acting Commissioner and O.C. Troops.

Raids and counter-raids were well understood by most tribes, as they had been accustomed to them for generations, but a real good knock-out was something new and was generally well remembered. In my experience, no punitive measure ever resulted in the killing of many of the enemy; they did not give one the chance, and as often as not they killed as many of the punitive force, and sometimes even more. Punishment was mostly confined to an attempt to capture their stock and, failing that, to the destruction of their huts and food supplies. The number of times a tribe laid itself open to punitive measures depended a great deal on the force of the knock they received; and also very largely on the time the punitive force remained in the affected area; a dash in, and a hasty return, even with cattle, had little effect. It was nothing new to them. But even a short stay, living in the country, and keeping them on the move, was something they did not like; and it at least showed them that the invaders were not afraid of them. The Nandi, admittedly, were an exception, as they received some fairly hard knocks on six occasions, and were only knocked out in the seventh round by a drive by three columns, extending over a period of many weeks.

The result of our punitive measure in Kamassia, though we crept and crawled along too slowly to capture their cattle, was quite effective, as we found and destroyed their well-stocked granary, hidden away in dense forest near the top of Martean Hill.

After the expeditionary force had returned to Uganda, the Kamassia made several attempts, at varying intervals, to sue for peace, through the usual channel, an old woman; but each time I declined to have anything to do with them, unless and until they excluded their alien, one-eyed 'lybon' from their councils, as he alone was the cause of their troubles.

What I expected was that they would bring him in and hand him over to me, when, as a political prisoner, he would have been deported to some other part of the Protectorate where he could do no harm. Instead of doing that, or packing him off to northern Kamassia, they killed him; and then, without so much as asking leave, a deputation of elders carrying grass and green twigs, came to tell me all about it.

Their story was that they had done their best to get rid of him, but he declined to go, defied, and even threatened them with his magic powers, so in the end they invited him to a carousal, made him drunk, knocked him and his son on the head, and threw both of them into a deep wooded ravine. It was, of course, a brutal act, but the fact

160

remains that the Kamassia never again gave any further trouble.

Ivory, bounty hunters, murder - all in a day's work

In 1907 Arthur Collyer was twenty seven years old; he had been brought up in the Home Counties and went to Oxford, he was the younger son of minor landed gentry in Sussex. It is hard to see how this gentle upbringing fitted him to be the District Commissioner of a largely inhospitble area of thorn scrub and grassland, peopled by different tribes, all with different cultural customs from each other, and very different from anything young Arthur would have been brought up to understand, but that was where his destiny took him.

The story of Mr. Newman's ivory gives us a glimpse across more than a century of the problems that faced this young man, and many like him, with no mobile phone or indeed any other telephone with which he could ask advice. He was thrown back on his own resources. His immediate superior was more than a hundred miles away – a journey that had to be walked or ridden – so not much help there; but nevertheless the PC, Bagge, in Naivasha wanted the whole matter investigated because he, in his turn, was being harassed to 'do something' by his superior, Mr. Hobley, in Nairobi. Mr Hobley was being harassed by a Captain Riddell who wanted to make a claim for the bounty on a cache of ivory.

Collyer was told to investigate; the ivory was hidden near the Uasio Nyiro River in Laikipia. A certain Mr. Newman (known locally as Nyama Yangu which means literally 'my meat') who lived by the Uasio Nyiro River, had become ill and gone to the coast where he had died. The essence of the story was that Captain Riddell reported that there was this cache of ivory hidden in Mr. Newman's hut and Riddell wanted to retrieve it and claim half its value. The young DC was asked to investigate.

It turned out that the heirs of Mr. Newman wanted his cattle and sheep, and the servants of Mr. Newman wanted their share, as did the local Chief. Two servants went to try and retrieve the stock from the local people and the chief was told to investigate the ivory.

161

The main characters of the story were Newman's "faithful servant", Karogi, two of his gun bearers, Basili and Muthengia, and a mysterious Marquis Hornvold, supposedly a relative of Newman's. Poor Muthengia was murdered on the orders of one of the local chiefs. No ivory ever turned up, to the extreme annoyance of Captain Riddell, and no doubt that of Marquis Hornvold.

Arthur's suspicion was that it was removed by a Somali caravan equipped with donkeys to carry the ivory, probably with the connivance of at least some of the local people. Somehow our young hero had to try and get to the truth and decide on the justice of a complex tale which took place several days' difficult and possibly dangerous walk from his base to Mr. Newman's settlement in order to visit the local chieftains and clan leaders. Reading his report over a hundred years later, it would appear that he came to the conclusion that to do more or less nothing, was his only option. He ascertained that there was now no ivory and he tried to reach an equitable distribution of the livestock between the local people and Mr. Newman's estate. He wrote a dry but reasonably detailed report for his superiors and hoped, perhaps, that it would gather dust in a government archive which is what it probably did. The absolute unvarnished truth was impossible to discover, and justice impossible to dispense. We must wonder as we survey that far away colonial landscape, what would we have done?

Setting up a new district

From those early days onwards the daily tasks performed by an administrative officer were extremely varied and because they were far from superior counsel they often they had to react quickly to the unexpected and fly by the seat of their pants. Colonial service was perhaps the most diverse employment that has ever been offered before or since. But most of them did not see it like that but as rather humdrum. Colin Campbell, was given the job of opening up a new district at Bungoma. I asked him what it was like. His reply was matter-of-fact:

To be accurate I was DO Kavujai, not Bungoma, in 1949. It was a chief's camp with a banda for visiting officers. Rather than hog it myself, I pitched and lived in a tent nearby. Also in a tent, not far off, was a Kenya Police Inspector who commanded a detachment of askaris.

Kavujai was a few miles from Bungoma which comprised a railway station on the Eldoret - Uganda line. When I was at Kavujai, a hospital was being built at Bungoma. This became the nucleus of a sub-station which was built round it and some years later the complex was expanded and hived off from Kakamega District and turned into a District in its own right.

My main role as DO Kavujai was closer administration of the main tribe, the Kitosh, to check any resurgence of the Dini Ya Msambwa [see Chapter 17'] My job was to travel round the area, liaise closely with the Chiefs, hold barazas and do any jobs allocated to me from Kakamega. These mainly entailed hearing land cases, which were appeals from the Native Courts. I covered a lot of ground hearing these appeals and also got off the beaten track. I don't remember having a bicycle but I probably borrowed one on a few occasions.

I also encouraged better farming practices. Kakamega had an outstandingly able and dynamic Agricultural Officer, Fergus Wilson, who had a number of schemes on the go, such as composting and planting vacant land on road verges with ground nuts. I also kept a fairly close eye on the progress of Bungoma Hospital on [Doctor] Howard Murcott's behalf, which was being built by an Indian contractor.

Another job was to supervise the work of the road gangs. A road network was the classic way of promoting closer administration. The gangs were directed and administered on the ground by a tough old Dutchman from Eldoret called Snyman, who, as so often happened with the Boers, got on better with the Africans than we did and was more on a wavelength with them. The labour was found from convicted Dini Ya Msambwa minor offenders and were really inmates of mobile detention camps without bars. Very few ran away and those that did were quickly returned by the tribal authorities. When I visited these camps I received very few complaints or shauris. [problems] I strongly suspected that discipline was aided by a kiboko [whip] but I received no reports from the labour, nor did I invite any!

There was nothing magical or romantic about starting up as DO Kavujai. It was just an extension of the safaris which all district officers carried out from HQ. I didn't set up an office as such, as the aim was to remain as mobile as possible so I presumably was pro-active!

I used to go into Kakamega most weekends to deliver reports, collect new law case files and to use the clerical and typing facilities there. I usually parked myself on your long-suffering parents and it was on one such weekend that I met Jackie who was hitchhiking with a girlfriend from Kisumu to Kitale, via Kakamega. The Agricultural Officer found them out on the road rather late at night and, considering this unsuitable, packed them into his car and delivered them to your ever longer suffering parents.

So indirectly there was some romance at Kavujai!

At about the same time Tom Watts was in Turkana *concentrating on the maintenance of tribal discipline and security by stopping intertribal raiding, killing and stock theft between the nomadic tribes along our Ugandan, Sudan and Abyssinian borders. There was tax to collect, an efficient way of keeping tabs on the male tribesmen. There was livestock to purchase with which to feed the troops down-country. Early on in my service with the Turkana I received a basic lesson in economics from an elderly tribesman who had been asked whether he had paid his tax. He looked at me disapprovingly and then replied, 'When have I had a chance to buy some money?'*

Keeping the Population Fed and Prosperous

Locust control was not usually the prime concern of an administrative officer but, of course, everything that happened in the district was his and his colleagues' responsibility. In 1942 the weather conditions of rain and warm sand created a particularly perfect breeding ground for these voracious insects in Turkana.

As Kenya was providing an important amount of food for the North African Campaign a great effort was made to kill the newly hatched "hoppers" before they reached maturity in the warm desert areas to fly away to devastate the crops in the agricultural areas of East Africa. A large expensive transport organisation was set up to bring in poisoned bait (the husks of the coffee berry) by the thousands of sack loads, and water with which to damp them before laying the bait across the path of the marching hoppers. Companies of the East African Pioneer Corps were employed not only on laying the bait but also in digging trenches across their path whose density was so great in places that they smothered each other in the trenches before they could

164

crawl out. The last line of attack, when the hoppers were reaching the final instar by developing wings, was to use flame throwers to scorch the almost mature beast before it could fly away in its vast swarms. It was deemed necessary even to burn war-time petrol in the attempt to protect the crops.

The Administration was the buffer between the tribes-people and the pioneers. Every effort was made to warn these simple people of the dangers of the poisoned bait but even so women gathered them up and boiled the coffee husks as food for their families, fortunately with no apparent fatalities. This campaign kept men in the bush for many weeks. One dreamt of these hoppers with their large eyes peering at one. During one night a band marched through my camp and tackled the bags of maize meal rations and made a meal of the puggree on my helmet.

After those early years when Sir Frederick Jackson burnt granaries as punishment, this policy went into reverse and district officers were required to inspect the granaries. If they were low it was up to him to ensure that corrective measures were taken, or to report to his superiors in order that the shortages could be dealt with in good time.

The dread of famine was a constant worry to many administrative officers, one of whom, in Tanganyika, said that *to allow famine to develop without early warning was the worst offence a district officer could commit.*

Mr Brian Carlisle, an administrative officer in the Sudan, faced a famine in Beja district:

The rains of 1947, 1948 and 1949 were all very poor outside of the Gash and the Beja started to suffer real hardship through lack of grazing and failure of their rain crops. In the summer of 1948 the Sheikhs brought in reports of some people really going hungry and some action was clearly needed by the Administration. Although still a very new boy I was acting in charge of the District and wondering exactly how to play it with Province H.Q.; I turned to the excellent filing system in force throughout and discovered lengthy correspondence about a previous famine situation some years earlier: this discovery assisted me to put up a cogent case for some free grain to be distributed through tribal circles. As the situation worsened more grain was requested and constant supervision became necessary of the worst hit areas.

Some administrative officers worked to improve farming techniques, even though there were highly competent and innovative Agricultural

165

officers who were more than up to the task. But land disputes were very much a district officer's area of responsibility and Reginald Davies, also in the Sudan some forty years earlier, found that:

Many of the disputes which were brought to me for settlement arose over gum-gardens, as patches of gum yielding acacias were called. They were valuable because the gum, which oozes from long wounds in the bark of the branches, made with a small axe, was the principal cash-crop of the region. These acacias have a curious habit of regeneration. The trees are cut down when they become too old to produce gum, to make way for grain cultivation. Five years later the land becomes too exhausted to produce grain and is left fallow. After an interval the acacias begin to reappear, without human effort, and in five years or so are big enough to be tapped for gum.

It was the job of the administrative officer to pronounce on the boundaries of the gardens. Davies would sometimes have to thread his way between the trees to mark the boundaries of ownership, listening and reacting to the protests and counter protests: "My God it is not thus!" while the other side were suspiciously silent. Thus were the boundaries drawn.

Keeping the Peace

Christopher Dodwell was the D.O. in Oyo, Nigeria in c1959. The Alafin told him, "The business of ruling is like a rabbit. You have to hold it close, or it escapes you."

At this time independence was appearing on the horizon and the political temperature began to rise in Oyo when two lawyers, who did not live there, decided to make it the centre of their power base. One of these, known as 'The Bulldozer', lived a hundred and twenty miles away in Lagos, while the other lived some thirty miles away in Ibadan.

These two would arrive in the small, peaceful township and hold meetings in the Atiba Hall, which was situated at one end of the market square. At the other end was the Alafin's palace and in between the two was the police station manned by a dozen unarmed Native Authority Police.

One morning Christopher Dodwell was summoned to the square to find a large and angry crowd of the Alafin's supporters drawn up in front of his palace. At the other end of the square, in front of the Atiba Hall was an equally large and angry crowd intent on forcing political change.

The noise of shouting and drumming at both ends of the street which ran through the market place, was deafening. Slowly the two factions began to advance upon each other.

By patrolling up and down between the two crowds with a couple of Native Authority Policemen, Dodwell managed to bring them to a halt. The problem was what to do next.

Apart from anything else, his desk back at the office was groaning with files which needed urgent attention. His solution, therefore, was ingenious. Sending for the files, he borrowed a table and chair from the police station and placed it in the middle of the road. With threats to strike the first man who passed his table he settled down to the business of the day.

Nonplussed by Dodwell's sang froid the crowds filtered away.

It was the dry season in Sierra Leone in the late 1930s and Pat O'Dwyer was out on trek collecting tax. He received an urgent message to say that the iron ore miners at the Marampa Mines in Lunsar were on strike and that he must go there immediately.

This was tricky. He was in the middle of collecting several thousand pounds worth of tax. All the chiefdom had gathered for the purpose, as well as to have their complaints heard and it was embarrassing for Pat to leave them; besides which the DC was always personally responsible for any deficit in the tax or any other revenue. Nonetheless he decided that he must trust his accompanying clerk, with the help of the Court Messengers, to go on collecting the tax and to bring it in to the Headquarters at Port Loko when it was completed.

He set off with a couple of Court Messengers to the nearest road and there he hired a lorry to take him some several miles on to Lunsar. As he approached the mine a number of palm trees had been felled across the road to prevent any vehicle approaching.

There was a highly tense situation beyond the road block in the mine.

167

Five thousand labourers were very angry; the considerable number of Europeans, mostly Scots, who worked at the Marampa Mines were forced to stay in their houses or they would have been attacked.

Road blocks in the bush are perilous places. The blockers have every advantage and the blocked are left stationary, pointing the wrong way and vulnerable. Nonetheless out climbed O'Dwyer from the lorry to parley. Despite his weak bargaining position, with two unarmed Court Messengers and a commercial lorry driver hired an hour or so earlier, it touched him that on recognising the blue band around his topi signifying that he was the DC, the strikers did not hesitate to accede to his request to remove the trees from across the road.

For several days Pat remained at the mine doing everything he could to persuade the men to go back to work and the company to negotiate. But the miners were adamant that unless they were given more money they would not pick up their shovels. Wages were indeed very low and partly paid in rice but the Company were equally adamant that it would not discuss wage levels under duress and the miners had to go back to work first.

Further pressure was put on Pat by the Provincial Commissioner in Freetown who ordered that the impasse must be broken and the men got back to work. Iron Ore was needed for national purposes: Britain was building up its armaments as World War II loomed.

As there was no way of persuading the Company to offer better wages until the men resumed work, something had to be done to bring this about, in both the miners' and the company's interests. Requesting another 70 Court Messengers from the Provincial Commissioner and a company of troops, Pat O'Dwyer devised a cunning plan which was going to be a long-shot at best. When the troops arrived the officer in charge was told that the soldiers were only in reserve in the event that the strikers went beserk, and they were to be well hidden from them. The somewhat gung-ho officer was disappointed but did as he was told and drew them up on the road about a mile from the mine well hidden in trees.

Having briefed the Court Messengers, O'Dwyer then sent a message out that it was very important to have as many of the miners as possible to attend a meeting on the football field. When they arrived he harangued them as he had done several times previously trying to persuade them to return to work, while the Court Messengers were scattered amongst the crowd. With the Company's approval, he told the men that if they did start work again they might stand a chance of higher wages.

When, as he expected, they refused once more to go, Pat gave a pre-arranged signal to the 70 Court Messengers who each grabbed the workman next to him and frog-marched him up the hill. *Damn me if the plan did not work,* he wrote. Having seen that the game was up the others on the field meekly followed the seventy frog-marched men and walked to the mine.

It would be nice to conclude by saying that there was a happy ending with all parties satisfied by the outcome but history does not relate the sequel.

*****

Roving bands of criminals, the most dangerous of which were personally led by a renegade brother of the Emir, were known to haunt the outskirts of large market towns, raiding and robbing as opportunity offered. ...Thus wrote Bryan Sharwood Smith in his book "But Always as Friends". He was writing of Gwandu, Nigeria in 1931 where the lack of roads meant that crime was difficult to check.

Together with Usumanu, 16th Emir of Gwandu and "one of the most dynamic and, at the same time, most lovable personalities with whom I ever worked", Sharwood Smith devised a plan to create a disciplined mounted police force which would make it easier to move around the roadless areas.

The Resident of Gwandu, Mr Daniels, was the very man to advise his DO, Sharwood Smith, and the warrior prince.

He was a hard riding character with a red wig, frequently worn askew, who loved horses almost as much as he loved the North and its ways, in which he was deeply versed. Not only did he give us permission to go ahead at once, he also told us where we could get second-hand saddlery and equipment...

As soon as it arrived from England, we started serious training ... Dickie Carr, our Education Officer, a tough ginger-haired little man, had done most of his soldiering in a lancer Regiment; this project of ours was right up his street, and he devoted all his spare time to ensuring its success. Evening after evening out trotted Dickie, jaunty and erect, while toward him, the dust billowing behind him, drove the Emir. Awaiting them, squatting on the grass by the wayside, were the new recruits, each holding the reins of his newly acquired mount. Then, for an hour, Dickie instructed while the Emir encouraged, or reproved, with blistering effect should anyone fail to put his heart into his riding.

After three months we had started show-jumping and tent pegging and gymkhana events in general. We then issued a challenge to Sokoto to send over a team of 12 to take part in a two-day competition, a challenge that was at once accepted. ... Our gymkhana was a great success, especially as the Gwandu team defeated Sokoto by a narrow margin. We were all delighted, for not only had they practiced very hard, their success made them feel that they were, indeed a corps d'elite.

Soon, in twos and threes, they rode off into the bush with orders from the Emir to harry the robber bands that had for so long plagued the peasantry until they found the land too hot for them. And so it was. After a fortnight or so, in twos and threes, they came jingling back again, and before them in handcuffs came their prisoners, the Emir's renegade brother among them. Crime in Gwandu had, at least for a while, ceased to pay.

Road Building

In his book "The Lunatic Express" Charles Miller quotes Bishop Tucker living in Uganda on the system of postal communication by runner before the advent of the car: *Huts were built at intervals of one mile along the principal roads ... A letter dispatched say, 100 miles in the interior is placed in the hands of a native runner, who at once, having tied it to the end of a split reed, starts at full speed holding aloft the missive and shouting at the top of his voice, 'A letter, a letter, it is burning in my hand – a letter, a letter.' As he draws near the first hut on the road he finds a messenger standing ready... For important communications such a postal service was invaluable. But... not infrequently I have been roused up at one or two o'clock in the morning with the cry, 'A letter, a letter – it's burning in my hand,' and upon opening the letter I have found it read something like this: 'TO MY FRIEND THE BISHOP. How are you, Sir, How have you passed the day? All is well here; there are no evil tidings to tell. Farewell. May God take care of you. I am, your friend who loves you, SAMWILI.'*

As cars became more prevalent the needs for roads were high on the to-do list. A near death experience on the part of Major Clarence Buxton and a veterinary officer, George Low, who was accompanying him, showed the extent of that necessity. They were trying to get from Narok to Nairobi across country and nearly died from dehydration and exposure. At the eleventh hour they crawled into a filthy cattle and game water-hole and drank their fill. This saved their lives but George Low nearly died from the diseases he took into his system from the water. Buxton was completely unaffected.

While he was at Narok Major Buxton tried to persuade the Masai moran to build roads into their location in order to open up trading possibilities with their neighbours. The moran turned against him and whipped themselves into a frenzy, they bore down on the camp where he and his family were staying. Buxton bundled his wife and children into the car with a guard, leapt on to his horse (a beloved Arab stallion called Forge) and raced out to meet the moran, which surprised them into silence. After a harangue from the DC on his horse the steam went out of them and they wandered back to their manyattas.

Eric Loveluck, an enthusiastic DC in post-war Tanganyika, was determined that his district should no longer be without roads. *I have got the whole African population behind the scheme. The chiefs are behind it and everybody is going to work for nothing, unless I have the money to pay them and if I do I pay them as and when on the never never plan and they would all trust me completely,* he informed the Governor, to whom he had, rather unusually, taken his request for a D4 caterpillar tractor with bulldozer blade. His Excellency, no doubt disarmed by the fact that Loveluck also had the complete backing of the Almighty ("I mustn't forget to say that") suggested that they put a line through a couple of pages of the district estimates and wrote: "To the purchase of one diesel bulldozer." Sharwood Smith and the Emir also enthusiastically over-spent their budget on building a road to the remote independent district of Illo, "an historical anachronism."

During the decades before the British occupation, successive Chiefs of Illo, protected by river, marsh and forest had successfully resisted all attempts by neighbouring Fulani to subjugate them. Thus when a British expedition laboriously poled and paddled its way upstream, intent on striking Northward in Fulani territory, Chief of Illo of the time was very willing to help in any undertaking that would embarrass the Fulani. For his services his independence was underwritten and he was made a 2nd Class Chief. The present Chief of Illo, however, though a most personable and magnificently built young man had a tendency, if left unvisited for long, to divert the revenues of his tiny treasury, into projects of a personal nature. There was another reason too, for making Illo more accessible, it lay on one of the oldest trade routes in this part of the world, and we were continually hearing stories of donkey trains being bogged down and of goods being lost on the journey across the marshes on their way to and from Dahomey and the Gold Coast.

One of the Emir of Gwandu's more endearing, but often disconcerting qualities was the speed and vigour with which he got to work on any project in which he took personal pride and interest. I had yet to learn that once such a project was agreed between us, unless I kept an eye on him, he would apply all his boundless energy and all the resources of the emirate in carrying the work through to completion. To problems of finance and accounting he was supremely indifferent. It was the D.O.'s business to look after that sort of thing.

And so it was the case. I returned from my reconnaissance of the Illo route to find the old man, very pleased with himself, waiting to tell me that not only had he pushed through a track to a ferry point on the Niger, he had actually got his own car down to the water's edge.

This was all very fine, but I, the D.O. must now explain it to a ruffled Resident how it was that our road 'vote', already all but foundered, was now well and truly overspent, and with three months of the financial year yet to go. And, in those days of exigence and highly centralised control, there were few sins that a DO could commit that were more nefarious than overspending a vote ....

So off I went cap in hand, to Sokoto, my head bowed to the blast that I felt to be inevitable, for L.S. Ward, who had taken over from Daniel, was reputedly somewhat of a purist in matters of native administration finance. However, I was let off lightly, for the Illo project appealed to his imagination. Not only did he secure approval for the release of Gwandu Native Treasury funds sufficient to cover the work which had already been completed, he also got agreement to the more elaborate and more expensive section across the marshes toward Illo. Illo and its troubles had featured so frequently in correspondence between Sokoto

and Kaduna in recent years that any scheme that would insure closer administration was welcome.

The crossing of the Niger opposite Illo, our main task, would have to be carried out in two stages. First there would be an approach road across the marshes to the point where deep water would give access to the main stream. Then would come the actual crossing by ferry. This would probably be alarming but not difficult. Our problem would be to reach the main channel, for the marsh at this time of the year was entirely under water except for a number of tiny islands. The only possible way across would be to construct a series of causeways connecting such of these islands as suited our purpose. These causeways would have to be revetted and bridged at frequent intervals to let the current through.

Fortunately the area was thickly studded with borassus palms, which made our task much easier. These great trees, thirty to forty feet high, played a vital part in our construction program. The male palms are impervious to white ants, where all other local timber would rot, they could endure for years, even when totally submerged. They can be used whole as bridge girders or split into sections for decking or revetting. But when we started to get down to business we ran into trouble at once. The river people declined to co-operate. They alone knew where the water was shallow and where it was deep and which was bog and which was submerged sand, but they felt, with some justification, that a motorable track across the marsh would put them out of business as guides and ferrymen. There was only one way of finding a way across and this was by personal exploration, using our bodies as gauges. So a small party of us by trial and error, wading now knee deep, now chest deep, now waist deep, found the shallowest route from island to island, staking the line as we went. It was a crazy thing to do, but I had not then heard of bilharzia and I was sure that there were not crocodile in such weed-clogged water.

Every fifty feet or so we put in a small bridge, and in the centre, as the waters began to run more swiftly, we constructed larger ones. Our first causeway was our longest, and it did not seem possible that we should ever reach our goal, a small hummocky island almost five hundred yards distant. But yard by yard the road snaked across the lagoon, enthusiasm mounting as the labourers got into their swing, each gang vying with its neighbour as it strove to complete its allotted section first. We employed a pair of drummers for every gang of twenty men, and these were often supplemented by unpaid volunteers. A gang working in time to the rhythmic beat of the drums and the chanting of the drummers, to which they themselves supplied the refrain, shifted soil and undergrowth with a speed that it was a joy to watch. They never seemed to pause from dawn to dusk.

Long before first light the thud, thud, thud of the drums summoned them from their encampments, and they hacked and stacked and carried, with barely a break for food and drink, until it was too dark to see. Then, still accompanied by their drummers, they wound their way homeward to where, by the light of huge fires, a gargantuan meal of meat and corn and rice awaited them. Then they feasted to the rhythm of the drums until, sated and exhausted, they flung themselves down by the fireside to sleep until first cockcrow heralded another day.

We all slept on the job, though I had to run back to Birnin Kebbi every few days to clear my office desk of the mail that had accumulated in my absence.

Measuring the gradients was an essential part of road building when there was a gradient to measure. In 1927 in Nigeria, a man called Bridges fashioned *a builder's spirit level screwed to a pole with one pin on the siting end, and 3 pins at the far end, representing 1 in 16 down level and 1 in 16 up. While Dike, the interpreter, kept an eye on the bubble I sited on a T-square of the same height as the spirit level, held by another assistant, the road maker driving in pegs to mark the line and level. The trouble was if Dike's attention wandered after a heavy lunch and the bubble wasn't where it ought to be.*

In 1928, Jack Flynn, a young DO in the Embu district of Kenya, remonstrated indignantly with his parents for describing his as being a 'roadless district.':

We've got lots of quite good earth roads, in fact more than we want because some of

174

them are hardly ever used and are a job to keep up. Lamb, who used to be DC here, was a surveyor originally in Uganda, and he seems to have spent all his time making roads. In reserves the roads are usually good because there is so little traffic: there are only 6 cars in the whole district I think, including a Hudson which Chief Runyengi bought for £50 from the duka about a fortnight ago: he keeps a chauffeur too.

The 'Knife thrust' of Kindness

When Hal Williams was in Mandera in 1933 Gerald Reece was in charge of the District, based at Moyale [See Chapter 8]. Some of Reece's letters to Hal show his character to be that of a mercurial martinet. Hal, though, was devoted to Reece as were almost all his subordinates and there was an extraordinarily compassionate side to his character which particularly came out when he was dealing with the people for whom he was responsible. Negley Farson wrote *he knew the personal character of nearly every man in the region and almost the whole NFD (Northern Frontier District) It was like watching a man weave a pattern, using human beings instead of wool.*

Also in Mandera with Williams in the early thirties was the Goan clerk Da Costa. Fifteen years later when the author, Negley Farson, was travelling with Gerald Reece who had risen to be Provincial Commissioner in the NFD , they went to visit Moyale and there was Da Costa, now retired and *doing a small commission business; previously he had been twenty-six years in the Administration at Moyale. Reece and got him the MBE when he was retired in 1942.* Farson said that he was a kindly-looking old man with grey hair, dressed in a worn but neatly kept brown suit.

Mr Da Costa found it very lonely in Moyale. "I have no one to talk to. My wife? Yes, sir. But ... occasionally one wants to talk to other men. I can't do that, sir. Perhaps it is the 'official consciousness,' sir - the reason why they won't talk to me?"

"Oh, you mean the - the white men here?" asked Farson.

"Yes, sir. I'd very much like to talk with them. Sometimes I get tired of reading. I have had thirty years, all told, in the service of the Government.... I took up business, my little commission business, because I must have something to do. I <u>can't</u> waste my time ..."

Negley Farson told Reece of his conversation who said to the DC as he

175

was leaving "Old Da Costa came over and showed Farson his MBE Says he's lonely. Got no one to talk to. Pity, isn't it ... faithful old chap like that - and nobody here will talk to him? Well, goodbye."

"It was," said Farson, "as pointed as a knife-thrust."

On the same safari with Negley Farson, there was a slender native woman *wearing just the scantiest of rags, leading a little girl by the hand. She was darting at anything that the Dubas might have left, although Reece was adamant about leaving a camping place undefiled. ...The woman dived like a hawk on any object ... then, with the most rueful expression, examined it. She was a scavenger herself as much as any pinioned hawk wheeling in the sky. When I came near to see what it was that she could possibly find of value, she walked closer to me and gave me a strange smile. ...*

'Most extraordinary creature' I said to Reece when he came back. 'She almost seemed to be flirting with me.'

His face fell. 'Oh is she here? She's mad. It's the only case of love that I've ever known in native life - true love, between man and woman. Her husband was a Gabbra, a very bad Mohammedan. He discarded her. He went off with another woman into Abyssinia. For years I tried to get him to come back - at any rate, to do the right thing by her. And I saw her - right before my very eyes - go mad from misery....Hell of a thing life is, isn't it?...' He walked over, and I saw the woman reach out and take his hand. They stood there like that for a little while, Reece talking gently to her. Then he withdrew his hand, put it into his pocket, and handed her a fistful of money.

'Uncle Reece' would also come down like a ton of bricks on wrong-doers. The story that Negley Farson tells of Reece's wrath shows not only this facet of his character but also how important it was that officials got out from their offices and travelled in their districts and sub-districts.

Reece and Farson were on their way south from Moyale - which is on the Ethiopian border - and they had passed Buna, following the road to Wajir, a much used camel route.

clunk-clunk ... these great 'ships of the desert' swung to and fro as they stalked majestically past us on the road to Wajir. ... there would be over 10,000 camels at the wells by the time we got there....That morning Reece and I came on a scene that showed all the avarice and brutality of Somali life. This was at a 'pan' where some envoys of a Wajir camel-sheikh were in camp, demanding money from incoming Somalis before they would let them water their camels there. If they did not pay, it meant that, with sixty miles still to go, and no water whatsoever in between, all the weaker animals, especially the fresh-born goats, would die before they could get to the Wajir wells. Reece, who took in the meaning of the scene even as we came up to it, went livid with rage.

It was one of the most impudent scenes I have ever looked at. For sitting comfortably under the wide shade of a wild fig tree was a knot of Wajir Somalis, with a couple of bearded, ferocious-looking headmen; and in the partial shade of a grove of acacia trees was parked a large herd of camels and goats, with some stupefied, weak Somalis debating what they were going to do about things. From some thick brush beside the wild fig, marabou storks, with their obscene flesh-coloured sacks dangling, were rising, and hundreds of doves were darting about - sign of the big pool of water there. ...

Reece, ominously quiet now, stepped from our car and walked up to the aghast Wajir Somalis, who leapt to their feet.

It was worth paying a ticket of admission to see such a set of scoundrels get such a thorough dressing-down. Without raising his voice or even making a gesture, Reece stood there facing the frightened sheikhs, and struck them blow after blow of verbal insults. He staggered them, literally. As he took each man in turn, the man fell back from him. In the meantime, at a snapped command, our Rendille Duba had gone across to the waiting camel clan and told them to begin watering. ...

The camels were standing dejectedly, silent, with their loads taken off them. They were terribly thin and emaciated, dirty from lack of water and even sufficient grazing that would have put them in good heart. They seemed immensely tall as they stood here and there among the acacia bushes; and some obediently sat folded up on the ground, from which their owners now began hastily to unstrap the four deep wooden red water-pots. Now a line of smiling, happy men and women began an instantaneous procession back and forth to the pan. Nobody talked. ...

An uninquisitive passer-by might not have noticed anything unusual in the scene, for, as I have said, the Somali has an immense dignity; and Reece, knowing just how to meet with that, was dignified even in his harangue that was taking the skin

177

off them. He just stood there quietly telling the Somalis who had been trying to hold
their brother Somalis up for bribe-money that they were the most mean-hearted,
disgusting set of thieves he had ever come across. The strangest part of the whole scene
was that there were two armed policemen there who were supposed to guard that pan.
Reece put the fear of God into them also.

'There, you see,' he said when we drove on again, 'is what happens when a DC does
not go out on safari enough in his district.'

Visitors

Frederick Jackson's book Early Days in East Africa, gives us a flavour
of how he went about his tasks before Kenya was a colony of that
name and these include contacts with his German counterparts in
Tanganyika in Uganda in 1894.

It was while I was acting between Colonel Colvile's departure and Mr Berkeley's
arrival, that Naval Lieutenant von Kalben, who was himself acting for Captain
Langheld, the officer in charge of the Nyanza Province in German East Africa,
paid me a visit.

Colvile and Langheld had been conducting a far from friendly correspondence on the
subject of the misbehaviour of our [African] canoemen in German territory, when
employed on water-transport work between Mwanza and Entebbe; and it fell to von
Kalben's and my lot to smooth over matters.

His first act, at my request, was to renew his correspondence in English, and he also
accepted an invitation to pay me a visit at some future date, to discuss various matters
of mutual interest and importance.

In those days it was difficult to notify ahead the actual date of one's expected arrival,
and my guest arrived and departed by steam-launch before his letter by runner reached
me. The result was that while he arrived resplendent in uniform, I received him in an
old flannel suit, and I am inclined to think that our mutual embarrassment, he at
finding himself unexpected, and I at his sudden appearance, helped greatly to foster
our spontaneous regard for each other.

I have always regarded Uganda as particularly fortunate in having as neighbours in
charge of adjoining German territory such men as Langheld, von Kalben and von
Strumer, with whom negotiations were always conducted in the most friendly spirit
and on the principle of give and take.

Among other things which von Kalben and I discussed and agreed to represent in the strongest terms to our respective Governments, were the disadvantages of the one degree of South latitude as our frontier, in place of the Kagera River which the former crossed and re-crossed in several places.

The small areas within the various bends were mostly marsh and of no value, but were regarded as a harbour of refuge for all sorts and conditions of 'wanted by the police,' who, when hard pressed, found it easier and safer to step across an imaginary line, and defy their pursuers, than to face a deep river full of crocodiles. However, no notice was taken of our pleadings and nothing was done. I have always understood that politicians at home like to have a little bit of land to play with, particularly if it is an annoyance to a neighbour; it may some day come in handy as a useful bit to exchange for a bit elsewhere. In the meantime, local annoyances, that might lead to unpleasantness, are of no account. [See Chapter 10.]

"The man who makes no mistakes does not usually make anything." E.J. Phelps (1822-1900)

In the first year of his service in Kenya, when he was 24, Hal Williams's inexperience found him taking a decision which he remembered with remorse to the end of his life. The incident occurred when he was temporarily stationed at Meru before taking up his post in Mandera.

I was sent out to evict some Boran from Isiolo who were alleged to be poaching grazing in the Meru district. When I located these Boran and moved them on, I allowed the Chief and Interpreter to persuade me that the wisest course of action would be to burn their village as they would return and continue poaching as soon as I had left. Having done so, although I knew it was wrong, the storm was not long in breaking. The Boran lost no time in making fantastic claims for many thousands of shillings, despite the fact that I was careful to make sure that the huts contained no goods.

My two superiors were men of great practical experience who resolved the matter and kept it within the family. Nonetheless, it gave me a nasty jolt and it could have had serious repercussions. It taught me never to accept the advice of interpreters and their ilk against my own judgement.

The Downside of Life

Loneliness in the outposts was indeed a problem. In 1941, Hal Williams, was transferred from Narok, where he was living with his

179

wife, Joy three year old son, Richard, to Garissa in northern Kenya. At that time the Italian Army was threatening Kenya's northern border and units of the Kings African Rifles and South African troops were being drafted in to defend it. Administration officers were given military ranks and the whole area was put on a war footing.

Wives were strongly discouraged from living in the Northern Frontier even in peacetime. It was a bafflingly masochistic policy which made life far more spartan than was necessary and no provision or thought was given to where the families left behind would live. For about a year after his transfer Joy lived in a variety of places: she rented a house for a while but that was too expensive, and for short periods she, the baby and ayah stayed with her aunt, Olive Collyer, in Kabete. Then she took a job as a nanny, which provided money and a roof over their heads. It was a difficult period.

Meanwhile in Garissa Hal was bored to extinction and very lonely. He wrote many letters to his young wife which still exist and overflow with misery over his enforced bachelor existence. Communications were difficult and haphazard. In one letter in 1941 he wrote, *This is just a note to tell you that my telephone is out of order. I am, however, going up to the Camp Commandant's this morning to see if I can get through on his as I am very anxious to hear what your plans are."* In another letter in July he said, *"Now, my sweet, I want to try and come down between the 1ˢᵗ and the 8ᵗʰ [of August] .... The question of transport is rather difficult and I may not be able to get any. In which case I shall just have to leave it until I come back from Kismayu. ... We shall have to talk about it on the telephone if I can get through."* Later in August 1941, he wrote, *"The military have given up collecting our mail bags, so do not know when I shall hear [from you] again.* He also reports that his wireless did not work and he wondered if his wife could find a second-hand one that they could afford.

He felt woefully cut off. Low morale sapped his energy and he was worried about money. On 14 March, 1941 he sent an official request for a transfer to

The Hon. Chief Secretary, Nairobi. Thro' Officer-in-Charge, NFD:

Sir,

TRANSFER. MR C.H. WILLIAMS
DISTRICT OFFICER

I have the honour to ask that the question of my transfer from Garissa be considered by Government.

2. The facts are that in October 1940 I was stationed at Narok when I was notified of my transfer to Garissa. In common with the great majority of the Administration I had applied to be released for military service but had not applied for Administrative service in the N.F.D. and had no desire to leave Narok involving as it did the keeping up of two separate establishments. However as I understood it, was a special case and that my services were considered to be of use to the war effort at Garissa [which was then a war zone] the situation was accepted without complaint and I was only too happy to stay as long as those conditions applied.

3. I would now submit however that these conditions no longer apply and would ask that my transfer be arranged as soon as is convenient.

I have the honour to be

Sir,

Your obedient servant

His request did not find favour at all. Hoskins, the Chief Secretary made him sweat for five weeks before replying on 26th April 1941:

PERSONAL & CONFIDENTIAL

Dear Williams,

I have deliberately delayed answering your letter of 11th of April for some time until I could have an opportunity of discussing it with Reece and also of making a cool and unbiased judgement on it.

First of all I like officers to write frankly and to say exactly what they feel and I appreciate the confidence shown in me by your writing so freely.

After five years of the most comfortable stations in the Colony you have been required to serve in the Northern Frontier District and you have been there six months and find yourself bored to death with no work to do. The work in the NFD and in other outlying stations - even in Narok - is what you make it. If you are content to wait for work to be forced on you there may be less than half an hour's work a day, but I cannot believe that in a district of the extent and population of the Garissa District there is not ample work, and surely a mass of arrears of work, to keep two men busy.

I am afraid that the North appeals only to a limited number of officers and that we have to require others to serve there even though it does not appeal to them. In wartime we expect every officer to put his heart and soul into any job to which he is sent.

As to the double establishment, your wife has, I know, relations in Kenya and my latest intelligence was that she was with you in Garissa.

You were certainly sent for a special purpose to Garissa but the war is not over though its focus has altered ...

Had you put your back into the job at Garissa, even though you did not like it, I would have done my best to have met your wishes over your next station, but the best advice I can give you now is work. Look for work and make yourself enjoy work with the consolation that you are doing the job that you are required to do in wartime.

Yours sincerely,

Although we do not have my father's reaction to this rocket, from the later correspondence it seems clear that it gave him a tremendous jolt. And the Chief Secretary was right, Joy had unexpectedly turned up in Garissa and without doubt that was the real reason why his spirits and his work improved dramatically.

Without letting him know, Joy had packed her toddler son and the ayah into the Ford V8 box body and headed north.

We spent the night at the hotel at Thika and here I went and saw the local policeman who was a friend of ours. I told him that I was going to Garissa the next day and as Hal did not know about it, would he telephone Garissa at about 5 pm to find out if we had arrived? The policeman was delighted to do this and he also asked me to take one of his askaris who was returning home. This was a good move for me too, to have a policeman with me. Also in the hotel at Thika were two army officers who, when they heard I was on my way to Garissa, asked me if I could take their driver back. He, they said, could help me with the driving. Actually it turned out that he had only driven staff cars and the old Ford defeated him. But he would have been able to help me change a tyre if necessary.

182

The road had been recently graded to accommodate the increased military traffic and the 228 mile drive went very smoothly. We crossed the Tana on the ferry, which was just below the house, and drew up at our door just after 2 pm. Hal, having an after lunch nap, opened an eye when he heard the vehicle. He thought he was seeing things when that eye seemed to light upon what seemed to be his very own car. His concerns about insanity or delirium changed to incredulous delight when he saw it was indeed his own family.

When the army headquarters heard of our arrival they gallantly offered to service the Ford and a driver came over to collect it. As he backed it out of the garage the fan belt broke. On opening the bonnet, there it was in ribbons. It just saw us there and that was all.

In July Mr Hoskins wrote a personal letter in his own hand:

Dear Harold,

Some weeks ago I wrote you a stinker in reply to a letter of yours saying that you were bored to extinction - couldn't find half an hours work a day to do.

You deserved it!

Gerald Reece is now in Nairobi & has told me that you seem to be putting your back into your work & to be liking it better. I understand that your wife is still with you - which may well make a difference to your outlook on life.

Anyhow Reece seems to be very pleased with the way you are doing the job & I want to thank you for the way you have got down to it.

Let me know if you like it any better. These days, I cannot hold out hopes of a speedy release which would merely unsettle you but you may be surprised to hear that I take considerable interest, not only in the efficiency but also in the happiness of administration officers.

Good luck to you both, don't let your wife stay too long as she hasn't quite got your robust frame.

Joy and Hal spent a supremely happy year together in Garissa. Her presence not only proved that she was quite robust enough to survive but that she was able to make life so much more comfortable for Hal and others in the boma. She sent down to Nairobi for a dozen hens and she also made a vegetable garden. She was able to nurse the sick and injured that arrived and she could help Hal on safari.

Her happy time in Garissa exploded the myth that women could not survive in the NFD and after that time most wives accompanied their husbands on such postings. Thus the spartan Beau Geste lifestyle began to give way to normality.

Hal and Joy Williams with their son, Richard, Garissa 1941

Many years earlier in 1923, Major Clarence Buxton did not want to leave Narok at all either. But a serious clash with his immediate superior led to a precipitate transfer. Buxton was to become closely associated with the Masai and fiercely to defend the tribe's interests. [see Chapter 10.] As one colleague put it, *He gallantly defied all encroachment both of Government and settlers, corresponding over his Governor's head with the Secretary of State, caring nothing for the ensuing rows or any personal consequences.*

But it did take its personal toll and at times his frustrations weighed him down. He wrote gloomily to his mother:

I havn't done a sketch for six months or more! The pressure of everything is too much and the Kenya ways of doing things more futile so that one's time and energies are just wasted. ... The pettifogging trivialities with which we fritter away our chance [is] appalling.

The row began innocently enough. He was, at the time serving at the District Headquarters of the Masai, working under the DC, Major Rupert Hemsted, who was very knowledgeable about the tribe, having studied their characterics for over ten years. Buxton had enjoyed working with Hemsted, carrying out his policy which was aimed *at the development of the power of the Native Councils so that they might restrain the hubristic habits of the Muran (warriors). The Masai elders agreed that the Muran were no longer required for the defence of the tribe and could not be employed for their aggrandisement by raiding, but they were unable to prevent the Muran from enjoying their old privileges or to divert their energies to peaceful industries. Consequently, the repression of cattle thefts, looting and murders which took the place of war was left to the European Administration, the Elders merely advising the Muran not to commit these excesses and being defied by the 'sirits' of lawless, lazy and licentious warriors.*

Buxton had been impressed by the "unswerving loyalty" of the Elders when some Muran had gone on the warpath, causing the European and Indian traders to flee in panic from Narok but he believed that the elders "lacked the means to exercise any effective control over the Muran who had defied them no less than the Administrative Officers. In order to achieve more effective control, Buxton asked Hemsted for permission to increase the number of Tribal Police that were under the direct orders of the Tribal Councils. The DC agreed to this because such a change would have been in line with his policy of indirect rule throughout Masailand and the plan was implemented. It meant, of course, that because the numbers of Tribal Police in the Manyattas were increased, there were less of them at Narok.

Major Buxton believed that the system worked well. He introduced a number of checks and balances which ensured that the Tribal Police under the control of the tribal elders were kept up to the mark.

Suddenly the policy was reversed. In June 1923 Mr Henry Horne took over from Major Hemsted. He decided to return to the system of concentrating all the Tribal Police at the Government station. Major Buxton objected strongly. At Mr Horne's suggestion he submitted his views in writing:

I am not prepared, Buxton wrote, *to reduce the number of Tribal Retainers with Councils unless I receive definite instructions to that effect.*

Horne responded that he did not propose to discuss the matter further and would go to the Secretariat and explain that he could not tolerate Buxton remaining in charge of Narok District. As good as his word, three days later Horne travelled to Nairobi and the following day Buxton received telegraphic notification transferring him from Narok to Kisii in Nyanza Province.

Down but not out, Clarence fired off a furious letter to the Chief Secretary. He said that he recognised that, "if a junior officer disagrees with his senior, it is best for the sake of social convenience and official harmony that the junior should be transferred." But he believed that both Hemsted and Buxton leaving the district at the same time would be detrimental to the well-being of the Masai, especially in view of the fact that there would also be a reversal of policy. He thought that: "as I had been in charge of Narok District for seven months I feel that I have a duty and a right to express my views on the administration of that district and to protest against the decision on a matter of such importance to the Masai."

His arguments were to no avail. Off he went to Kisii.

Although Buxton returned to Masailand to fight another day, precipitate transfers such as this could cause great bitterness. In his book "Kenya", Dr Norman Leys described another transfer during the First World War which produced the worst result of all.

A certain district officer refused to carry out an order that he thought involved injustice, was naturally rebuked, and was transferred in disgrace to a lonely post usually kept for those unpopular with authority, and shot himself in the head.

This particular suicide may explain the presence of the ghost who was often seen at the District Commissioner's house at Kipini in Tana District.

Suicides were very rare, despite the privations and the loneliness. [See Chapter 4] "We were always extremely busy." was Johnnie McCall's response when I asked him if he ever felt overwhelmed by solitude.

J.A.G. MCall on board his official launch the "Dorothy" – Nigeria.

"Then the mosquitos – phew!" – The discomforts of service in the outposts

Most men who served in the Colonial Service can remember the excitement, the fascination, the friendships, the hard work and the achievements but they have played down the loneliness of living day after day far from home, often in considerable discomfort and surrounded by people who were very different from themselves.

During the Second World War J.A.G. McCall was posted to Brass in Owerri Province, Southern Nigeria; an area which he covered by launch (when it was working), car, canoe or bicycle.

On 6th September 1941 he wrote home:

The last week I have been in Brass, and it has been a pleasant change after weeks of constant travelling. The other evening I was surprised to be disturbed after nine in the evening by the whole of my staff who had come to pay me a visit. They came to 'beg' me as they say in this country. On this occasion their begging consisted in asking that there might be less travelling. I rather sympathised with them, they don't get much chance of home comforts; they are always on the move, and only see their wives for less than a week every month.

At the time Johnnie was not married himself and he lived a very solitary life during the war years, relying on his Pye radio which brought him war news and classical concerts. He was not able to accede to the request of the staff to travel less, and the following day:

I am off on tour again. This time I am doing an unusual tour. I am going to Degema as usual, but there I am abandoning my launch for three days and am going into the Ahoada division .... I can reach the most distant parts of this district more conveniently through Ahoada than from any other direction.... It will be a change to travel on roads and by car.

He adds rather shyly:

It is not good to be always entirely on one's own. It is a well known fact, and it is pathological as well as pathetic, that the less a person in a lonely station sees of his fellow kind, the less he wants to see of them. There have been cases of chaps stationed in very lonely stations who have fled to the bush when they have heard of the impending once-three-monthly visit of the European Medical Officer. I don't want to get into that state. And as the doggerel rhyme puts it, 'black men's ways and black men's faces' are apt to get a bit nerve wearing at times, for certainly their ways are as different to those of the European, as the colour of their faces. No Administrative Officer lives closer to the Native than does the AD, [Assistant District Commissioner] *Brass.*

But keeping up a cheeryness, he adds: *Oh, but it's a great life and here I am after a year in Brass, still liking it as much as ever.* It is only reading between the lines of his letters and imagining what it must have been like minute by minute of every day that one realises that sometimes he may have dipped into despondency.

Perhaps especially this was so when he was not busy. As the song puts it, "For there's nothin' like a Sunday, makes a body feel alone."

My Sunday timetable, he wrote on 5th October 1941 from 'The Consulate, Brass,' *is different to that of other days, as of course is the Sunday programme of most people. I get up at six. That is normal, unless I want to lie-in but that is not very necessary in a place when any late night on Saturday is out of the question. I go over to the office and either work or write letters until ten, when I have my breakfast. Then I return to the office as now, and do not have my lunch until four in the afternoon. Lunch on Sundays consists of palm oil chop - the dish célèbre*

188

of the West Coast of Africa. This is chicken boiled in palm oil, and served with all manner of titbits such as local red pepper etc. It is an acquired taste, and I did not like it at first, but now that I think of my coming lunch today, my mouth waters. It is undoubtedly the best meal of the week, and I should have it every day, if it were not so very rich, and thus fattening, and this is a question to be reckoned with in Brass when one never gets any exercise. Chicken, chicken, chicken ... every day and every meal. Unless you open a tin, there is no other staple food to eat. I refrain as far as possible from opening tins, particularly in wartime, when tins mean imported articles.

One of the places on McCall's beat was Nembe, *which is surely one of the last places it was ever intended that a white man should live. It is a town lying in the midst of a mangrove swamp, and in the wet season it is difficult to find a dry spot in the Rest House Compound. The town is a collection of the most ramshackle, tumble-down houses that ever you saw in your life. Most of them are built of "pen" (corrugated iron) and were put up in the palmy days of the last century when the Nembes controlled the oil trade in these parts. Now they have lost all that trade and much of their former wealth. There is little prospect for their future, and they have become an idle and discontented people torn by dissension and intrigue. This attitude to life is reflected in the condition of their town. There can be nothing uglier than a broken-down, and rusty corrugated iron house, and as they were built quite indiscriminately, and close together, the picture of ugliness, dirt and stink has to be seen to be believed.*

I think I have already described to you the rest house. It is a mud wall building with a corrugated iron roof, and it also is falling to pieces. (The Nembe Native Administration has no money to repair it.) Inside, the floor is perpetually covered with a green slime, and the floor has cracked and sunk, and looks as if it might at any moment fall into the creek. There are large gaps between wall and floor, and also large holes in the walls. When darkness falls the rest house becomes alive with crabs - crabs large, medium, small and tiny. They run all over the place, and Easten [the auditor] who was having his first taste of the delights of Nembe, played games with them and even tried to arrange races between them. Then the mosquitoes ...whew. Unless you want to be eaten alive you just have to go to bed.

Not every officer lived in such places in the outposts with unappealing

189

animal life but one in the Sudan Political Service living in Renk on the Upper Nile had a daily routine during the rains of *walking down a cleared path to the river before breakfast, picking the leeches off his legs, wiping the mould off his boots, followed by breakfast, after which he would proceed to the office where he spent his mornings giving his clerk a thorough grounding in the mysteries of the Civil Secretary's filing system.* The clerk subsequently rose to the top of his profession.

The sun burns and the hot winds blow
In pitiless accord
And we who serve the sceptre know
We may not draw the sword.
From aching eyes and bitter hearts
Deliver us, O Lord.

Richard Owen in Western Kordofan in frustration at not being able to
join up in World War II

Chapter 15

COMRADES IN ARMS

When the 1914-18 war began, *Colonel von Lettow-Vorbeck had less than 5000 men under arms, including a few hundred Europeans. Later, however, by utilising every conceivable resource, he brought into the field at various times nearly 4000 Europeans and over 20,000 warlike 'Askaris'. The East African campaign was therefore a SERIOUS MATTER and the problem was increased by the incredibly difficult nature of the country where thick bush, particularly in the South, gave every advantage to the defending force.*

The two World Wars did much to break down the barriers between African and European. Sir Philip Mitchell, in his book 'African Afterthoughts', saw this when looking back on his experiences in the East African Campaign in 1914 against General von Lettow-Vorbeck:

Another thing the war did for many hundreds of Europeans and thousands of Africans was to introduce them to each other, so to speak, in a way and with a completeness hardly to be achieved otherwise. First-line transport was exclusively by porter and it took three porters to keep a rifle in the first line, even with an African infantry regiment, so that a column on the march and in camp was in fact a large mass of Africans with whom their British officers and N.C.O.s marched, slept, ate, washed and had their being in a physical closeness of a quite exceptional kind.

On patrol on the frontier in 1914 and 1915 and in German and Portuguese East Africa from then until the armistice everything that I had and used, including four days' rations, clothing, bedding, knife, fork, spoon, plate and mug, had to go into two porters' loads, restricted in most King's African Rifles battalions to forty-five pounds each; in that shape I rubbed elbows with my African comrades in a manner which did me a great deal of good and for which I have been grateful ever since.

Rations were, of course, simple; normally bully beef, or, in cattle areas (which were relatively few), tough fresh beef, weevilly biscuit, coffee, or tea, salt and sugar; jam more usually yesterday and tomorrow than today! And often ... we had to make do with anything we could get - buck meat, zebra, even giraffe or hippo, sweet potatoes or cassava, or maybe a little maize, rice or millet, green bananas, occasionally river or lake fish and wild honey. All shared alike, of course, officers and men, and all frequently went very hungry for weeks on end.

The military contribution to the war effort in both World Wars by both West Africans and East Africans was magnificent and has not been fully acknowledged by most historians. One distinguished officer of the Kenya Administration, Lt Col Oscar Watkins, CBE, was given the task of raising the Carrier Corps for the East African campaign. In 1919, in his report he wrote:

From small beginnings, learning its lessons as it went, it has entered on its registers nearly half a million men. From Somaliland in the north, from Portuguese East Africa in the south, from Nigeria, Gambia and Sierra Leone in the west, from the great lakes and the headwaters of the Congo and the Nile, from the snow-clad peaks of Kilimanjaro and Kenya, came contingents to the Corps. Men who a few years ago had never seen a white man, to whom the mechanism of a tap or door-handle is still an inscrutable mystery, have been trained to carry into action on their heads the field wireless or the latest quick-firing gun. ... Men of the cannibal tribes of the interior, sons of the Arabs who filled Africa with the agonies of villages raided for slaves, Hausa and Mende, Somali and Galla, Kavirondo and Kikuyu, Wanyamwezi and Wanyika and Wakua, and countless other tribes besides have learned that they had a bond of union in the 'Carrier Corps' as they called it and fearless champions in its officers and NCOs.

When the Second World War broke out, Kennedy Trevaskis was serving as a junior DO in Northern Rhodesia. Shortly before he arrived he had voted for the motion in the debate in 1933 at Oxford *that this House will in no circumstances fight for its King and Country"*, which was carried by 275 votes to 153. However, when war broke out in 1939, he put his pen down on his desk, walked out of his office and joined up in the Kings African Rifles. The battalion was sent to serve in the in what became known as the Abyssinian Campaign, to drive the Italians out of Somaliland and Abyssinia. His unit was one of the first to arrive in Somaliland and a military bungle saw the unit captured by the Italians.

As a prisoner of war, Trevaskis, led by Shaukat Hyatt Khan, spent his time digging a tunnel but one of his African soldiers, Private Kenani, wiled away the time sewing together little pieces of material that he came across:

It was on April Fools' Day 1941 when one moment we were passing the time in our customary fashion and the next gazing intently through the barbed wire at a small column of armoured cars approaching us. Could they be British armoured cars? No sooner had we asked ourselves the question than a head popped out of the leading car wearing an unmistakably British steel helmet. A few minutes later we were shaking hands with our liberator, a young British Bimbashi of the Sudan Defence Force. What an April Fools' Day that was!

Our captivity was at an end but, as the curtain came down, an unforgettable little scene took place. We were all shouting, shaking hands and thumping each other's backs when suddenly somebody pointed to the flagstaff which towered over the camp. Looking up, I saw Pte Kenani, the bad boy of my platoon, shinning up it. On reaching the top, he tore down the Italian tricolour and then replaced it with his handiwork, a diminutive homemade Union Jack. 'Long live Bwana King George!' he shouted. 'Long live British Empire!' Sgt Kabanda appeared at my side. 'We all knew that we would win', he said. 'The British always do!'

But only a few Administrative Officers were allowed to join up and it caused great bitterness amongst some. In the light of what happened to him later this bitterness was never quite forgotton by Pat O'Dwyer right to the end of his life. [See Chapter 13]

He was *on the reserve of the RWAFF (Royal West Africa Frontier Force) and each year I had done an attachment with them either in Freetown or in Daru. Things started to blow up (in August 1939) and I was wondering whether and when I would be called up. One evening I was shooting with Peter Youens in Port Loko and the international news was very bad and the next morning I got the wire ordering me down to Freetown...*

In the RWAFF I was given a platoon. Up to then the troops had never worn any boots or puttees, instead they polished their shins and feet. Now War had come it was thought that they must wear boots and puttees. Having just been issued with these I was ordered to take my platoon up to French Guinea to liaise with the French Commandant. This meant going up through Port Loko and Kambia and a lot of marching. The troops' feet got so sore that they all took their boots off and hung them round their necks. We marched through French Guinea and the people in the country seemed so quiet and morose and I could not help comparing them with the happy and laughing Africans on our side. Yet when Independence came to all the African countries years later, the erstwhile French colonies seemed to behave much better than our old colonies.

195

The task of the RWAFF for the time that I was with them was to man the beaches against a possible attack by the Germans from the sea. The fear was that the Germans would take over Uruguay and launch an attack on the West African coast from there. In between sojourns on the beach with my platoon we use to do some training in the bush. One day we were in thick bush just off Jumley Beach when we were attacked by the most vicious swarm of bees I have ever come across. The troops were carrying heavy equipment such as Lewis guns when every single one of us was attacked. The troops had to chuck all their equipment away and run for it. I defy the Brigade of Guards or anyone else to stand up to wild bees when they are angry. I joined the troops in running and we all made for the sea with bees buzzing and biting us as we went. Only when we all got under the water did we escape from the onslaught.

In August 1940 the RWAFF was posted to Port Loko and Pat O'Dwyer was redesignated DC there.

Detachments of troops came up from Nigeria and the Gold Coast and were posted there. ...The Army had to defer to me for anything they wanted in connection with the African or the country side. In this way I felt quite important but I felt awful when they all left on their way to Burma to fight the Japs, and in spite of my efforts to join them I was not allowed to do so.

Interest amongst the civilians in the fortunes of the Allies during the Second World War varied. In Bornu Province, Nigeria, where some of the district Heads were of such ancient lineage that they could trace their families back a thousand years, the enthusiasm for the war effort was considerable.

Every Tuesday evening wrote Rex Niven, *I would go to the Middle School to talk to the boys about the war news. I drew on the blackboard and showed them the maps. The boys took a great interest, and asked intelligent questions. ... After the Middle School I would go along the Dandalo to the Shehu's gate and there sit down in a circle of townspeople and tell them too about the war news. Great was their interest. I gave the news in Hausa and a 'shouter' yelled it in Kanuri. Oddly the crowd varied with what sort of news it was: if we were doing well there might be two or three thousand people, if not so well it would dwindle to hundreds.*

On another occasion Rex Niven was asked to act as umpire - flying in a Blenheim - to the French Air Force who wanted to test two navigators:

It was a good flight and they reached the points indicated. At Biu we came down to a few hundred feet and circled the town, flying low over the streets. I had been able to send a message to the Chief so that the people would not be alarmed - it was the first time that anyone down there had seen an aircraft. The people were delighted and

196

waved: later, of their own accord, they collected some hundreds of pounds for the 'Spitfire Fund' - the official theory of which was that £3,000 would buy a new Spitfire fighter. Bornu in all raised enough for three.

In Brass District South Western Nigeria, on the other hand, in June 1941 Johnnie McCall was not having quite the same success. He held eight flag days in eight different places over the period of eight days in aid of the Red Cross. Brass District was a very scattered area and the third flag day was held in Oloibiri, at just about the point where the mangrove bush merges into the rain forest.

There is a Native Court and a Rest House here," he wrote in a letter to his family in Scotland, *"placed on the only solid piece of land in the neighbourhood. It is a typical creek station, with the ebbing and flowing waters of the tide, instead of the running waters of the main branches of the Niger, as in many other places of the Brass District. There are thirty-two villages under the Ogbeyan Clan, and most of them seem to have come in today.*

...The programme started with a Service in the local Church. There was a packed congregation. After the Service, everyone moved up to the Court Compound, and when I say everyone, I include about thirty two schools. ... Nearly every school had a band, and moreover each band was anxious to show its paces so each band was playing at the same time, but different tunes and with different time. ... Add to it the singing of all the scholars, several hundred of them, the shouts of the spectators each shouting at the other at once and you have a fairly accurate picture of the African really enjoying himself.

There followed a speech by myself - the only time during the day that I could hear myself speak - the sale of Red Cross Flags, musical drill by the scholars and they are very good at this - due, I suppose, to the Native's innate sense of rhythm - the opening of a new Dispensary, a Red Cross raffle sale which I conducted, break for lunch, Native dancing in the afternoon followed by a further raffle sale, until the party finally wound up with a mammoth Native dance in which everyone took part - you know, I have described them to you before, everyone waggles round in a circle with posteriors going back and forwards to the rhythm of the drums. ... We havn't counted the money yet, but when I do I shall let you know how much was collected but don't expect too much because the collection is almost entirely penny penny, if not halfpenny halfpenny.

When WWII war ended Rosemary Dowson was in Garissa in Northern Kenya with her husband John. He was on safari when she heard that Churchill would be announcing that the war was over. Not wanting to hear the announcement on her own, she wrote a polite little note to the only Europeans in the station at the time, two Italian prisoners of war, inviting them to come to her house to hear the announcement with her. The Italians equally politely refused. Rosemary, therefore, listened to Churchill's long awaited announcement and then went into the kitchen to celebrate with her cook, Ikuna.

"Ikuna!" she said "Isn't it wonderful, the war is over!"

Ikuna was in the process of taking a tray of scones out of the oven, he glanced over his shoulder to her and said, "Yes! ... Who won?"

J.A.G. McCall presiding over a heated land dispute at Otako, Niger Delta, 1947

Chapter 16

TRANSPLANTING ENGLISH LAW TO FAR OFF LANDS

I Promise to do right to all manner of men, without fear or favour, affection or ill-will."
Part of a colonial Governor's oath.

Before the arrival of a British colonial administration the enforcement of law and order varied from tribe to tribe but on the whole punishment was prompt without such niceties as proving guilt or innocence.

In Uganda the Banyoro were, we are told by Sir Harry Johnston, *an honest race - the exactions and raids of their chiefs and kings excepted. ...Theft is peculiarly rare. ... and they are honest to a degree which is exceptional in the Uganda Protectorate, where, as a rule, the people are a very honest lot. ... Under the old native Government, if a case of theft took place in the daytime, it was punished by a fine, but if at night, the culprit was left to the mercy of the people he had robbed, and this usually meant his being beaten to death with clubs and his body thrown on to the main road.*

On the western side of the continent justice was, if anything, harsher still before the advent of British law. In Ondo State in Nigeria the native punishment for murder, burglary, robbery and slave-dealing was death *usually by crucifixion in the bush*, and sedition was punished by cutting off the offender's lips and ears *after which he was chained to the town gate to act as toll-collector. And in some towns in Awka Division punishment for murder was the fine of one woman.*

In the 1940's Hal Williams found himself discussing with the local leaders how to mete out justice to some maize thieves in Kwale on the

Kenya coast. His suggestions, which were of course in accordance with British law, met with disdain: "When we caught someone stealing maize," he was told severely "we would cut off one hand and if he was caught again we would cut off the other."

Trying to transpose English law to Africa was not, therefore, an easy matter as Lord Justice Denning observed in 1955. (Quoted in the Corfield Report)

Just as with the English oak, so with the English common law: one could not transplant it to the African continent and expect it to retain the tough character which it had in England. It had many principles of manifest justice and good sense which could be applied with advantage to peoples of every race and colour all the world over, but it had also many refinements, subtleties and technicalities which were not suited to other folk. These off-shoots must be cut away. In those far-off lands the people must have a law which they understood and which they would respect.

The task of making these qualifications was entrusted to the judges of those lands. It was a great task.

Magistrates were usually District Commissioners or District Officers who were designated as Class I, II or III Magistrates and there were limitations in sentencing imposed according to the Class. There were also some magistrates who travelled from district to district. In Kenya one District Officer, Jack Flynn, was struck down with multiple sclerosis fairly early in his career. (It was a double blow because he had been an athletic man who had represented Britain as a hurdler at the Olympics.) When his illness had been diagnosed he became a roving magistrate.

Often the first step people made in seeking justice was using the device of the petition. It was a popular method of making people in authority aware of a problem and sometimes it could be resolved at that point. Mervyn Maciel, a clerk in the Kenya Administration was of the opinion that the petition was a helpful way to get a grievance off a petitioner's chest and even if the DC's solution was not to his advantage, the petitioner could at least go home relieved that the problem had been resolved one way or the other. The reasons for a petition could be minor, and quaintly phrased, such as this one told by Reginald Davies in the early days of the Sudan Administration:

To his Excellency the Governor. The Bash-Shiwash [Sergeant Major] of the Police has my wife, my God how annoying! and it ended sadly, *Ah! and ah!.*

Many people employed the services of the professional letter writer and strict rules applied and M.C. Atkins tells us that:

The amount which they were allowed to charge was laid down by law according to the number of words and the number of copies required and it was a criminal offence to charge more than the fee prescribed.

Serious petitions were dealt with sympathetically and a strict, if cumbersome procedure was followed when such a petition was received. He goes on to say

Petitions came to the DO in the first instance but the addressee might be the DO himself or, in ascending order, the Resident, the Chief Commissioner, the Governor, the Secretary of State for the Colonies, or His/Her Majesty. Each petition addressed to an authority higher than the DO had to pass through the officer(s) below on both the upwards and downwards journey. The number of copies required was the number of stages through which the petition had to pass, plus one; a petition to the DO had to be sent in duplicate whereas one sent to the Monarch or to the Secretary of State (who were regarded as the same for practical purposes) needed six copies. Petitions to the Governor would receive a reply usually within nine to twelve months while one addressed to the Secretary of State or the King would take up to 18 months; as often as not the reply would simply be that His Majesty, His Excellency, or His Honour had nothing to add to the advice given by the DO to the petitioner. ... Petitioners were always addressed as Sir or Madam and accorded the following ending:

I have the honour to be,
Sir/Madam
Your obedient Servant

Probably the most prolific letter-writer and certainly one of the least inhibited dwelt in Abeokuta. During the course of a single year he filled seven files averaging 200 pages each with petitions on his own behalf and on behalf of his clients. He was also perhaps the most mendacious. In one of his own petitions he accused the DO of assaulting his wife, raping his daughter, falsely imprisoning his brother and using such bad words on the petitioner himself that he could not even understand them. The letter ended, 'From all the above, I can only conclude that the DO does not love me at all.'

The claim to fame of one of the Warri letter-writers rested mainly on the headings to his letters. Two examples are:

'Mr X, an incompetent drunkard'
'Lt Col Y is a goat'

The DO described as an incompetent drunkard, is said to have shown the letter to

the Resident with the remark that it was the first time that his competence as a drunkard had been called into question.

While the DO was the commonest recipient of petitions, no government official, trader or commercial could expect to escape altogether. One received by the Manager of Elder Dempster Lines was a claim for compensation for damages from a dock labourer. He had fallen into the hold of a ship and according to him, had suffered a long list of injuries to head, neck, ribs, waist, legs and feet. The last injury listed was: 'One private member (slightly bent).

Petitions could also be made in person and this could stretch the resources of the Administration considerably. In some places such as the Sudan, in the very early days local elders were brought in to help but Reginald Davies wrote:

It was flattering, but irksome, that petitions always seemed to want the attention of the British Inspector. As one of them, making his way reluctantly to the panel of elders, cried out picturesquely, 'The turban will not ease me! The tarbush will not ease me! I want the helmet.

Debt is and always has been a universal problem. In Sierra Leone all cases of debt were brought before the DC followed by interminable distress warrants issued when the judgement had not been fulfilled. Finally court messengers had to distrain on the property of the debtor.

In the early days of the British Administration in West Africa and indeed prior to its arrival, recovering a debt often involved pledging a debtor or a member of a debtor's family. In Sierra Leone, for example, domestic slavery was legal until 1927. After that date it became illegal, but pledging and slavery continued. When the slave had the courage, he or she would complain to the DC who would order him to be set free. Their masters were of course always Africans too and many of these were chiefs. One Nigerian man I knew had been pledged to a chief to repay the debt of his dead father. This was a great misfortune for our friend who was an intelligent man but he almost totally missed out on his education, working for his father's creditor.

It was sometimes awkward to disagree with a chief's ruling because good relations were valuable but where misdemeanours such as adultery were punished by pledging there was no choice:

Very often a man would pledge himself to the husband of the girl with whom he had committed adultery because he had no other way of paying damage. This form of pledging one's person was illegal, but the chiefs for the most upheld it and indulged in it themselves because a peasant really had nothing to give but himself when he got into

debt. This was one case when we often had to overrule a chief and set the man free.
Native courts presided over by the chiefs, heard civil and criminal cases using procedures based on their own native laws. The chiefs' powers varied in each colony but generally they were empowered to imprison, in the District gaol, for up to a period of six months, confirmed by the DC and with appeal permitted to the DC, the PC or the High Court. These native courts worked well. O'Dwyer says that in Sierra Leone *the DC was always wary of upsetting the chief's sentence, for if he undermined the authority of the Paramount Chief in his own Chiefdom, he could bring disorder which he, the DC would have to repair.*

Julian Huxley, who was asked in 1929 by the Colonial Office Advisory Committee to go out to East Africa to advise upon certain aspects of native education, discussed in his book "Africa View" the pros and cons of indirect rule. With this in mind he considered how the law would be affected:

Under direct rule he wrote *an overburdened white man attempts to deal with the legal affairs of tens of thousands of natives. In spite of finding his energies overtaxed, he knows if he reflects a little, that only a fraction of the accumulated litigiousness of the people actually finds its way to him. Either violent or illegal means of settling disputes must be increasing, or the old traditional methods of native justice, although unrecognized by white authority, are dealing with the bulk of cases out of his sight, below the surface. ...*

But under the full system of indirect rule, not only are Native Courts recognized, but they are recognized as the mouthpieces of local law and custom, only to be interfered with or modified if these conflict with certain fundamentals of white justice. Thus the law which regulates the dealings of a native people with each other is no more imposed upon them from without than is the chief who rules them; it is their own law, an indigenous product.

In the Musoma district I was given an example of how under indirect rule the natives get the law they like, and not an alien code. The people here are very frightened of witchcraft, and take great precautions to conceal their excrement, nail-parings, and so forth, for if an enemy got hold of such products of their bodies, there would be no limit to the harm he might do. Recently a man was caught stealing another man's urine. The presumption was that he wanted it for magic purposes, and the Native Court inflicted the heavy fine of 10 shillings. And the District Officer, when he went through the records, upheld the judgement. According to certain standards, he was wrong to confirm what he knew was based in error; but granted that the territory has embarked on the policy of indirect rule, he was perfectly correct.

Did the people "in those far off lands" have a law which they understood, respected and above all which worked? Pat O'Dwyer, who wrote a comprehensive description of the justice system in Sierra Leone thought so:

In capital cases of murder, arson etc. the DC took depositions from all the witnesses and committed the prisoner for trial in the circuit court. For this a Puisne Judge would come up from Freetown and go round the districts about every six months. If the trial was one in which a native was involved, the DC got hold of two Paramount Chiefs to sit with the Puisne Judge to advise him on the native law. He was not bound to take the advice of the chiefs and there was no jury. For the most part I think justice was done all right.

Elliot Balfour considered that the colonial penal system *placed a great deal of power in the hands of a single individual, but seldom, if ever, was this power consciously misused.*

Brian Carlisle hopes this was so in the Sudan:

Whilst in the Districts in the Sudan in the forties one was properly pitchforked into the DC's work and, looking back, I am amazed to see how soon I was put on trying judicial cases - I trust no great injustices were done. In Kassala Province no Province High Court Judge was appointed until late 1947 and even then a lot of judicial work still fell on the Administration, particularly the Magisterial Enquiries that still had to be held for commitment for trial by Major Court. For the first few months an interpreter was at hand but after that one coped on one's own. My records show that in this period the cases I tried included the...beating up of a policeman, selling a short measure of cloth, insulting the Police by a prostitute, having a dirty coffee shop and smuggling.

In 1931 Margery Perham spent a morning in an "A" grade native court in Oyo, Nigeria:

It is, for tropical Africa, the usual open-sided building which attracts the crowd. Spectators were divided as to sex, about thirty women on one side, about a hundred men on the other. The clerk at the table was writing in what I observed over his shoulder to be very dubious English. Seven Judges reclined on the ground upon a slight dais. They wore flowing robes with large blue and white patterns and baggy trousers. The president had conceived a striking attitude in which one foot was raised above his head, a pose I have only seen upon a Chinese print. The clothes heightened the Chinese impression, the round heads, some slanting eyes and a couple of top-knots in pure Chinese fashion.

The form here of greeting one's superior is to fall flat on the ground and put your face almost in the dirt. Whenever a new judge joined the bench all the others collapsed, a rather tiring and insanitary form of greeting. One of the young British cadets introduced me with a nervous speech which was not received by the court with much enthusiasm.

A clerk sat next to me and breathed an interpretation into my ear. The women litigants were shrill to the point of hysteria. When the judges were shouting down their colleagues and the goats at issue in the case were bleating and the hens clucking it was not easy to follow the legal niceties of the proceedings. When they wished to confer together the chiefs rolled into a heap in the middle, wallowing like a school of walruses. One old gentleman, following excellent Western precedent, was fast asleep. As so frequently happens in African courts, no case ended; each was adjourned for further evidence: a sign of thoroughness or lethargy?

Hearing cases was, of course often a tedious job, particularly as in most places it involved interpreters:

...all non-summary trials in the Sudan *were recorded in English and read over to the witness in the presence of the accused in whatever language they used.*

A.F.B. Bridges in Ondo 1934 alleviated the boredom by bird watching:

An enterprising couple of swallows had been able to build a nest on a beam over my desk. Apart from a leisurely sweeping of the floor daily, the office boy's principal duty seemed to be to put a clean sheet of paper on my desk each day to catch the droppings. It was a pleasant interlude watching the family being fed when complaints were particularly long-winded.

J.A.G. McCall, a DO in the Niger Delta, presiding at court 1947

207

It is hardly good sport to sit in a court
While weather is dripping and sultry
And trying to channel the facts for law panel
Re customs and local adult'ry

We - um and we - er about him and her
And the state of a fully bought wife,
Or such pregnancy fees to be paid as we please,
Divorces and marital strife.

(Recording Customary Law)

Rex Niven demonstrated what *The Times* in 1959 described as, *the extreme difficulty of applying the cold logic of British Judicial methods to the essentially imprecise undertones of much that goes on in Africa."*
Quite unwittingly I committed an injustice in a case I was hearing. A man was charged with burglary in a long room, a sort of lodging house, where he had been seen in the middle of the night walking with a lighted lantern in his hand. In my simplicity I thought that this was a sign of innocence, for a guilty person would surely not be so blatant. But according to all the local experts, I had been wrong in acquitting him, as the fact of the lantern showed his guilt. The first thing a good burglar would do was to blow a magic powder under the door and give it time to do its work. Then he would enter with his lantern and rob at leisure. The powder would be sleep-inducing and everyone would be in a deep sleep. The police used to find these powders when they arrested people, also a wad of cotton-wool, which was for invisibility, and a little pot of grease to get out of the handcuffs. When these had been placed out of reach, they would say 'he is now helpless', and he certainly was.
Justice, in Niven's case could also include guile:
Kabba was badly split into factions regarding the succession to the chieftancy. One day members of 'section A' came streaming up to my office in great agitation. They said that the leader of 'section B' had been seen placing a stone in the thatch of the biggest roof belonging to the leader of 'A'. The stone was produced, a smooth piece of granite shaped like a spearhead so that it would stick in the thatch. This stone, they all swore, would attract lightening - for which the area was notorious - and so set fire to his whole compound and with luck burn him up with it.
Unfortunately British law, thorough and painstaking as it is, had never categorised attracting lightning with intent as a crime. I could have fallen back on the old charges of intent to commit a breach of the peace and the like, but the 'crime' was too nebulous for that. So the only thing was subterfuge.

208

I took out the impressive leather-bound Record Book, huge and heavy, and a pile of legal volumes. The leader of 'section B' was then charged with attempted murder - it seemed better to do the thing properly - and the rest of the day was spent taking down depositions, reading them over and getting them signed or attested.

The Court (myself) then explained to the assembled public that the accused had so far not actually done anything. The stone they gave me was solemnly wrapped up and sealed in the presence of all, marked 'Exhibit 1', and locked away in the safe. The accused was bound over and warned that all that had been written would be taken into account should another squeak come out of him. They went away very thoughtful and no further trouble arose. The loose sheets on which I had written the depositions were put into an envelope - I had written nothing at all in the great Record Book. I wondered sometimes what my successors thought of that stone. Maybe it is now in some museum.

How much crime there was in Africa during the period of British Administration from a statistical point of view is an impossible question to answer without going into more detail than would be interesting. Crime existed, of course, but the flavour of writing and interviews from people who were there at the time, seems to demonstrate that the general trends of crime were not a matter of great concern.

Stealing on the farms in Kenya was fairly common (and difficult to resolve) but life for all the races was not ruled by fear of crime and our memory is that there was a much more laid back attitude than exists today which probably demonstrates that crime was not very prevalent. Cars and houses were seldom locked prior to the Mau Mau. At one time in Nairobi the criminal fraternity discovered a rather ingenious method of petty stealing with the use of poles. These pole fishers used to push their poles through the windows and silently hook out items of value from the house. They were rumoured to be extraordinarily dexterous. There was one story, which may be apocryphal, of the man who awoke to find his wife's handbag sailing passed his face on the end of a pole. He plucked it off, shouted "Go away!" and turned over and went back to sleep.

In July 1922 Olive Collyer was attacked in her bedroom when she was sleeping. Simultaneously the man slashed her on the head with a knife and bashed her on the knee with a heavy stick. She jumped up and said, "Nataka nini?" (What do you want?) He said "Nataka rupia." (I want rupees)

"Oh do you!" she said and jumped out of bed to go for him. He fled and was not seen again. She called up her servant, Nathanial who found her streaming in blood from a horrid gash on her head. Her knee swelled up like a cricket ball. They dressed the places and she went to sleep soundly until morning. The next day she stayed in bed but the day after that she motored herself 120 miles to the Nakuru races.

A.F.B. Bridges commented on crime in Nigeria in 1921/22:

There was on the whole, surprisingly little thievery in the country outside the big towns, considering that bush houses never had locks or doors and internal walls were only about 6 ft high, without ceilings.

In the Sudan during the period 1908 to Independence in 1956 it is recorded that only four members of the Sudan Political Service were murdered by Sudanese. In Beja district in the Sudan Carlisle says that *Crimes were largely those of a pastoral society particularly animal theft, affrays and the occasional murder. Criminals were pursued relentlessly and where after some months of trying we could not arrest a really wanted man then with the Nazir's and DC's approval the Police could resort to temporary apprehension of his mother or other women folk which nine times out of ten did the trick and led to the wanted man surrendering himself to the authorities within 24 hours.*

Although it would seem that criminal activity during the colonial period was not a major worry, within the secrecy of tribal rites dark deeds were done which were sometimes impossible to trace or get to grips with. Julian Huxley mentions in his book *Africa View* published in 1931, that *the traditional native institutions tenaciously continued to live a subterranean life.* And this included killing people. Elspeth Huxley describes graphically how when she was duck shooting one evening as a child, it seemed that one of two young men who had appeared to be larking about in the water, had drowned. When she went back to the area a few days later the man she was with, Njombo, refused to admit that a blanketed body floating in the water was a corpse and nobody, not even the local chief would admit to anyone missing or even discuss the matter *The man in the vlei seemed to have dropped out of existence without so much as a ripple on the surface of the life around him. Considering that every Kikuyu was embedded in a solid matrix of family, that no one ever stood alone, this was peculiar.*

A curious case of what is known today as serial killing took place in Ndola in Northern Rhodesia in 1944 told by Chiripula Stephenson.

A Standard VI African Constable murdered five or six fish sellers. He would stop a man on the pretence of examining his loads for customs. Then he would take him into the bush and kill him by wedging his head in the fork of a tree and strangling him with his belt. The constable would sell the fish and use the money to buy a correspondence course in the detection of crime. The series of murders was discovered when one man he left for dead recovered and came to the police station to complain. At the interrogation the interpreter was none other than the constable. There was a dramatic moment when the African was asked if he would be able to recognise his assailant and he pointed to the constable interpreter. After police investigation the constable not only confessed to the murders but to the theft of cash from the police station the previous year.

When it came to sentencing, Bridges describes the difference between an Assistant District Officer's powers of punishment and those of a District Officer in Onitsha, Nigeria, 1922-23:

An ADO's powers in the Provincial Court were: civil cases when the dispute was for a value of £25 or less, and criminal cases where a maximum punishment of £25 or three months imprisonment was considered adequate; the DO's powers were: £50 fine or two years imprisonment in criminal cases; and a Resident's powers: £100 civil and £100 or 5 years imprisonment in criminal cases. All members of the Court had to send a monthly return of cases tried to the Chief Justice, and these returns acted as an appeal. The Chief Justice could reduce or quash a sentence, and as one never got any reasons from him for this action, we never learned what mistakes we might have made.

O'Dwyer tells us that in Sierra Leone, but as far as we can ascertain nowhere else, if a convicted prisoner was sentenced to fourteen days or less, he would be placed in the Chief's stocks. These were known as alligators and consisted of two planks of wood hinged at one end and padlocked at the other. The prisoners would sit on the ground and their feet would be imprisoned by the alligators.

As Lord Denning observed, some aspects of English law did not suit folk in far off lands and one of these aspects was, in the case of some people, imprisonment. In the Sudan Davies was concerned about putting the nomadic Arab into gaol and wondered at first if it was not tantamount to sentencing him to death. However, one Arab whom he sentenced to prison in Khartoum for ten years, after serving seven and a half was released early and thought he would pass the time before his train left, by calling on Davies, then in Khartoum.

'How did you get on in prison?' Davies asked him. 'By God, that prison is wonderful. They teach everything there. They taught me carpentry.' He glanced round the room and his eye fell on a cushioned wooden settee. 'I made that' he said, 'with this my hand. And that,' he added, pointing to the visitor's arm-chair.... He spoke

as though he were happy to have been able to make some slight return to a benefactor. So much so that I was misguided enough to follow that lead and say, 'As you are now a skilled carpenter, would you like me to help you get a set of tools so that you can set up a shop in El Odaigo, or even Nahud?'

He was staggered by the suggestion, but not with gratitude. "I a carpenter?" he said, 'I?' He laughed heartily. 'They have given me a ticket, fourth class, to El Obeid, by train. It goes tomorrow. From there I'm going straight back to Dar Homr, to my cattle.'

'With safety!' I said, when he asked leave to go.

'God keep you safe!' he replied.

Nonetheless ,confining people who lived unfettered and wandering lives was a very real problem. Philip Mitchell records a tragic case involving the little wild men of the Uganda forests.

One of the forms that sorcery or witchcraft takes is the digging up of dead bodies to obtain certain parts which are believed to have a special potency in necromancy; the genital organs mostly, but also the fat at the base of the thumb and other bits. It is ... especially common in Toro, and the usual thing was to engage a Mwamba, who are little wild people from the Congo border west of Toro, pigmies in fact, forest dwellers ... as watchmen for the graves of the newly deceased relatives until risk of desecration was past. One such little man, hired by the local chief, standing guard at night, saw two men and a woman, stark naked as they always are on these expeditions, come to the grave and start digging. He crept upon them and shot an arrow, which killed the woman, the two men ran off into the darkness.

In the morning, conscious of duty done, the little man called on the chief and showed his handiwork. He was at once arrested and later committed for trial by the High Court for murder, tried by the Chief Justice and sentenced to death. How such a thing could be, I cannot tell. It was certainly the law, for the Attorney General must have indicted him and the Chief Justice tried him - and then made a strong recommendation for mercy. The little man, who of course had no language in common with the police, counsel or court, took it all very well; I suppose he thought rather a fuss was being made of a very ordinary bit of archery. He was understood to have said that if, incredibly, it was now thought that he had done wrong, he would be happy to return the goat and few chickens which had been his fee.

He was, of course, reprieved and a sentence of imprisonment (for five years) substituted. A few months later the Chief Justice wrote to me in great distress and said he had been back to Fort Portal and found that the Mwamba was dying. ... At that time there was nothing the matter with him which could be made the subject of release on medical grounds, he was just pining away. He had tried once or twice to escape, and had been retaken; now he would just die. So I had a private talk with the appropriate officers, hoping that he might be helped to escape, but without result. He was at last released on completion of sentence went home to Bwamba and died of tuberculosis.

It is true, though, that morale in the prisons was generally high. In Kenya prison was often said to be referred to as the 'Kingi Georgi Hoteli'. Prisoners were kept busy and I have childhood recollections of playing in the garden while prisoners cut the grass with their long sharp scythes within feet of us, while they gossiped and laughed.

One lady recounted:

It always amused me so much when the prisoners came to do one's compound. They were with their machetes, which they sharpen like razor blades. There were the prisoners cutting the grass with these machetes and the man in charge of them just had a truncheon. ...There was one occasion when things went wrong in Lagos. The prisoners were clearing some ditches and two prisoners whose families were against each other, were working together, and got into a furious conversation, and one just swiped the other's head off! Whereupon all the prisoners and the warders legged it back to the prison as fast as they could go.

Hazel Carlisle remembers her regular prisoner/gardener in Rumbek in Southern Sudan. He was a Dinka man and he arrived at the garden each day in his prison uniform. He would then decorously go behind a bush to take it off (that was the titillating part in his mind), fold the clothes carefully and then stride out stark naked and get on with the gardening.

The prisoners were employed keeping government houses in good repair and the gardens clean and tidy. They emptied the latrines where sewage pipes had not been sunk and carried water to houses where there was no running water. One wife in Nigeria effected a rather clever swap with a missionary who lived in the vicinity. In return for something he wanted she received a water tank which she had erected on stilts. From then on the prisoners shinned up the ladder with buckets of water each day thus providing her with the untold luxury of running water in her hand basin.

Of course disaffection did exist in the prisons but it did not loom very large in the scheme of things. When Hal Williams was a supernumery DO at his first post of Kiambu, the prisoners were employed building themselves a new prison. It was a long, single story building with the main door in the centre. One morning a prisoner shut himself behind the central doors with a pile of rocks and proceeded to lob out the rocks if anyone came near him. The only thing he would yell at them was that he wanted to speak to 'Bwana Kidogo '(Mr Small). Now, in Swahili the word 'mkubwa' means 'big' or 'large' but it also translates as 'important'. The word 'kidogo' - or 'small' - is also used in the context of 'unimportant' or 'least important' although this meaning is not quite so commonly used. In Kiambu the DC - or Bwana Mkubwa - happened to be a short man while the most junior DO - or Bwana Kidogo - was Hal - a tall man.

Confusion reigned while the prisoner continued to throw missiles out through the door. The short but important DC - Bwana Mkubwa - was sent for but the rocks rained down on them; then the senior DO arrived to no avail and so on until, finally the very large, very junior supernumerary DO, Hal, was sent for and the prisoner came out like a lamb.

Rex Niven tells a story of a disaffected prisoner being held in Kaduna in Northern Nigeria. Niven was at the time Resident in Jos when the Superintendent of Jos Prison telephoned him to say that he had received a parcel of prison clothes through the mail. There was no message or covering letter: what should he do?

I suggested that he ring Kaduna Prison. He did so and was told that a prisoner whose name was written on the clothes had escaped from a working party and they were looking for him. I said we had heard nothing from the Native Authority, and it was possible that he might be following his clothes. Sure enough in a day or two he turned up at the Jos prison and knocked at the great entrance door. He said he did not care for the food and amenities in the Kaduna Prison and understood that things were better in Jos, and so here he was. He had, he added, come 140 miles in mufti and on foot to avoid recapture. For the sake of discipline he had to be sent back to Kaduna, but before long some hard heart melted and he was formally transferred to Jos.

During the first half of the twentieth century capital punishment was not considered unusual and throughout the British Empire hanging was the sentence for murder. However, in the case of some nomadic tribes the confiscation of camels, cattle or flocks was also imposed.

Whether one is for or against hanging, it is a tragedy. To recount the story of a man's death feels almost like an intrusion, but I would like to think that all the participants of the following account might agree that their story should not be lost in the mists of time.

Some splendid rivers crossed the Southern Division [Plateau Province, Nigeria],

214

and over the millennia had carved through the edge of the high plateau, leaving in one place a great flat-topped hill, standing alone and impressive in the plain.

This solitary massif was inhabited by people singularly ungracious compared with those in the plains. This is what I thought then, but maybe this attitude expressed a deep resentment at interference with their ancient liberties, which included being captured as slaves by the Fulani raiders. Their neighbours did not like them and called them Mada. I never found the real meaning of that word or even in which of the several possible languages it originated, but they didn't like it, so it must have been uncomplimentary. They themselves pressed for the name of Egon: 'The Men'. One fine clear morning fifty years ago [c 1930] two young Egon men were sitting on a rock high up the hillside, watching the trade-route far below them. They saw a figure appear on a distant bend in the road. They watched carefully and could see no one with him. 'There's a Hausa', said one, 'and he's alone,' said the other. 'Come,' said the first, 'let's kill him.'

They were wearing little and did not show up as they slipped down the rocky hillside. They moved fast and reached the path before the lone traveller. They hid behind a huge rock and some greenery and waited for him. He passed them oblivious of their menace. They crept out and moved up on him from behind in absolute silence. One blow on his head from a heavy stick: a great shriek and then silence.

Some days afterwards a European surveyor called Buckingham came into my office in Wamba. He was a very good-looking man, and always wore pale blue shorts - to match his eyes the ladies said. He was doing some mine surveying in a camp to the north, where there was a certain amount of tin and where mining had been going on for years. He said that one of his labourers, Musa, was missing. ... Musa was a good worker and doing well, and there was no reason for his continued disappearance. He had been given a short leave to go south to see some relatives who lived across the Divisional Boundary, and had not returned.

Meanwhile, in a village on the edge of the Mada Hills near the scene I have described, the two young men were beginning to get worried. It was a firm belief in those parts that the ghost of anything killed would haunt the killer unless steps were taken to prevent it. There was a simple juju remedy to be had on application to the right person on payment of the right fee, which would afford complete protection - it was usually hunters who wanted it. If all this was necessary for the death of a large animal, what, they wondered, must you do to protect yourself against the haunting of a dead man? The two got more and more anxious. Inspite of their bravado they had never before actually killed a human being. And so they took cautious action.

The Village Head went to the District Head, a wise and experienced man. The Village Head said that two young men had come to him asking for a 'medicine' called *lahubu*. This was a very special medicine, nowadays never asked for, but which had been much in demand in the past. They had been discreet but also frightened. And well they might be, for the medicine was only given to protect a killer from the avenging soul of his human victim. Neither of them knew of the search for the Survey labourer Musa. The District Head sent the information on to me.

I went with him on a long walk to the village of these people, sited in stupendous scenery in the glory of the hills. He searched the houses of the two young men and found nothing. My head messenger, who also was not without experience, said, 'Let us not leave before we have had a look at the grain bins.' In most of the villages of that area, and indeed of many other areas, these were built like great vases in the finest mud.

The messenger took a small calabash and started to scoop out the grain into head-pans. After about a foot had been moved he struck lucky. There was a white Muslim skull cap, with four pence in coppers in its folds. And on the edge of the cap was printed the name 'Musa' in the neat movable type that the Survey use in their original map drawings.

At this point the younger of the two boys broke down and said that he would show us where the body was hidden. The other remained grim and scowling. I had with me a small police escort armed with rifles and bayonets. Now realising the seriousness of the situation, they formed themselves of their own accord around the two boys and myself. We went down the hillside, not by the route the young men had followed as they ran down to the kill, but by an easier and smoother track.

When we reached the trade-route in the valley, we moved south for some distance and then the youth stopped. It was here, he said, that they hit the man and he fell. But there had been no blood stains or marks of struggle when the original trackers went that way some days before. The youth smiled and said they had thought of that. He knelt down and started to turn over flat granite stones - like paving stones, flat on both sides - that made the footway. The undersides bore the marks of dried blood....

We followed the youth, now tied to the Corporal with a piece of string. Not far away we climbed up a vast smooth boulder and at the top found that two other boulders joined it. Over the join was a pile of brushwood, looking as though it had fallen there years ago. The messenger dragged it away and uncovered a hole like a manhole. He looked down and said, 'There's a body'.

The two prisoners were charged and committed for trial by...the Resident of the Province. He came especially from Jos, and drove up into the Mada Hills. This was in the days of the old Provincial Court and though we were all members of that Court with varying powers, he alone had the ultimate power of life and death.

The two young men were sentenced to death and the sentence was to be carried out

216

near the scene of the crime. This was for obvious reasons: it was essential in those days for the people concerned to see that the law had taken its course. The African population being in a more elementary stage of life, took these things in their stride, with a polite interest and a mild wonder that so much trouble was taken in ending the life of a man, who was obviously qualified for a sudden and painful death.

The finding of the Court went to the Governor for approval in Council, or rather for an expression of the exercise or non-exercise of His Majesty's clemency - a complex way of saying a simple thing. We were not a little surprised to hear that the sentence on the pleasant young man was confirmed and that the law should take its course but, owing to a legal technicality the surly accused was to be released. This kind of result merely confirmed once more in the Nigerian public their firm belief that the white men were basically mad. There was, of course, precisely the same amount of guilt between the two of them. So he was released and we awaited the Warrant with the great black seal to deal with the other.

By the time it came we were in the Rains and the Commissioner of Police, Graham Callow (later a judge of the Nigerian High Court), and myself, the condemned man and a considerable police escort made our way into the heart of the Mada Hills and stayed the night in a rest house. The difficulty was getting a doctor to attend. You cannot execute a man without one present. We had no Medical Officer in the area; the nearest lived to the south at Lafia and had to come on the night train to Gudi. Then he was to be driven to the nearest point on the road, from which he had to walk some miles to the scene. It was a tight schedule and it seemed that something was bound to go wrong. Callow and I and this motley crew started off from the rest house at daylight to walk the twelve miles to the village. After a while it started to rain.

The police were on tenterhooks as it was their duty to get the man there and carry out the execution, and at the same time stave off any attempt at rescue. This was a very real danger. We had no idea whose side the public were on; they were non-committal and tight-lipped, and there were plenty of them, all armed. To make matters worse, the narrow paths in those parts ran between steep dry-stone walls, in many places ten feet high. In other circumstances we would have admired the ingenuity of their construction, but as things were they were merely a menace. The 'path' was just wide enough for feet in single file, the walls curving away to take bodies and loads. Many fields were divided by similar walls at right angles to the path. There could not have been worse territory. The police threw out flank guards on each side but they were out of our sight and if they had been attacked it would have been extremely difficult to concentrate the fire of the main body of police, strung out as they were in single file. All this was passing through Callow's mind. I admit I was worried too. Further, the prisoner himself had to walk with his escort in front and behind him and not on

217

either side.

The rain became heavier as we went along. The 'path' was soon a small stream in most places, with irregular stones and small obstacles invisible below the water. The policemen were strangers and could not speak any of the local languages, and scarcely anyone at all could speak the prisoner's native tongue. It was a nightmare journey. And there was no doctor in sight.

After what seemed an interminable trek we reached the village of the two youths. Fortunately the rain now slacked off and eventually stopped. We decided in everyone's interest, specially the condemned man's, that the job should be done without delay. Callow and his Sergeant were used to these things and set about preparations briskly. I stood with wet feet feeling definitely queasy. I had seen a great many men killed in action, [in WW I] but this was quite different.

He was hanged off a huge branch of an immense local bean tree, about thirty feet above the ground. Behind the tree the ground fell away sharply into the valley of the murder, and beyond was the magnificent vision of the Plateau escarpment. In another direction were bold rolling hills, tree-clad in every shade of green. No one could have asked for a more dramatic place for his ending. I shall not go into the technical details; they were simple and very effective. The police made it as easy as they could for the young chap and handled him as tenderly as a baby. From the time he stood under the branch to the time his neck broke was just twenty-five seconds.

The youth conducted himself with the greatest courage throughout that miserable last morning of his life. He was much more cheerful than we were. There were some hundreds of villagers in a huge circle round us, perched on every vantage-point. They were quiet and motionless. There was a low groaning sound at the last instant and that was all.

Andarobo of the Rift Valley.
Taken by Sir Harry Johnston, GCMG, KCB 1902.

Chapter 17

"WE AND THEY"

We eat pork and beef
With Cow-horn-handled knives.
They who gobble their rice off a leaf,
Are horrified out of their lives.

We and They by Kipling

Darkening Skies

The story told by Frederick Jackson about the old 'Andorobo' called Teriko, offers an insight into life for a district officer at the turn of the 19th and 20th centuries faced with the immense gulf which divided and baffled the two races. It also shows that there was considerable goodwill on both sides of that gulf.

An old Andorobo, Teriko, his shrivelled-up wife and his family of two grown-up sons, two small boys and a pretty little girl of about nine, lived in the forest close by the Ravine station in funny little bowers of green branches neither rain-proof nor wind-proof, at the foot of some giant trees. They knew that vast forest from A to Z and all about everything that lived in it, and subsisted almost entirely on colobus monkeys, honey and any flour they were able to obtain in exchange for the [colobus] skins at the station. One day I went out with the old man, two sons and the little girl to see how they hunted the monkeys and saw them kill three, with their barbed wooded-pointed arrows freely smeared with poison.

When a small troop was sighted and began to disperse each of the party followed and kept their eye on a particular monkey, but no attempt was made to shoot until it stopped and tried to hide itself. To anyone who knows little or nothing about them, colobus monkeys, though a very distinct black and white, are extremely difficult to see in the giant treetops, as they generally lie along on a bough, with just their face and drooping tail showing on one side or the other. Black as their faces are, they are very far from easy to 'pick up', but the practised eye of the Andorobo spots them at once. It is then necessary for the bowman to manoeuvre until he stands practically plumb under the peeping monkey, in order not to lose the arrows in case of a miss. If he misses, the shooter cocks his head on one side and intently listens for the arrow to fall. That day not an arrow was lost. While the old man and sons had been fully occupied the little girl kept calling at intervals, as she stood guard below the father of the troop of monkeys who was lying flattened out on a bough a little too thin to hide his bulk, and a bulge in his stomach showed up rather prominently. The first two shots at him were misses, but the third pinked into the bulge, and stuck. For five minutes or so the poor beast never moved, but then began to get fidgety and after several distressing attempts to retain his hold, he toppled over.' I hoped he would crash to the ground and have all life knocked out of him. But it was not to be as his fall was broken by the thick 'boxwood' undergrowth. Then followed a struggle between him and the suddenly transformed and fiendish little barbarian of a girl who finally strangled him. It was one of the most revolting sights I ever witnessed.

That little girl was later taken into service by Martin and his wife. They were both kindness itself, fed and clothed her well and she had a warm hut to sleep in; but in less than six months the call of the forest was too great and she returned to savagedom.

Outside the forest Teriko and his sons were absolutely useless. They were, I believe, afraid of being out in the open. I took them out several times hoping to pick up a few hints on stalking and bush-craft and even carried a notebook so as to jot anything down of interest on the spot. But all they thought about was honey, and they were far more intent on listening for the chattering call of the honey-guide (Indicator indicator) than on keeping a look out for game. The last day the old man and a son were out with me I was suddenly prompted to give them a real good fright. We had cut the quite fresh spoor of a rhinocerous leading up-wind, and I at once noted that they were very averse to following it. However, I decided to do so and although the country was open, and there was no possible chance of blundering on to it, they went very slowly, hesitated and played the fool generally, until the spoor suddenly changed about and led direct down-wind. Then they plucked up courage and stepped out gaily, heading straight for a large bush in the far distance that looked a likely spot for a midday rest; we found, a little later, that the old rhino had walked round it, and then gone on. When within a couple of hundred yards, and with a strong wind behind us, the old man began to try and impress me with the importance of extreme caution and absolute silence by walking on tiptoe and making a variety of signs with his hands, sometimes pointing to his ears. Dear old Ramazan [Jackson's foreman] was by that time inclined to be a bit restive, but was checked in time, for I was as anxious as he was to bring such tomfoolery to an end, but in my own way. We advanced to within some sixty or so yards of the bush when the silly old ass began to stoop and to signal me to do likewise; but instead of doing so I gave vent to a screaming yell, as unearthly as I could make it. Those two Andorobo received, at that moment the fright of their lives. Later on I heard that they had declared that they would never again go out with Lambala (my native name) but as I had no intention of asking them to do so it did not matter. Silly old man though the head of the family was, an incident occurred while I was at the Ravine in 1896, in which he proved himself to be the real hero of a little romance.

At the time, the Kamassia, through the machinations of the one-eyed lybon, were openly hostile, [See Chapter 14: Service in the Outposts] and I had had no communication with them for a week or more, when old Teriko came in to tell me that his wife, who had gone in to exchange monkey skins for food, was held as a prisoner by them and was closely guarded in a hut, and to ask if I could help him to obtain her release. I had to admit frankly that I could do nothing, and he went away very disconsolate.

However, about a week later he came in again with a beaming face, and accompanied by his more than ever emaciated and shrivelled-up old wife, also beaming. Their joy was so obviously genuine as to be almost pathetic.

And this is what the old man told me. He had started off by himself, and by lying up, hidden in the bush, near huts and listening by day, he located the position of his wife, and eventually found the actual hut, one of a small group, in which she was confined, with the door shut and fastened with two men on guard outside at

223

night. By crawling round to the back of the hut and scratching on the wall, he attracted the old lady's attention, made a little hole, whispered instructions to her, returned next night, and directly the two guards were asleep silently approached and unfastened the door; and all was then plain sailing. The old man wound up by saying he had been sorely tempted to kill the guard as they slept, but considered their own chance of escape would be imperilled if a hue and cry was raised. He also informed me that the real reason for detaining his wife was that the Kamassia were preparing for trouble as they were moving their food supplies into large granaries hidden in the forest and were busy making fresh arrow poison, and they did not want it known.

All this subsequently proved to be correct.

Although there was little antagonism between the African and British cultures on a day to day basis, it did cause frustration at times, as well as antipathy and this sometimes led to revolt. The Dini Ya Msambwa was one such example which began to take hold in the mid-1940's on the Kenya side of the slopes of Mount Elgon near the frontier with Uganda and the home of the Kitosh people who now have renamed themselves, the WaBusuku.

The brave woman, Bahati, who was found by Frederick Jackson, when the tribe had been targeted by Arab slave raiders was a Kitosh. [See Chapter 1] The first District Commissioner in Kisumu, Hobley - known as Hobley-Bobley - considered them to be "a mystical and bellicose people" who, having lost the opportunities for fighting and raiding, directed their "turbulent blood" to a heady mixture of ancestral gods, Christianity and nationalistic fervour. Interestingly, he also had to deal with a religious fanatic in the District whose teachings were not subversive, but he forecast great trouble ahead when one such subversive leader arose.

The story of the Dini Ya Msambwa was told to me by Edwin (Teddy) Eggins who was a DO in Nyanza P;rovince, Kenya, with responsibility for the Kitosh area.

The Dini ya Msambwa('the faith of spells') has been described as a Cult of the Ancestral Spirits; one of those storms, or perhaps a mere shower, of fanaticism - partly social, partly religious, partly nationalistic - which pass from time to time across the landscape of history. It centred around a person known as Elijah (pronounced Eleejah) Masinde. He lived at the Friends Africa Mission but was evicted after he had taken a

224

second wife. He became an obsessive reader of the Old Testament and believed that there should be a black Christ with Christianity for black men which would allow polygamy. He alleged that God replied that the request was reasonable but so long as there were Europeans in the land he could not grant the request. Once the white men had been driven out of the country, then the Black Christ would appear and all would be well. Further, Elijah said that the missionaries were all wrong about the customs of the Kenya tribes. Of course a man should have two or four or twenty wives, if he can afford them; and of course, men and women should be circumcised, since this is right and customary.

Elijah Masinde was estimated to have been born in 1910. He was a strongly built man with eyes which were concentrated and peculiar. He displayed a certain talent for football (a half back) and he captained the Kimilili side. In 1930 he played for Kenya versus Uganda. However, various responsible people such as Chief Amatullah and head of Elijah's Omubachi Clan, Tomas Warianla, thought him more or less mad.

Elijah's first appearance as leader of the Dini appeared to have been at a baraza held at Kimilili in 1943 by the District Commissioner, Mr. Hislop, when Elijah rose and fired a series of questions at the District Commissioner with great intensity. The incident was dramatic and Elijah's prestige was greatly enhanced.

In 1944 the movement gathered impetus and its following began to increase. During that year Elijah was accused under Native Authority Ordinance 2/37 Sec. 8(e) before the Kamutiong Native Tribunal in Criminal Case 374.44 of failing to obey the order of Chief Amatullah to desist from conduct likely to cause a breach of the peace. He was sentenced to three months hard labour and a fine of Shs 100/- or I.D. (in detention) a further three months hard labour. He appealed to the Native Appeal Tribunal and his appeal was dismissed. He appealed further to the District Commissioner and the conviction was upheld but the sentence reduced to two months hard labour and a fine of Shs 50/- or I.D. a further two months hard labour. The fine was paid and the sentence served.

He next came into the limelight in October 1944 when he and two of his closest adherents forbade an Agricultural Instructor from entering their shambas [fields] in order to carry out an inspection of the Mexican marigold weed, and he threatened to kill the instructor if he insisted. On the 30th of October Elijah and ten other men ambushed a government party, Liguru Jonathon and two civil conscription askaris, who had gone to serve summonses on Elijah to appear at a baraza. The ambushers used pangas, clubs and sticks and all three of the Government party suffered injuries, the askaris having to spend several days in hospital. At this ambush a cry was raised, though by whom is not known, to mutilate the Government party by cutting off their penises. It seems that this has never been a local custom in inter-tribal war and, as some of the ambushers demurred, fortunately the deed was not done.

He was arrested again and, this time, as he was being taken away to prison, he declared, "I shall come back; and when I come back that man [the Assistant Agricultural Officer] will have gone and his house will have been burned down!" This prophecy was duly fulfilled by some of his followers, to the further prestige of Elijah.

While serving this sentence, he kept demanding to be taken to see King George, and his behaviour was such that an enquiry was held on his mental state. During the enquiry the Provincial Commissioner came to see him, whereupon he exclaimed "You surely do not claim to be King George?" Despite this, it was decided on the evidence of a Medical Officer that Elijah was mentally unbalanced and he was committed to Mathari mental hospital. When he was considered fit for discharge in 1947 the Provincial Commissioner failed to find a way to keep him away from the location and his activities intensified.

By June 1947 Elijah had collected about 5,000 followers and he led them to the old fort near Lugulu where a battle had been fought earlier in the century between Government forces and the Kitosh. One of his objects seems to have been to exorcise the ghosts of the men killed in that battle and a sheep was sacrificed according, he said, to ancient custom. He cut up the sheep, giving each man a small piece. Then he made a speech on the eviction of Europeans and said he would have to ask God to show him how to get rid of them.

On the 10th of February 1948 the Assistant Superintendent of Police, Mr. Walker, went to Malakisi and saw a large and ugly crowd in the vicinity, which appeared to be making for the government camp. He immediately went ahead of them to the camp and when the crowd arrived he tried to reason with them. A few of them attacked him and he was felled by severe blows to the head. He fired in his own defence and was knocked down again, whereupon general fire was opened by his Police party. The crowd disappeared leaving 7 dead and 13 injured.

A week later Elijah was found by another Police party with about three hundred followers. He gave himself up without further trouble and he was shortly afterwards deported to Lamu.

For a year or more the activities of the Dini ya Msambwa were confined to outbreaks of arson and destruction. But in 1950 one of Elijah's disciples, a man by the name of Lucas, with a gold tooth in his jaw which he said that God had given him, was preaching Elijah's doctrines to the wild people of the Suk, who lived around Lake Baringo. In the name of Dini ya Msambwa, he proclaimed the overthrow and ejection of the white men, the appropriation of their lands, the shedding of European clothes, a return to tribal ways, and an era of fertility and plenty in the fields, among the cattle, sheep and women.

Rumours of this propaganda were reported to the British authorities. The DC, and his soon-to-be successor, together with a detachment of armed police went out to meet the Dini band. About two or three hundred of them were found on the 24th of April near Baringo. Some of them were dressed in warlike array, with shields and spears (which Africans were not allowed to carry.) Fighting started. The in-coming DC, two British and one African police officer were killed. On the other side some twenty were killed and a good many more were wounded. Lucas of the Divine Tooth was identified to have been among the slain. With Elijah Masinde in exile in Lamu, this battle signalled the end of the Dini ya Msambwa.

This was not the only cult which was springing up. A section of Kikuyu, styling themselves "Watu wa Mungu" (Men of God) speared a European assistant police inspector and his two African constables in 1948. *They had mutilated the bodies in a most gruesome fashion, slashing the inspector's face open across the eyes and mouth; ... and one poor native, with his hand half cut off, they had paraded around the village, telling him that he was on his way to a ceremonial execution. He was saved by a reinforcement of police, which had been rushed to the scene."* [*Last Chance In Africa* by Negley Farson]

And other sections of the Kikuyu tribe were brewing another fanatical, nationalistic and even uglier movement, the effects of which were so far-reaching as to ruin many lives, rock the Government in Britain and bring turmoil and bitterness to the reasonably ordered lives of many members of the Colonial Administration and to those of all races who lived and worked in Kenya.

Perhaps the most tragic aspect of the Mau Mau was the fact that it split the Kikuyu tribe asunder. By far the largest majority of the tribe were against the Mau Mau and *some 1,800 are known to have died, but the true number will never be known.The Origins and Growth of the Mau Mau* by F.D. Corfield]. Only 58 civilian European and Asians were killed and even with the total casualties of the security forces - African, Asian and European - of 167, the effect of the tragedy on the Kikuyu was profound.

Enormous pressure was put on members of the tribe to sign up. In his survey of the Mau Mau F.D. Corfield described exactly how frightful that pressure was.

[A Kikuyu Catholic woman] *was dragged by night from her house to a hut. After she had refused to take the oath she was stripped and beaten and informed that she would be killed and those present would drink her blood. She still refused and after again being beaten she was hoisted off the floor at the end of a rope until she lost consciousness. When she partially regained her senses she was compelled to drink some blood from a bottle and to perform the other disgusting rites constituting the Mau Mau oath-taking ceremony.*

There are many stories of loyalty and courage *of the brave, often lonely, Kikuyu and others, both Christian and pagan, who, with so little thought for their personal safety and so little effective help from government, sought to oppose Mau Mau.*

At the beginning of the Mau Mau emergency Arthur Horner who worked in the Secretariat in Nairobi, remembers his Kikuyu houseboy rushing into the sitting room, when he was standing at the window admiring his garden, drawing the curtains and saying fiercely to him "Never do that Bwana." Later the houseboy was removed, along with virtually all the Kikuyu, as much for their own protection as for the protection of the Europeans, into a detention camp. His family were all massacred by the Mau Mau and after the Emergency was over he went back to see the Horners, a broken man.

Kit Taylor who, together with her husband Charles, farmed coffee outside Nairobi [See Chapter 12] described the period as:

Absolute anguish. It was a battle between love and loyalty to the Europeans that they worked for and the terror of dying for the oath....I know one man who knew his boy was absolutely loyal and he asked the people who had arrested him to allow them to have five minutes alone together during which the servant said 'Bwana don't stop

*them taking me away. I want them to take me because if they leave me here I may
have to do something terrible.'*

It was not uncommon for house and farm servants to feed a gang in
the forest from European produce in order to prevent them having to
murder their employers and Kit Taylor believed that some of their own
people did this in order to protect the Taylors' lives. This staunchness is
beyond all praise when one remembers the huge differences between
the two races - the We and They aspect - the extremes of fear and torn
loyalties that were being suffered. But it was the norm rather than the
exception.

*Elizabeth Cooper rang us to say that she could see a gang coming our way up the
valley."* Wrote Kit Taylor. *"The women in the gang were carrying guns of two
[European] teenage boys who had been killed. (Stupid parents had given their sons
airguns to shoot birds in the middle of the Mau Mau and the gang had killed the
boys and kept the guns.) The bibis [women] were rushing up the road with the police
in hot pursuit. Old Gichuru walked up and down outside: you could see his throat
working. He passed us twice before he could get out the words 'Keep in the house'.
We did and the bullets started whistling through the garden.*

The Mau Mau in Kenya was described in the Corfield Report as *the
violent manifestation of a limited nationalistic revolutionary movement confined
almost entirely to the Kikuyu tribe.* The paper deals sympathetically with the
strains imposed upon people who were having change thrust upon
them at an almost unprecedented rate.

*The individual is brought up in an environment of the old tribal culture, but with
adolescence he comes into contact with a different culture, which makes nonsense of his
primitive beliefs. Once he goes into the outside world, he has lost most of his
traditional moorings. His magic modes of thought persist, but the old restraints are
gone. ... He often becomes rudderless and it is too easy for him to identify his trouble
with the European, who has indirectly brought on his troubles, but it should not be
forgotten that such mental conflict and confusion is not a peculiarity of the African
mind, it is apparent in the incidence of mental disturbance in modern cities.*

*This rapid transition has also produced a schizophrenic tendency in the African mind
- the extraordinary facility to live two separate lives with one foot in this century and
the other in witchcraft and savagery. This has often been noticed, but Mau Mau
revealed the almost inexplicable lengths to which it would go. A Kikuyu leading an
apparently normal life would, in one moment, become a being that was barely human.
A most notable manifestation of this was the murder of the Ruck family at the end
of 1953. Mr Ruck's groom, who led a gang of terrorists, enticed Mr. Ruck from his*

229

house at night on a spurious statement that a gangster had been arrested. He was battered to death in front of his wife who had come out to assist him, and she was then murdered. On the instructions of the groom, their small son, aged 6, hiding in terror in the house, was then slashed to death - a typical Mau Mau murder. The groom, who led this attack, had only a few days previously carried the boy tenderly home some miles from the house after a riding accident.

It is widely accepted that the land question was at the root of the resentment of the Kikuyu tribe. Negley Farson, in his book *Last Chance in Africa* reporting on a visit to Kenya in 1948 alerts the world to some unpalatable truths about land in the Kiambu District outside Nairobi where the Mau Mau movement is thought to have begun:

Here are some facts from inside the reserve. The Kiambu district of the Kikuyu Reserve is its most prosperous district, containing, as I have said, some of the best-watered and most fertile valleys in all Kenya. Yet today its land is so overpopulated, overworked, over-grazed (and badly farmed) that, it is admitted officially some of its 28,500 families must be moved elsewhere. Forty per cent. of its 196,181 population is already landless. And an official report runs: 'On the assumption that 40 per cent. of the population is already landless and that 10 per cent. of that figure are engaged in non-agricultural work, on the present density in Kiambu some 90,000 persons might become without means of support within a short time: something which cannot be faced with equanimity.'

In conversation with me Arthur Horner was of the same opinion:

I think Mau Mau was caused to some extent by land - land hunger and the desire for more land, and being told that the Europeans just went along and took it. But nobody could get land in the land units from 1939 onwards; it was impossible to buy land in the Native land units.

But the African believed in European land annexation and at a combined meeting of the Kenya African Union and the East African Indian National Congress in May 1951 (before the Mau Mau Emergency was declared), Mr Eliud Mathu said:

It is on the land that the African lives and it means everything to him. The African cannot depend for his livelihood on profits made through trading. We cannot depend on wages. We must go back every time to the only social security we have - the piece of land. The land stolen must be restored, because without land the future of the African people is doomed. God will hear us because that is the thing he gave us.

But the Provincial Commissioner, Central Province, countered this by pointing out:

It is easy to say, for it is true, that the African must learn, like all other races of the world, that he can no longer expect by right of birth to have the world provide him with a farm whatever the circumstances of his father; the surface of this planet cannot expand, whatever the universe may be doing, and the addition of adjacent lands would only be a palliative for a few years to this problem.

When the British settled in the area which was to become Kenya, vast tracts of land were empty and untouched because the population was so small. However, the control of disease both in humans, crops and livestock created a great increase in the population and this in turn increased pressure for land. Added to this, many Africans both in East and West Africa, used the slash and burn method of farming. After two or three crops the soil would weaken and crops would be light, forcing the farmer to clear another area to till in order that he could leave the first patch fallow for several years.

It is true to say that land was never 'stolen' it was bought or negotiated by treaty and in a few instances land was confiscated. However, as we have seen in Chapters 7 and 10, strict fairness was not always upheld. An example of confiscation was the area around Fort Smith, where a fort near Wyaki's village, had been constructed by Major Eric Smith in 1891 to accommodate members of the Imperial British East Africa Company on their way to or from Uganda. Some years after it was built, a Kikuyu clan which had attacked and murdered some occupants of the fort were punished by having their land expropriated.

But it was not only the need for more land which caused resentment. During the late forties other tensions manifested themselves, particularly among the Kikuyu. There was resentment over a government order to encourage the women to terrace their land in an effort at soil conservation and in the political arena there were angry debates over a national registration. Arguments also flared up over the number and make up of delegates in the East African Central Assembly.

The sparks of resentment were also being fanned by those outside the country who were against the British colonial presence in Africa. People began to believe that the African was quite capable of running his own affairs and they considered colonial government a gross imposition. These siren voices telling Africans visiting the United States, the Soviet Union or Britain, that they must act must have been tempting indeed and the young, educated Kikuyu did not resist.

Since the twenties young hotheads had formed associations and agitated but recruitment in the form of oathing ceremonies appears to have begun only in 1948. These ceremonies, based on primitive superstition, which in the most extreme cases involved intercourse with sheep and adolescent girls, sucking a dismembered penis and mixing semen, publicly produced, with menstrual blood and sheep's blood. The oaths (the most extreme were never published) resolved adherents:

 (a) *to burn European crops and kill European cattle,*
 (b) *to steal firearms,*
 (c) *if ordered to kill, to kill, no matter who is to be*
 *   the victim, even one's father or brother,*
 (d) *when killing, to cut off the heads, extract the*
 *   eyeballs and drink the liquid from them.*
 (e) *Particularly to kill Europeans.*

The participants were filled with such ghastly terror that they believed they had no choice but to obey the rules of secrecy and murder.

Philip Mitchell wrote in 1954:

*Oath administration goes on and becomes continuously more hideous and revolting, more obscene, bestial and filthy, involving practices which would be simply incredible if they were not proved beyond doubt to be true. It will be necessary for a plain account to be written and published, for they **must** be told the truth; but the unhappy man who has to do it will hardly be able to restrain his vomit as he writes. That persons of some education, who could ascertain the facts from official sources, should describe this monstrous, nauseating wickedness as a 'resistance movement' is intolerable...*

The Mau Mau in Kenya cast a sinister shadow over the life of European and African alike. Hatred and tensions flared up between African and European, African and African but also between the officials and the settlers which were, at times, venomous. Settlers thought they knew it all (a common settler failing, I admit, even though I partly come from settler stock) and young DOs and DCs found themselves trying to obey orders, unravel a tangle of vested interests and stay alive in a newly menacing and violent world.

In our own very minor way as small children we could feel its chill over our lives at our boarding prep school in the highlands. Great loops of barbed wire were laid around the school perimeter. Companies of British and Ugandan soldiers were given a paddock nearby in which to pitch a rest and recuperation camp in return for which they would patrol the school bounds. Most of the staff took to carrying pistols: some were hung on belts, whilst others were, fascinatingly, tucked inside female bosoms.

The African sports days which we had all enjoyed so much were stopped and instead of fire practice we were drilled in Mau Mau practice. At a given signal - I think it was a siren - the children in the dormitories facing the outside of the grounds had to rush into the inner ones and hide under the beds. (As the nights were cold and the beds themselves short of blankets, the inner dormitories became rather coveted.)

Farmers organised themselves all over the country into patrols to try to protect themselves and their neighbours. It was forbidden to travel anywhere without one's firearm. This was to prevent Mau Mau gangsters from breaking into the temporarily empty houses and stealing guns. Going into church on Sundays was not merely accompanied by the organ but also by the clatter of gun butts on stone.

It became common practice to lock servants out of the houses before sundown. This way they could not be coerced by gangs to let them into the house. One family did not follow this practice, keeping the servants in the house to serve supper. The only survivor of the ensuing massacre told me that one minute there was a cheerful, chatty atmosphere around the dinner table and the next a fearful chill silence fell and into the room filed a gang of wild looking men with pangas. They circled the table in complete silence and then they fell upon the diners howling as they did so. The sole survivor who was in her teens, was badly injured and left for dead but she managed to crawl through a wheat field to a car which she then drove (despite never having driven before) for help.

Perhaps now, over half a century later, the Mau Mau may be seen as a heroic struggle to throw off the bonds of the oppressor. But I do not believe that many Kikuyu saw it that way at the time. It was too ugly, too sordid, too terrifying to be heroic.

Hal Williams was awarded a CMG for his work as Provincial Commissioner, Nyanza Province. The citation said that it had been awarded for his contribution to preventing the Mau Mau from spreading into Nyanza. His way of doing this was to ensure that every chief and local leader was supported and listened to. He told me that he had said to each and every leader of every level that if they were at all concerned or worried they could telephone him whenever they wished and his door was always open to them. In addition, he and his DCs and DOs travelled constantly to every area to encourage, listen and support.

Years later just before Independence, when he had retired from the Colonial Service and was farming, Hal was approached by a member of the Agricultural Workers Union who asked him if he could stage a union meeting on the farm. Hal readily agreed and a date and venue was set for the meeting. The farm labour force were all told that the Agricultural Workers Union representative would be in a certain paddock at ten o'clock on the appointed day.

The day arrived and, to Hal's embarrassment, only he and the representative turned up. At the evening milking he remonstrated with the men. They listened politely but without comment as they leaned their heads companionably against the flanks of the Ayreshire/shorthorn cows they were milking. Finally, he picked out Mechemi, and said "Mechemi, you are an ex-Mau Mau, you of all people should have been interested in what the trade union representative had to say."

"Not I" he said firmly. "I have had societies of all kinds. They take your money, they do nothing for you and they make your life a misery. No more societies for me!"

McCall meeting "a few of the natural rulers" in the Niger Delta 1947

Chapter 18

THE LEOPARD MURDERS OF OPOBO

Lycanthropy: Transformation of witch into wolf; form of madness in which patient imagines himself some beast & exhibits depraved appetites, change of voice etc
                                        - The Concise Oxford Dictionary.

Intense fear of the occult can cloud the truth. Take the case against Billy Eshiet. . . .*[a] mother reported that her child had been seized and taken away by a leopard. About four weeks later, she made a further statement that it was not a leopard but a man who had seized her child, but she could not recognise his face as it was covered by a cloth. Then, at the Preliminary Enquiry before the Magistrate, she said that it was Billy Eshiet who had run into her compound and seized the child; she saw it was Billy Eshiet clearly because he had no cover over his face. Billy Eshiet was subsequently condemned to death.*

Apart from Billy Eshiet, seventy-six people were condemned to hang for the so-called 'leopard murders' in Opobo District, Eastern Nigeria. Only sixteen were reprieved. It was probably the most puzzling and distressing predicament faced by any administrative officer in British Colonial history. Johnny McCall, District Officer, Opobo and his Assistant District Officer, Wing Commander Gibbs, questioned conclusions reached by the Police and stood up for the condemned men. The Government was far from grateful and McCall was hustled out of the district under a cloud of secrecy in something akin to disgrace.

All over Africa people believed that certain of their number could turn themselves into lions, baboons, leopards or crocodiles and attack their enemies, dragging them into the bush and mauling them to death. One can see how such beliefs could arise. An old predator whose teeth and claws were almost useless would become a man-eater and attack a villager - usually a child or a woman. A member of the clan, or perhaps a group of people, would seize the opportunity to plant the idea that the attacker was a particular person, in the guise of the man-eater. Or sometimes it was the other way around where a man became convinced of his own powers to implant only his spirit into an animal.

In Sierra Leone Pat O'Dwyer came across this phenomenon at Makeni in the early forties:

I had not been alone in charge of the station for long before a dead body was brought in from the country very much disintegrating. You can imagine that a dead body would not last long in the tropics. The chief's messenger, who brought it, said that the chief's view was that the man had been the victim of a secret society and that it was murder. The body had obviously been clawed about and the first thing for me to find out was what the doctor thought about the body's injuries. The corpse was taken, therefore, to the doctor who said that it was so decomposed that he could not really tell. However, the claw marks could be those of a leopard, or they could be imposed by metal claws and inflicted by man. I held an enquiry and the most feasible thing seemed to me was to return a verdict of accidental death. I concluded that the man, who was a farmer living far out in the bush in a hut on the edge of the forest, had been the victim of a real leopard's attack and had thus met his death.

After the verdict I heard murmurings by the Court Messengers to the effect that really he had been murdered by a secret society. Well, this is where the African's mind becomes very confused. There is no doubt that secret societies did exist, which were really murder societies: for example, the Leopard Society, the Alligator Society and the Baboon Society. The allegations were that members of each of these societies took very secret and binding vows and associating themselves with these animals, simulated their methods of killing their selected victims. Thus, the Leopard Society would dress themselves in leopard skins and attach to their hands and feet metal claws. They would then lay in wait for their victim and pounce on him, clawing him to death. The Alligator Society would similarly attire themselves and wait by the water side and drown their victims and the Baboon Society would batter their victims to death.

It was well known that the real animals would also attack human beings and kill them, particularly children, out in the bush.

A further possibility which the Africans believed in was that a member of these societies had the power to direct his soul into the body of a leopard, alligator or

238

baboon and conduct that animal to attack the victim of his choice.

A little while after this time there was trouble in the Kenema district where members of the baboon society were put on trial for murder. The evidence against them was very strong, and the accused themselves added evidence to prove their own guilt, [by believing in their ability to put their spirits into baboons.] *They were found guilty and sentenced to death for murder and the sentence was carried out.*

It was only later, too late, that it was decided that these poor men were not guilty but only believed that they were.

Back in Opobo, Calabar Province, Nigeria, Johnnie McCall was learning his way around his new district in June 1947. He was a gentle, sensitive and intelligent member of the Nigerian Colonial Service. Photographs of him in his khaki shorts, show a man a little under six foot, with glasses and his friendly smile was evident when I visited him and his wife in their home south of Edinburgh in the early nineties.

During the course of the hand-over from Colonel Schofield, McCall and Gibbs visited the prison where several remand prisoners approached them. These men were awaiting trial as "man leopard" murderers and they told the two officers that *they were all innocent and that they were there in prison, charged with murder, only due to the malice of their enemies.* McCall came away from the prison deeply disturbed by the incident.

I have been an Administrative Officer in Nigeria for eleven years, he later wrote to the Resident in Calabar, "*and most of this time has been spent in the bush. It would be strange, considering one spends most of one's time trying to discover it; if one did not acquire some ability to distinguish between truth and untruth in the spoken word. I felt that these men were speaking the truth. Incidentally, it may here be mentioned that the majority of those unconvicted prisoners who said they were innocent have since then been discharged by the court, by the Judge or through Nolle Prosequis.*

Between the years 1943 – 1947 which was prior to McCall's arrival some two hundred to two hundred and fifty people were killed. These mysterious killings were initially assumed to be the work of a wild leopard. However, the District Officer at the time became convinced that a 'man leopard' society was operating in his division, a view which the Governor accepted and a force of 200 police was sent to Opobo.

As the killings increased and the terror gained momentum, the "Leopard man" problem reached the ears of the English press. *This is the strangest, biggest murder hunt in the world.* wrote Graham Stanford in the

Daily Mail on June 30, 1947 writing from *Leopard Land,* Nigeria. The article stated:

In the grim words of a hard-bitten senior English police official, 'The stage has now been reached when every single male adult is a potential leopard murderer.'... Real leopards prowl through the thick, 6ft high bush which fringes the twisting dusty tracks. But 'man leopards' with a blind belief in their primitive cult, are now taking human lives at the rate of more than one a week in this blood-stained patch of Africa.

Since the hunt began nearly two years ago 81 proved leopard murders have taken place.

Every afternoon at four o'clock there is a curfew in 'Leopard Land'. In almost every case the leopard-men strike at dusk. But still, about once every week - often more - people huddled in villages hear screams from the bush.

By the clawed, mutilated body of the victim will be the pad marks of a leopard. And only the distinctive claw marks on the face and body tell the killing was done by man and not the beast.'

Today three European officers and nearly 200 armed African policemen patrol 'Leopard land' by day and night.

Camps stud the country and mobile patrols roam the bush during the three murder hours between four o'clock and seven in the evening.

The police sleep in different villages every night in order to hear the hushed gossip of the bazaars and markets. But still the leopard-men strike - sometimes within a few hundred yards of the police patrols. For these killers believe so strongly in their powers that they are not frightened of the men who hunt them.

The police go after the leopard-men fully armed since the day one of their men was murdered by this nightmare method.

When the hunt first started in 1945 Senior Assistant Superintendent Fountain was sent by the Government to make a complete enquiry.

Fountain, an expert on the life and customs of the country, investigated scores of cases, visited every village in 'Leopard Land'.

At first he worked on the theory that the killings must be the work of a murder society, since the killings were all so similar. After long enquiries that theory was discarded, and in a factual report of several thousand words which he made last year he stated:

'We are fighting nothing so tangible as an organisation but rather an attitude of mind. Purely preventive measures haven't succeeded. They have not disturbed the leopard-men'.

... Patrols have been strengthened, curfew imposed, wholesale arrests have been made,

240

and some forms of ju-ju have been banned. But the leopard men still lurk in the bush and the cult has grown so strong that the police believe the word of no man. Every man in the Ibibio and Annang tribes of 'Leopard land' is suspect.

Stamford then chilled his readers:

The method is first to stun with a heavy stick and then to jab a yam-spike or needle-like knife into the neck and upper part of the body. Mutilation then takes place, to give the impression that the victim has been mauled by a leopard.

With the luxury of hindsight, 'attitudes of mind' may well have been proliferating in that overheated atmosphere. Did the police really not explore sufficiently the possibility that man-eating leopards could be at large? That would-be murderers, doubtless aware of the numbers of police in the area, would be less likely to attack near them than a leopard who only knew he was hungry? Or that the wounds on the cadavers made from "needle-like" instruments could have been made by animal claws or canines, the normal imprint of which might have been altered by broken teeth or damaged pads?

After he had taken charge of the division, Johnnie McCall and his ADO, Wing Commander Gibbs, discovered some significant facts. One was that the leopard killings did not occur north of the Qua Ibo river, *a deep, wide, fast flowing river with only one bridge across it.* Not much of an obstacle for humans but a difficult river for animals to cross and re-cross.

Why then, were people in peril south of the river but perfectly safe on the northern bank? McCall said that Police convictions showed that in practically every proven case there was a motive. *Marriage customs, child betrothal, adultery and so on have been listed as the main reasons for 'man leopard' murders. Yet north of the Qua Ibo River not a single person has been killed for one of these reasons.*

Furthermore, the availability or otherwise of normal leopard prey had a direct correlation to the numbers of human deaths. In the southernmost part of the division where game such as deer and monkey was plentiful, people were able to go about their business outside their villages in safety but in the areas where the least amount of game existed the most "murders" occurred.

Wing Commander Gibbs wrote:

The depredations of leopards in the area are not, I think, generally realised. Not many weeks ago I found out by dint of travelling through the affected areas that two cows, two pigs, one duck, one sheep and twenty one goats had been killed by leopards in the space of nine days. The fact of the matter is that in the 'Man-Leopard' area the natural food of leopards has been trapped and shot out of existence; a few herds of pigs which are not easily attacked by leopards, the odd duiker and antelope alone remain.

At about this time Gibbs acquired a leopard cub.

A further clue emerged bearing out Gibbs' belief that there might be too many leopard hunting too little game. In the area where the most people were being attacked it was found that the villagers had not shot many leopard in recent times due to the difficulty of obtaining arms and suitable ammunition during the war years.

In the tangled web of tension and anxiety McCall and Gibbs began to conclude that at least some of the killings that were causing so much terror and police activity had been perpetrated by the genuine article: man-eating leopard. McCall reported his findings to the Governor and his Council who listened but did not agree with him. They did, however, make some funds available to help in a leopard-trapping operation.

A serious difference of opinion developed between the two district officers on the one hand and the police on the other. McCall and Gibbs, responsible for the well-being of the people they administered, were concerned to ensure that all the facts were uncovered, unclouded by fear and preconceptions. The police, for their part, no doubt aided by their informers, dismissed the man-eater theory, despite the fact that the villagers said that "when the leopard-men kill they roar like wild-animals." On the other hand Fountain and his men, according to Stamford of the Daily Mail, "*the best brains in the police service*" firmly believed that if a few murderers were hanged, the others would be frightened into ceasing their activities.

Moreover, their convinced belief in hysterical murder seemed to affect the collection of evidence. But the study of hard facts in many cases was cursory and conclusions were muddled. Some of the sites of the kills were not visited and in others vital clues, such as excreta containing bone, were ignored. In one case, though, the police did send the pathologist some excreta found near the body of a victim. It contained a piece of bone on which he had found human African hair and leopard hair. The Pathologist's rather odd conclusion was that the bone was not human because he believed that it was too large to pass through a leopard and it would seem unlikely that a leopard would pass a fragment of non-human bone, human hair and its own hair all at the same time. The Police rather airily decided that the excreta was not from a leopard anyway. This irritated Gibbs, who was convinced that its description tallied exactly with the excreta his own leopard cub produced, and he pointed out that the policeman concerned *would be the first to agree that his knowledge of leopard excreta is meagre.*

The police stuck to the lycanthropy theory and went so far as to say that the villagers in one part of the division did not approve of the leopard trappings initiated by McCall and Gibbs. Wing Commander Gibbs was ndignant: *This is exactly the reverse* [of the truth.] *There is much rivalry as to who is to set traps; the killing of a leopard is a red-letter day in the life of an Annang or Ibibio village and the hunter is bedecked with Mkpat leaves, while the leopard is taken round the town. The affair is accompanied by much drinking and eventually the meat is apportioned out. A hunter who kills a leopard receives special honours at his funeral.*

During the process of trapping, one particular kill gave McCall and Gibbs further reason to believe that it was man-eaters, not man-leopards that were attacking the people.

Just a fortnight ago McCall wrote, *two persons were killed [at Ikot Odoro]. The day before they were killed, two large leopards were seen in that particular bush. I instructed Mr. Gibbs to send a trapper there. Close to the place where the two persons were killed, the trap was set. On the very first night, this large male leopard was killed. It was very old, and of its four fangs, two were broken down to half their size. One of its paws was mutilated, one pad being missing. This mutilation had clearly happened long ago.*

It is, of course, well known that the large predator cats can become man-eaters due to old age or injury. *This leopard was suffering from both.*

After he had been dispatched, the killings in the area stopped. However, to McCall's intense frustration men were continuing to be condemned to death. He and Gibbs appeared to be helpless to defend the people they were dedicated to protect both from attack and miscarriages of justice. And he was unable to convince either his superiors - far away from the district - or the police on the spot of what seemed to him to be worthy of serious investigation. Tension rose between the two administrative officers and the police.

His report was quite properly addressed to the Resident in Calabar but he requested that it *should be brought to the notice of His Excellency, the Governor. In doing so I am deeply conscious of my junior status in the Colonial*

243

Administrative Service. I would therefore emphasise at once that I write with the greatest respect. As the subject matter of the Report, however, concerns government policy and action of the most fundamental importance, a degree of frankness of writing may be inevitable.

He stated that the evidence against the so-call leopard-men indicted for murder simply did not add up and his report catalogued each case with the questions that the evidence posed, *From the study of dozens of cases, I must affirm what I firmly believe that I place no reliance whatever on the 'eye witness' accounts of 'man leopard' attacks. I have yet to read one which I believe. Judges Pollard and Ademele have evidently shared this disbelief in many cases.*

McCall's report makes grisly reading. He described the nature of the wounds found on the necks of the victims, the cleaning out of the victims skulls and whether or not the private parts were interfered with. It was all written carefully and clearly. He concluded:

Miscarriages of justice have occurred and innocent men have been hanged. I fear that, with present methods of investigation, miscarriages may continue." And he added *Despite the meticulous care with which Justice Ademele has heard recent cases, I heard condemned to death the other morning a man who I believe is innocent.*

I have come to my conclusions in this terribly serious matter unwillingly. .... Mr Gibbs, Assistant District Officer, has come to the same conclusions equally unwillingly. We both wish most sincerely that we could agree with the other point of view. We have no desire to stir up a scandal. But we are the men on the spot and I am myself an Administrative Officer of eleven years experience of the Eastern Provinces of Nigeria. Possibly the West African climate has affected my reasoning powers and led me to the wrong conclusions in this matter. The same cannot be said of Mr. Gibbs, whose distinguished war service as one of the youngest Wing Commanders in the Royal Air force and a DSO. to boot do not suggest a man of a completely irresponsible type and outlook. Yet of different character, temperament, training and ability, we have formed the same opinions and reached the same conclusions. We are the only Administrative Officers who have travelled extensively in the 'leopard' area. The opinions and conclusions of this report therefore are the opinions and conclusions of the men on the spot, and as such I think that they deserve at least the consideration of the highest authority in Nigeria, and if considered necessary, of the highest authority in the Empire.

It has been said that attention in this matter need not be paid to the past. But the Warrants of Execution of twenty persons odd have already been signed. In the light of consideration of the facts, opinions and conclusions recorded above, Government must decide whether to go on with these hangings.

I consider that, to say the least, the gravest doubt exists as to whether there have been many or any 'leopard type' murders. In existence of this grave doubt, which may soon be resolved one way or the other by the killing of wild leopards, I most respectfully recommend that all death sentences be commuted to terms of life imprisonment. If killings cease with the killing of the wild leopards, consideration in the future might then be given to the exercise of the Royal Prerogative of Reprieve by His Excellency. I would observe that the great majority of those convicted have already been awaiting execution for five or six months, and any further delay in their execution, pending the resolving of this grave doubt, would appear to be contrary to justice.

The killings did cease with the trapping of wild leopards but Mr McCall was given twenty four hours to leave his division with orders to proceed to Calabar and not to give anyone the impression that he was being transferred.

On 29th December 1947 the chiefs and representatives of the people of Ikot Akan, Opobo addressed the Secretary of State for the Colonies, Downing Street, London, and His Excellency the Officer Administering the Government, Government House, Lagos. They were writing in a foreign language; nevertheless, this remarkable and powerful document is a credit to the intelligence and confidence of the signatories as well as a testimony to McCall's loyalty to the people he served and his determination to defend their interests.

We the undersigned are directed by all inhabitants (men and women) of the Ibibio (Opobo) Division, which comprises Ikpa, Ibekwe, Ete-Okon, Nung Assang, Minya, Nung Asetang, Ibeku, Ikono, Abak-Idim and Ibesit/Nung Ikot Native Authorities and by the Central Executive of the Division to bring to the notice of the Government with a view to allaying the justifiable anxiety of the Division and particularly of the members of the community immediately affected, the universal dissatisfaction and disappointment caused by abrupt transfer of the District Officer in charge of the District in the person of Mr. J.A.G. McCall which transfer has incontrovertibly been engineered by the inconclusive evidence collected by the Police despite our protest through the Resident, Calabar, to the Government.

The petitioners are of the opinion that the Government has in recent times been endeavouring hard to extirpate the existing terrible depredations of the leopard society, having apparently overlooked the acknowledged facts that real ravenous beasts themselves as its accompaniament have been jeopardising both lives of poor members of the community and those of domestic animals during the past few years; that the most successful officer in extirpation is necessarily the most efficient and intelligent one who by his regular interference enlists whole-hearted cooperation of the affected area to detect the difference between man leopard and bush leopard; that close contact with the people and study of the difficulties confronting them with a view to ameliorating the conditions militating against their progress is the point to aim at for achievement of the true goal and that highhandedness, robbery, indiscriminate arrest and destruction of properties methods of which have been employed by the police force with intent to extort confessions played but little part in achievements.

The proofs that exclusiveness and aloofness have been the stumbling-block of many really clever officers who could have marketed their ability had they gone about it the right way and that most of the deaths attributed to man leopard have been caused by ravenous animals lie in the fact that reasonable percentage of unfortunate victims are children of tender age and women and that ever since trapping and hunting of the beasts in the area through brilliant effort of the District Officer and suit death rate has been remarkably small. The proposed transfer from his appointment of District Officer on the grounds of injudiciousness of his reports in man leopard investigation, in our opinion, is in the nature of punishment either to the area or the District Officer and such an action is liable to incite repercussions. If investigating Officers or District Officers are punishable by the Government when they give reports which though correct in fairness and equity, are displeasing to police or not in consonance with police instructions, to burke the fact the petitioners are left in the conviction that the Government will oblige every District Officer in the area to consult police authority before his conscience, practice of which will weaken popular faith in the continued existence of great qualities of high reputation of British Justice, fairness and equity and cause most of the British ideals to lose their original fervour today on account of their exponents being unable to soar above petty inclinations. And may we add without offence that if it is intention of the Government to penalise the area and burke' sole origin of prolongation of the menace, we prefer posting of police force in the area for massacre.

Whatever happens we require back our District Officer, Mr MacCall [sic] in whom our complete confidence has been vested and demand that in future District Officers with sympathetic heart be posted to the area.

"We have the honour to be, Right Honourable,
    Your obedient servants
   1. Chief Ntuen Ibok   His mark
   2. Chief Umoren Akpanta   His mark
   3. Chief Ayara Akpabio   His mark
   4. ? Jonah Ndife ?   His mark
   5. James Ukpon   His mark
   6. Japhet Akpan Udo   His mark

7. *S.O. ?*   *His mark*
8. *Lazurus Udo Akpabio   His mark*
9. *William ?*   *His mark*

Post Script

I am indebted to Mr McCall for allowing us to publish this story and others; also for contributing the photographs of him throughout this book.

The Governor at the time of the leopard killings was Sir John Macpherson. It is known that the leopard killings worried him deeply and his friendliness and support to John McCall after he had left Opobo District indicate that a, perhaps, troubled soul thought that McCall may have been right.

Burke – to stifle the truth

J.A.G. McCall visiting Ngo-Andoni market. Niger Delta 1947

Chapter 19

SING A SONG OF PRICES

Sing a song of prices,
A marketful of gum;
At Kaka in the crisis
Things began to hum.
When the markets opened
There wasn't much perhaps;
Now there's several thousand 'kant'
To set before the chaps.

DCEJ *Eastern Jebels (Sudan) Monthly Report*

Trade was, of course, a major reason for the European nations to take over the administration of Africa. In many places the potential was mouth watering. The land looked so rich it was hard to credit. Sir Harry Johnston GCMG, KCB in his ravishingly illustrated book *The Uganda Protectorate* wrote enthusiastically of the commercial possibilities in 1902. *Amongst the extensive collections of rocks and minerals which were made by my expedition, or on its behalf by officials of the Uganda Protectorate, only one amongst all the specimens of quartz shows any signs of gold. On the other hand, specimens of rocks from Unyoro. ... would seem to indicate a formation in that district analogous to the gold-reef rocks of the Transvaal. The country abounds in haematite iron, and in ordinary iron ore; there are graphite or plumbago mines, and there is perhaps a little copper. Some of the rock specimens collected by Mr. F.W. Isaac in the Baringo District indicate the possibility of precious stones existing in these formations. Salt of very good quality is obtained from the salt lakes. Whether this salt would be worth*

249

exportation is a matter of doubt, but it circulates throughout a good deal of Central Africa as a valuable article of barter.

He then went on to list ivory of the very best quality, *so long as the British Government can determinedly enforce the Game Regulations.'* He also suggested that the vast marshes and leagues of forest should be protected for the shelter of the elephant and he described zebra *"in countless swarms"* and fine large asses which might be exported, as well as giraffes and antelopes for sale and transmission to zoos, ostriches with their fine white plumes and honey bees.

The troublesome tsetse fly was only touched upon:

Either there is no true tsetse fly anywhere in the Uganda Protectorate or it is not able to obtain and introduce into the bodies of domestic animals the malarial germs which cause tsetse fever. Therefore, theoretically there is no part of the Uganda Protectorate in which cattle, sheep, goats, and horses cannot be kept. But he went on to admit to the existence of pleura-pneumonia which came down from the *Dinka countries in the Egyptian Sudan* and which caused devastation to the cattle of East Africa.

On the subject of produce from the soil he was even more enthusiastic.

Turning to vegetable productions, we have, in the first place, coffee. Whether originally introduced or not from Abyssinia, coffee is at any rate native now in a semi-wild form to the better forested regions of the Uganda Protectorate, its berries producing coffee of excellent flavour. Not only might the wild coffee be gathered and sold by the natives, but it would seem as though this country was singularly well adapted for coffee plantations, as the forested regions have a regular and ample rainfall, the soil is very rich and an abundance of shade trees exist. Coffee could be grown on the lake shore all round the northern half of the Victoria Nyanza. Steamers could carry the coffee to the railway terminus on Kavirondo bay, and it is probable that by steamer and rail, and steamer again from Mombasa, coffee could be landed at the European markets charged with a freight of not more that £2 10s a ton.

Regarding the soil of Uganda proper and the adjoining Districts of Busoga and Toro, Mr Alexander Whyte said:

Generally speaking this soil is a reddish loam on a subsoil of rich red or chocolate clay, sometimes of a great depth. At times patches of poor, gravelly soil crop up, more especially on the hilltops. The question generally put is, 'What will not grow and flourish in Uganda?' The furze and the broom grow so well that we are making hedges of them. Tomatoes grow quite wild. One plant was left by the boys when weeding my compound. It flourished so amazingly that I determined to keep tally of the fruits picked from it. The yield in two months has been 3,000. It still goes on bearing clusters of lovely fruits, and covers a space of twenty feet square.

205. A SUNFLOWER WITH NEARLY 300 BLOSSOMS ON IT AT ENTEBBE

The Uganda Protectorate by Sir Harry Johnston (Pub 1902)

Debate, however, was raging on the ethics of commercial exploitation. Johnston had no doubts that all would benefit. He said that critics such as *the editor of 'Truth', ... are asking now with renewed force whether the statesmen of both parties between 1885 and 1894 did not gravely blunder when they yielded to public sentiment and assumed for Great Britain heavy responsibilities in tropical and unhealthy Africa. These critics point to the wars which have occurred between British forces and the natives as a proof that our protection was not desired and had to be imposed by force. They single out an individual atrocity as a sample of the white man's daily conduct, and having thus shown the fallacy from the philanthropical point of view of our expensive efforts to administer an area in tropical Africa which equals the united extent of Europe without Russia, they brush aside the question of commercial gain either by declaring it non-existent and not likely to come to pass, or by alleging that it is no justification for that shedding of blood which seems to have been inevitable in the founding of these Protectorates.*

He countered that argument by saying that in Uganda:

If one reads the works of Speke, of Stanley, of the Rev. W.P. Ashe, of Lugard, and Colville, one realises what a bloody country was the Kingdom of Uganda before it came under British control. The flow of human blood must have been such a common

251

sight as to render the Baganda singularly callous. Speke gives a pathetic account of Mutesa's wives being hurried off to a cruel execution for most trivial reasons, raising their wailing cries of 'O my lord, O my master.' as they passed him on the way. Sometimes the reasons for these death sentences were that a wife had failed to close the door as she passed out of a courtyard or she had pulled the door to, when to do so was a breach of native etiquette.

If every adult male native in these Protectorates paid 8s a year in taxation, there would be little, if any, need to resort to the Treasury of the United Kingdom for funds to supplement the cost of administration. There would also be no cause for the British taxpayer to complain if coffee or rubber, gold or ivory, or all these substances combined, failed to provide a lucrative commerce for the British market. The Protectorate would then be administered purely in the interest of the black man. He at least, in the climate of the country wherein he was born, does not suffer from the diseases which afflict the European who attempts to settle in parts of tropical Africa; he at least is happy and content if he can maintain flocks and herds of cattle, sheep, and goats, and grow food-stuffs suited to his country and his palate. He can only earn money by working, say, for a month, or by collecting and selling rubber, coffee, or some other saleable substance, which he can acquire without robbing other people; or he may breed cattle for the provision market, or collect oil which is sufficiently valuable to meet the cost of transport to the European markets.

Johnston goes on to propose that Africans who are *by no means wanting in enterprise* should be encouraged to give their services *at good rates of pay* to working for European enterprises.

I know at first sight that certain people in England, keenly interested in the welfare of the Negro, and whose interest may sometimes border on sentimentality, will exclaim that the theory I am propounding of turning Central African labour into undeveloped South Africa, and South African money into unhealthy Central Africa, is but a disguised revival of slavery. A little reflection, however, will convince the really honest Negrophiles that this is not the case. A class of missionary now nearly extinct was bitterly opposed to the enterprise of non-missionary Europeans in Central Africa, and to any steps which might result in the Central Africans leaving their homes to go far afield for employment. This type of thinker, narrow if earnest, would have preferred that the Central African native should remain in modified savagery, without any wants or tastes than those which could be met by the simple instruction and pleasures of the mission station.

Sir Harry emphasised that no compulsion should be exercised to oblige people to go far afield for employment but in retrospect it is, perhaps, fortunate that his proposal did not come about, although people south of Tanganyika were often attracted to the South African mining industry.

But the question of reverting to slavery was a very real concern. On the 18th of August 1909, Sir Arthur Conan Doyle wrote a passionate letter to *The Times* about the exploitation of Africans in the Belgian Congo:

Sir, We live in the presence of the greatest crime which has ever been committed in the history of the world, and yet we, who not only could stop it but who are bound by our sworn oath to stop it, do nothing? The thing has been going on for 20 years. What are we waiting for? Our guilt of national acquiescence is only second to that of the gang of cosmopolitan scoundrels who have been actively concerned in turning all Central Africa into a high slave State, with such attendant horrors as even the dark story of the slave trade has never shown. In the slave trade the victim was of a market value, and to that extent was protected from death or mutilation. In this case the State is the owner of all, so that if one be dismembered or shot another is always available. ....

Every day that passes fresh crimes are committed. The rubber has been coming faster than ever to Europe this year, and the rubber can only come through the system and the system can only be enforced by terror. Consul Thesiger, in his report published this year shows that the screw is ever tightening, that new tribes are being drawn into the slavery, that they are worked in such a fashion that they have no time to plant their crops, and that a great famine is threatened in the future. Conan Doyle points an accusing finger at the Belgian Colonial Minister who had financial interests in the Congo.

How did it all turn out then? *One of the main tasks of the British administration* wrote a biographer of Sir Philip Mitchell, a distinguished administrator in Uganda at that time *was to develop crops to take the place of the trade in slaves and ivory. The local diet rested on bananas, particularly the plantain which could be turned into banana flour called matoke. This with grain crops and livestock supplied a subsistence agriculture in the fertile and well watered southern half of Uganda; but the twentieth-century protectorate needed more from its agriculture than subsistence farming. .... The extensive lakes made cheap water transport available elsewhere for the movement of agricultural produce; and the railway through Kenya linked Uganda with the sea. The Lancashire textile mills needed cotton, and cotton was a product which Uganda was ideally fitted to supply and it soon became the leading export crop.* It became a matter for concern that the economy relied so heavily upon cotton, though robusta coffee and sugar were also produced by Ugandans.

Further East in Kenya much of the export agriculture developed and was in the hands of the European settlers who produced tea, arabica coffee, beef, wheat, barley, oats, pyrethrum, mutton, wool, dairy and pork products. The exceptional quality of butter, cheeses and pork products competed successfully against the best Danish produce: the top quality European producers in this field during the colonial period.

Africans provided the labour on these farms which was always something of a thorny issue. Some Africans enjoyed getting away from stultifying customs or nagging wives and earning some cash but others resented the need for money and the breakdown of the tribal unit. European farmers were worried by the lack of good labour and the petty crime which went on, and over which DCs seemed unable to exert sufficient control. And those looking on from Britain were often shocked by the low wages paid to farm labourers in Kenya.

On our own family farm which was fairly typical, families lived in traditional huts, their children went to school on the farm, the farm paid for a school master and each family had a plot to till. There was also a small shop selling basic items at cost price and our mother gave medical help when it was required. Margaret Collyer's book *A Vivid Canvas* gives a good description of that farm in the early part of the twentieth century.

A very real concern for the officials was the soil erosion and environmental damage which many African farming practices caused.

The sad fact is wrote Sir Phillip Mitchell, *that with few distinguished exceptions, among whom pride of place must go to the Chagga of Kilimanjaro and the Kara of Ukara, as soon as a population reaches a certain density in East Africa and Central Africa it destroys the soil with a devastating ruthlessness. ... Compared to it the relatively trifling areas of land in occupation by Europeans and Indians are of negligible importance...* (About 13% of all land in Kenya was farmed by Europeans.)

West Africa did not allow European settlement but it was a powerhouse of commerce. Writing in 1945 Rex Niven describes West Africa as being:

divided into the Grain Coast (Nigeria), Ivory Coast, Gold Coast and Slave Coast (Dahomey). The grain was pepper.

Prior to the implementation of the Produce Marketing Boards, the produce was bought by a Licensed Buying Agent, or LBA, on behalf of the trading companies. A.F.B. Bridges, a D.O. in Onitsha in the twenties provides a snapshot of the old style LBA:

On the 6th March I was sent down to Atani on the river below Onitsha to go into a complaint from the Niger Company that the local people were trespassing on the company land. The agent gave me lunch. He was a young man of about my own age and [one of] several agencies up and down the river. Some managed to stick it - others did not and, not long after, one at another station committed suicide. Not only were the stations lonely, they were hemmed in by thick bush on the land side and the muddy river on the other, swarming with mosquitoes and other biting insects, hot and depressing. Further, the firms then had a system of fixed prices for trade goods and if the agent could find buyers at a higher price he was allowed to keep the balance. In this way the lucky or astute ones were able to make quite a lot of money and it was a fairly common experience to be standing talking to an agent on the riverbank at Onitsha and seeing a sternwheeler passing downriver, to be told 'There goes so-and-so - he's made his pile.' In the circumstances one can hardly grudge them their success, though it was a ubiquitous system and was later abolished.

Nigeria covers an area bigger than Belgium, France, Switzerland and Italy and in 1945 had a population of 22,000,000 which produced huge quantities of palm oil, cocoa, ground nuts, pepper and minerals.

After the Second World War responsibility for the marketing of Nigeria's principal agricultural products was handed over to a number of marketing boards. They paid a fixed price each year which was lower than the world market price, thus building up reserves which were used to cushion the farmers when world prices fell or to assist in times of hardship. And by appointing selected commercial firms as their buying agents, the marketing boards began to use their reserves for the development of their agricultural industries. Sharwood-Smith wrote

Thus in 1949, three quarters of a million pounds had been spent in the North on introducing mechanized cultivation, on artificial fertilizers, and on access roads to underdeveloped areas. The political significance of the new policy was even greater than its economic advantages. A quota of Nigerians was appointed to each board and to its advisory committee and to the marketing company in London. .... The same policy applied also in other sectors of Nigeria's industrial framework. One by one the Government-run coal fields, the electricity undertakings, the Nigerian railway, and the administration of the ports and docks were removed from the control of government departments and handed over to public corporations. Here Nigerians and Britons served side by side under expert chairmanship.

The genius behind this economic revolution was the late Sir Sidney Phillipson, formerly Financial Secretary to the Nigerian Government. Small in stature, sandy-haired, sparsely built, his self-effacing manner gave little outward indication of the

inner fires that drove him. The importance of "Sir Sid's" personal share in the peaceful transfer of responsibility over the whole field of the country's economy from British to Nigerian hands cannot be over-rated.

Angus Ferguson CBE was a highly respected lawyer in Nigeria during the colonial period and he continued to practice there until illness forced his retirement in 1988. The letter he wrote me provides a rather whimsical flavour of the commercial scene in the fifties, sixties and later:

Productivity of the ordinary man - the man on the Onitsha mammy-wagon - was not very high. The Nigerian way of life was generally attuned to a leisurely tempo. In the rural areas this was the pace required for subsistence farming which is what most of life was about. With increasing exposure to the Western way of life and the need for cash, and therefore for cash crops, the pace probably increased a little.

Increasing urbanisation provided a market for local consumption and the rapidly expanding market in export produce (groundnuts, cocoa, cotton, rubber, palm oil, oilseeds, timber) with guaranteed prices for primary produce provided an incentive to higher productivity. It is noteworthy that while guaranteed prices were fair there was high productivity; when prices ceased to be fair (after independence) productivity dropped off.

You will know, of course, that Nigeria was self-sufficient in food under the colonial yoke and depended on the export of agricultural produce for its foreign exchange. Thanks to the Produce Marketing Boards which had the export monopoly, the farmers were paid a fair price, Nigeria fared well in the world markets and agriculture flourished. For example, a million tons of groundnuts in one season.

Licensed Buying Agents (LBAs) were appointed by the Produce Marketing Boards to go into the bush and buy the produce for cash. LBA's were mainly, but not wholly, foreign or expatriate companies such as Levantis, Lever Brothers etc. and they needed finance.

The British banks at the beginning of each produce season would lend out millions of pounds (when pounds meant something) knowing that their money would not come back until the produce had been bought, tested as to export quality, shipped and sold. Branch managers did this every year without a qualm. Would that we had such managers today. What Bank Manager today would cheerfully watch a kit-car rumble off into the bush over-laden with bags of shillings (the only payment the farmers would accept)? Those were the days!

In the Sudan where cotton was a major export, another correspondent of mine, A.G. McCall B.Sc (Agric)NDA, described how he and his colleague K.L. Lea-Wilson B.A. (Agric) A.I.C.T.A. began a project in

Zandeland in 1945 to try to persuade the Zande people to grow some cash crops. It was a pilot project which, if successful, was hoped would pave the way for the social and economic development of southern Sudan. The instigator of the project, Dr. Tothill, had hoped that *in the course of some 30 years a happy, civilised, prosperous, even if not wealthy peasantry would be built up, economically self-sufficient and taking an ever increasing part in the management of its own affairs.*

Zandeland was chosen for this experiment because the area had good soils, a comparatively large and concentrated population and a people amenable to organisation and noted as knowledgeable and industrious cultivators. But it involved a fundamental change in their way of life.

We had deliberately to introduce the Azande to the heretical idea of a permanent homestead, to replace shifting cultivation by a settled form of agriculture providing for cash crops in rotations that would preserve the soils, to replace barter by a cash economy, to establish new levels of education and health, to direct a small fraction of the tribe into the even more revolutionary worlds of industry and town.

The idea was to grow cotton, citrus, guava, custard apples, paw paws and limes on a commercial basis. But the experiment was not a great success. The attractions of cash, as opposed to barter, did not appeal. Chronic sicknesses and subservience to a feudal heirarchy, magic, witchcraft and tribal custom *"sapped their energy and dulled their minds"* and once the initial novelty wore off the people lost interest. A certain amount of coercion was exerted to persuade the tribe to set aside a proportion of land to cash crops. Bonuses were suggested *springing from* complaints [presumably from the men] *in every sub-division, in the provision of a prize for the women. This may sound far-fetched but they, after all, do a great deal of the work and it would not cost a lot to issue say a cheap aluminium bowl or plate as a woman's prize.*

However the lasting benefit to the area was the establishment of weekly produce markets at village centres all over the district. These flourished and became an essential of normal life. Prior to these, *the bush-shops were the only countryside marketing agency, albeit untrustworthy and inefficient, and they are still the main channel for the disposal of farms' grain, oil seeds, chillies, honey and beeswax.*

Because Agricultural Officers were very active and deeply involved in the administration the British colonies and protectorates, commerce was not a major part of the administrative officer's working life. It is important to realise, however, that the colonies thrived. A great deal of

257

enthusiasm went into the enterprises to try to enrich all who took part. There was for example, in Asijiri, a small village in Nigeria in the late forties a "Welsh crusader" called Mr Price, who was not an administrative officer but who flung himself into the task of improving commercial practices and *who with all the fervour, eloquence and fanaticism of his race ... embraced the cause of co-operative societies. Largely at his instigation, the cocoa-growers [were] organized into thirteen Co-operative Marketing Unions, which between them [had] produced 180,000 bags of cocoa [in a] year. [The Mottled Lizard* by Elspeth Huxley]

Wherever it was in British administered Africa, great energy, ingenuity and fairness went into this immense commercial enterprise. This glimpse does it no justice. Not everyone was successful but countless people - Africans, Indians, Lebanese, British and other Europeans - prospered and there is no doubt that the foundation stones were laid for the countries under British rule to go forward and grasp the opportunities for themselves.

The Government's wise and the Government's good,
It loves hard cash as a Government should,
And it taxed all creatures that walk or creep
Save Addax, Leucoryx and Mountain Sheep.

From A PASTORAL by B.K.C.   Sudan 1924

Chapter 20

TAX COLLECTING AND TOURING

The phenomenon of taxes was not entirely new in Africa when the British arrived. Tribute to the chiefs in the form of days' worked, slaves or produce was normal practice. But in the early days in East Africa it was the need somehow to acquire money in order to pay the tribute that many people found difficult to grasp. This was because currency in the form of cash was unknown by most. As late as the time of the great slump in 1928 people were still somewhat baffled by the whole concept. Phillip Mitchell wrote in his book *African Afterthoughts*.

I remember going to a Chief's village near a place called Singida on the central plateau and being told that he had gone into the town to try to buy shillings for his people to pay tax with. 'But' said his clerk, 'shillings are now very expensive and even for a cow the cattle traders will only give very few, so that I do not know how we shall pay the government tax.'

Another chief, an important Sukumu baron and rather a special friend of mine, said to me, 'I quite understand the situation. Do you remember about three years ago some white men came to Mwanza and started a shop called 'Banki'?' Yes I did remember. 'Well' he continued, 'they started them to buy the shillings; now they've got them. That's all!'

In Machakos district, Kenya, in 1920 Clarence Buxton and his sister, Lucy, went out on a tax collecting safari. They had a fourteen hour trudge through the thorn scrub when they found they had missed the Christian Mission that was near the village of Kangunda where rest houses had been prepared. They turned back and after a mile or so reached the village where they were *never more thankful to sit down.*

Our troubles were not over, however, for a good deal of our kit had not arrived and we had only one tent and three beds amongst five people and one knife and spoon for us all to eat with. On the camping ground were two thatched huts but not ideal to sleep in as the walls were just reeds far apart and no protection, while the front was open altogether!

Having borrowed cutlery from the American mission, the resourceful cook, provided a dinner of *excellent soup, boiled eggs and cocoa.*

Miss Buxton reported that the hut tax had just been raised from 5 to 8 rupees.

Streams of people, she wrote *arrived at the camp. The different figures in their weird and scanty garments, most of them carrying their chits in a split stick - as they carry any letter in this country. Clarence says often an old woman comes along putting her tongue over her teeth, talking as if she had none, to show she is too old to pay tax. Another constant trick is that a man who has brought several taxes puts a handful of money down which is minus 2 or 3 rupees and which he hopes won't be noticed. When it is, he says they must have dropped on the way. Finally, to his great surprise, the missing coins are discovered in a corner of his blanket.*

*The money that is collected in a day is sent back to Machakos next morning, in boxes of 1000 rupees. The first instalment went off this morning at 6.30 in the charge of two askaris [*police*]. There are eight or nine askaris with the safari. They look very fine, as they are all tall men and wear the high red fez with a long black tassle, dark blue sweaters and puttees and khaki shorts - and of course full equipment when on duty.*

In the evening Clarence organised an archery competition. A target was nailed to a tree and first the small boys, then the young men shot their bows and arrows. The boys were much the best and the audience were very enthusiastic. Finally, Clarence caused much hilarity by having a go himself and missing the target altogether.

After their marriage in 1935, Hal and Joy Williams, were posted to Meru in Kenya which was a heavily populated district north of Nairobi. Because Hal was the most junior DO, he and Joy went out on tax collecting safaris most of the time. They would drive to the locations by car with an accompanying lorry which transported the specie (collected tax) boxes back to Meru. Until then they were chained under the camp beds of the DO and his wife *using us as bait so to speak* Joy said. In Meru District the whole village would come to pay the tax. The people would dress in their best and they would approach the camp singing, dancing and waving a contribution that would help to sustain the members of the tribal police. This contribution may have been a piece of wood, an egg or two, a hand of bananas or even a fowl and the chief would bring a goat or a sheep.

Some British wives not unnaturally found this noisy crowd advancing on the tax collector disconcerting, or even frightening but Joy was not so easily daunted. Besides which she was a straightforward and practical woman who enjoyed good company of any race or rank. When she went out on safari she would take with her their wind-up gramophone. A great favourite was *O For the Wings of a Dove* sung by a boy with an exceedingly high and pure treble voice. This would send the Africans into paroxysms of laughter and they would beg to hear it again and again. She would patiently rewind the gramophone and play it again while they rolled around in helpless mirth.

As well as the music she would take with her plenty of Ellermans Horse Embrocation which she rubbed on the rheumatic muscles of the old men and women which they found blissfully relieving. On the work side, once when the crowd of tax payers threatened to overwhelm them, the interpreter suggested that she was press-ganged into writing tax receipts. Hal was dubious to begin with - those were days when women had a strictly different role from the men - but the interpreter insisted and so she sat down and joined in.

In some distant districts Joy would submit to being prodded by the African women who were intrigued to see their first white woman. In Kisii district one day Hal was happily splashing in his canvas safari bath when he caught the sound of giggling. Peering through the tent flap he found a line of maidens thoroughly enjoying the impromptu show.

After World War II in the Sudan Brian Carlisle also tried to make tax assessment a less painful duty for all concerned.

To trade, he wrote, *a person had to apply for a Trader's Licence which I believe cost £4. If a trader's profits were deemed to be in excess of £150 a year he became liable to Business Profits Tax (BPT) which went up gradually on a sliding scale to 30% or 40%. Very few people kept books of account which they were prepared to produce to Government; so profits had to be assessed by a local board which was chaired by the DC and was composed of local merchants plus perhaps the odd notable. Fortunately it was considered quite*
an honour to sit on the BPT Board but allied with this was an obligation to shoulder a reasonable assessment of your own profits.

One of the qualifications to obtain a shot gun licence was to have a BPT profit assessment of I believe, £350 and this was quite a carrot to some merchants to accept assessed profits of this level: I believe there was another higher level at which you were entitled to something else but for the life of me I cannot remember now what it was. Although I appreciate that paying tax is no laughing matter I used to try to keep the meetings from getting too serious.

In the far west, in Sierra Leone, tax collecting was rather more adventurous. As a junior officer, Pat O'Dwyer had a superior who dispensed handy hints to subordinates who were about to set out on tax collecting treks. *Always keep your carriers with you or they will lag behind. Accept the 'dash' given by the chief where you stay and then repay to the treasury in cash. As you will only be a 'small boy' the dash will not be great but the going rate is one shilling for a fowl and a penny for an egg.*

Sierra Leone is a land criss-crossed with rivers and O'Dwyer used to watch nervously as the porters crossed the swaying liana tie-tie bridges, carrying specie boxes and chained together to prevent them making off with the cash, defying the ever watchful crocodiles beneath them.

Pat liked to shoot on the way splashing through water and swamp, which meant he would arrive looking dishevelled. This embarrassed him as the Chief and his elders always greeted him in their best. They would escort him to his house where pleasantries were exchanged and a pole found upon which to run up the Union Jack *to show that justice could be obtained if anyone wanted it.* The carriers were expected to bring firewood and water before they were paid off; the Chief Messenger would bring the 'dash' and then at last he was able to rest.

At the first rest house he ever stayed in, Pat had just thankfully lain down on his camp bed, when, *I looked up and, coiled around the rafter, was a python. I took my 12-bore shot gun and shot it at very close range. The snake fell down, but the shot must have hit a nail or something because the grass roof ignited. It was in the middle of the dry season and everything was tinder dry. As the grass caught light I called the Messengers for help and they were magnificent. All the houses were very close together so they and some of the villagers got on top of the neighbouring houses armed with palm fronds and water and stemmed the flames. Had it gone on it would have burnt down the whole village which would have been a dreadful blow to my career in the Colonial Service.*

In Northern Rhodesia Edwin Thornton considered himself privileged to have been able to experience the sights and sounds of those early mornings in the bush when camp was struck soon after dawn and the chill was still in the air. They would set out on bicycles:

with one's Messengers, the Chief, and Native Court, Treasury officials, and so on, along narrow footpaths amongst forest trees or through 'dambo' grasslands or maizefields, and all the colours and sounds seemed to be enhanced by the cold clarity of the morning atmosphere. Or one was punted across a dangerously crocodile-infested river in a twisted dug-out with no freeboard, by an old ferryman with a broken punt-pole, possibly a prototype for the chap who will take one across the Styx; but then at the other shore one rode triumphantly into the village amongst lines of village women and children ululating in, perhaps, spurious pleasure at the Bwana DO's visit. Even though one may have doubted their sincerity and their motives, it gave one a lot of pleasure to be welcomed by smiling faces.

Village tours lasted about two to three weeks, wrote Dennis Frost, who also served in Northern Rhodesia. *When the Boma acquired its first three ton lorry I used it to carry us and our camp equipment to the starting point of the tour but we still relied upon our bicycles thereafter. Before each tour a Messenger was despatched to the chief to notify him of our plans and to secure his availability to come with us. Others went off to recruit porters to carry the luggage, both domestic and bureaucratic paraphernalia, from camp to camp during the tour.*

The ritual was more or less the same at each village. Having been warned of our approach we would be met about half a mile out by all the small boys and girls in the charge of the school teacher or one of the elders, clapping their hands and singing out a greeting to us as they fell in behind our bicycles. A little further on we would come across the maidens in a bevy who joined in the singing and general jollification; then the married women and finally, at the entrance to the village the men and elders, male and female, would be assembled to accompany the chief and myself to the 'nsaka'. This was an open shelter in the middle of the village normally used by the elders as a meeting place to discuss affairs, maybe to eat their meals together, or just to while away the time. There, stools or chairs and, if the village ran to it, a table was set out for our use.

Once all were gathered and the chief and I and our assistants were safely seated, the headman led the village in a formal greeting, all going down on their knees and gently clapping their hands, wishing us well and hoping we had travelled safely. Then the villagers would squat on the ground, the menfolk gathered around the nsaka and the women and children seated a little way off but near enough to listen and chip in when they thought fit.

We in turn made small talk before getting down to the job on hand, giving ourselves time to recover our breath by asking the headman and elders if they were well and whether the crops or rains were satisfactory. We greeted anyone we recognised in the assembled throng; maybe a question to a pensioner from government service, or a joke exchanged with a newly released offender whom we had housed in the Boma gaol until recently, who had collected our water or firewood whilst awaiting Her Majesty's pleasure.

Once the formalities were over the names on the village register were called out and additions and amendments made as we proceeded to record, in the case of absentees, where they had gone, the numbers of people in the district working elsewhere, and those who had not paid their taxes. In this way we had some idea of the movements of people between villages, or those who were working in the mines or elsewhere, and we were able to keep a check on potential tax dodgers. In the evenings and again at the end of each tour I consolidated these records of movements, together with a count of the number of taxpayers, traders and others on our books in an attempt to produce a profile of life and activity within the district as an appendix to my tour report.

After the roll call I would refer to the notes of the last visit to the village and ask what action had been taken to put into effect the suggestions or instructions issued at that time. This usually led to a general discussion during which questions were asked, complaints laid and information exchanged concerning everything from new government regulations to the state of the crops, the rains or garden raids and other matters of mutual interest.

Sometime in the course of these proceedings the young men wishing to apply for identity cards and the old men applying for tax exemption would be brought forward by the headman to be examined by the chief and myself and a verdict given. If there were any litigants or complainants their cases were dealt with on the spot or they were told to follow us to our camp where they could be attended to in greater detail by the chief's court or by myself at the end of the day.

After these formalities had been completed it was usual to tour the village and village gardens in order to examine the state of the huts, latrines and rubbish pits as well as the gardens, crop storage facilities or anything else which came our way. The chief and I would be accompanied by the headman and elders, and a motley collection of small children and pi-dogs, the latter merely out of curiosity, but the former so that they could relay our instructions and words of wisdom to the whole village.

All this took up to an hour depending upon the size of the village, after which we mounted our bicycles, said our farewells and proceeded along the way to the next village, followed by expressions of good-will and assurances that what we had decreed would be carried out.

266

So some of us chivvy the slaver,
And some of us cherish the black,
And some of us hunt on the Oil coast.
And some on the wallaby track:
And some of us drift to Sarawak,
And some of us drift up The Fly,
And some share our tucker with tigers
And some with the gentle Masai.

Kipling *The Lost Legion*

Her Majesty Queen Elizabeth II unveiled in Westminster Abbey this plaque commemorating all those "who served the Crown in the Colonial Territories"

Chapter 21

UHURU!
Independence

If independence were to be hell, it would be little consolation to tell the victims that the fire had been lit by their fellow-countrymen.
Sir Arthur Richards, Governor of Jamaica circa 1940

We sailed wherever ships might sail;
We founded many a mighty State;
Pray God our greatness may not fail,
Through craven fear of being great.
Sir Arthur Richards, GCMG, First Baron Milverton of Lagos and Clifton in the City of Bristol and Governor of Nigeria from 1943 - 1947

We now come to the last snapshot of this briefest of episodes in the ancient story of Africa.

In 1957 Hal Williams decided to retire from the Colonial Service. He was Provincial Commissioner, Nyanza Province at the time. He had been awarded a CMG for his success in keeping the Mau Mau out of Nyanza. He did this through maintaining a strong communication network with the people of Nyanza and their representatives. When his retirement was announced, he received the letter over the page.

Looking at that great continent today (2014) where wars and corruption have created upheaval and tragedy on a massive scale - something which would have been unimaginable during the colonial period - we need to ask ourselves three questions. Was the timing right? Why was it that independence happened so unexpectedly and so swiftly? Did the people understand the implications of independence?

When African soldiers returned home from the Second World War they had a new confidence in themselves and a new belief that if they could be successful soldiers in the jungles of Burma, the wrecked towns of Europe or the deserts of Africa then surely they could administer themselves? There is much to commend this view. We, the British, asked a great deal of the people of Africa and many of them delivered a hundredfold in courage, blood, coin and loyalty. Without doubt in the late forties the time was approaching when self-determination for the colonies and protectorates should have been, and indeed was, a matter for discussion, debate and planning.

When Sir Arthur Richards went to Nigeria as Governor in December 1943 his remit was to plan a constitution for the country *which would be* wrote his biographer, Richard Peel, *best suited to Nigerian needs.*" It was a herculean task. *Nigeria was larger than France, Belgium, Holland and Italy together with a population well in excess of 30 million which consisted of ten main tribal groups and a myriad of smaller clans* many of which spoke their own language. The Governor could only achieve a workable constitution with the constructive help of the people, and at his swearing in ceremony he called on them to join with him in the post-war planning *for the road from tutelage to responsibility must be paved with self-help.* And Richard Peel comments that whatever road was chosen, tolerance and mutual respect for one's neighbour and a knowledge of his character and his culture were essential. Sir Arthur coined the phrase *'Unity In Diversity'.*

Planning for a hand-over began in the war but perhaps this was not translated swiftly enough on the ground. A few African administration officers were appointed but it was a drop in the bucket and there appears to have been no concerted drive to put Africans into positions of responsibility under the guidance of British staff. Recalling the rhythm of life then, we can understand the reasons for this; the everyday administration had to go on, the local current problems resolved, the reports written and the books balanced - and, besides, what was the rush?

At that time, the period of British administration in Africa had only been, in broad brush terms, about sixty years. During that period the

270

continent had been transformed from, in the main, a wilderness of scattered tribes; a vast, beautiful but often inhospitable land which had no roads, no hospitals, no schools, no world trade except in slaves and ivory, and no government in the modern sense: if you like, it had consisted of a myriad of tiny, weak disparately run nations. During the fifty years of her administration in the continent, Britain had found herself caught up in the maelstrom of two world wars in between which she - and practically every country in the world - had suffered the effects of the greatest economic slump that the world had so far seen. There was an enormous amount to sort out both at home and abroad. British politicians, people and civil servants can be forgiven for feeling that time was not of the essence to prepare for the hand-over of power to the African peoples they administered.

We also wonder if Africa needed more time too. As with most of us, many Africans are resistant to change. They were learning to weld themselves into greater national groups; to be countries - imperfect as many of the borders were - rather than tribes with ever shifting boundaries. They were accustoming themselves to modern communications, to new working habits and skills, the rule of law and to the opportunities which education brought them on an ever increasing global scale. We can speculate that had the mass of the people of Africa been given ten more years to equip themselves for the responsibilities of running their own affairs, and if the British administration in Africa had prepared better by driving forward a planned handover, much of what has happened since might have been avoided.

For whatever else may have been on the minds of the great and good - and usually distant - politicians of all races, the well-being of the 'man on the Onitsha omnibus' was not, at that time, the primary concern. For that lack of thought Sir Arthur Richards, by then Lord Milverton, at a meeting at the Royal Institute of International Affairs in December 1950, roundly criticised governments pressing ahead to make the colonies and protectorates independent:

Is it not a fact that the real point of developing Africa is the welfare of the African, and what do you mean by that? Welfare according to whose idea, the Africans' or ours? Does it not mean the break-up of the existing social and economic system, does it not presuppose the integration of the African into Western economy, a thing which means the complete change of the whole range of his life? That is not the outlook of the average African today, and I do suggest that the speed at which development, in the currency of democratic words today, is being forced upon the Africans is highly dangerous. . .in fact that system cannot be worked until the people appreciate what personal liberty, personal initiative and personal responsibility mean.

Those were prophetic words and history has shown that the welfare of the African was not well served by the unseemly acceleration to independence.

We now come to the question of why Britain divested herself of her colonies so swiftly and - for us who were there - so unexpectedly?

At the end of the war the United States and the Soviet Union, for their different reasons, wanted to see the end the British Empire. However, *The first step* wrote Robin Neillands in his book '*A Fighting Retreat*' *came even before the United States entered the war [WWII]. In August 1941, Winston Churchill and the American President, Franklin D. Roosevelt, met and drew up a declaration of their shared political views, a declaration which came to be called the Atlantic Charter...Clauses in the Charter covered freedom 'for all the countries of the world' and the Americans soon made it clear that these clauses applied as much to the colonies of their allies, the Colonial Powers, as they did to the Nazi-dominated states of Europe.*

This was undoubtedly a driver to early independence at the end of the war.

The feeling amongst Europeans in Kenya, where we were growing up, was that the good name of the "colonial", be he or she settler or administrator, was being sullied with false charges of racism and dictatorial rule. These charges began an unstoppable tide of world opinion which was coupled with, as Sir Arthur Richards put it the *advancing demands and ambitions of loud-voiced and self-appointed African leaders, whose methods of violence and intimidation silenced the dissentient voices of their own people and misled the ignorant majority.*

One of those methods of violence was, of course, the Mau Mau in Kenya. Although it had its origins in resentment over land, the lack of it, farming methods on it and the clash of cultures between tribal land customs and the western title deed system (or tiddly-dee as it was known,) the Mau Mau was later perceived as part of the "struggle" for freedom. The world's clamour to end colonialism was led by the two super-powers, the Mau Mau as a freedom movement fitted into this narrative. Detention camps full of resentful terrorists, and the deaths at Hola Camp left a stain and made people wonder if Britain (and

272

Portugal, France and Belgium) was right to "rule" another race in its own country. Britain, shot to pieces as she was both economically and emotionally, lost interest in administering disparate and far flung places and could not raise the will or the finance to resist her critics.

There were many in the Colonial Service throughout the British dependencies who believed, like Lord Milverton did, that MacMillan's 'wind of change' was more of an expedient to shed Britain's responsibilities rather than answering a pressing demand from the indigenous peoples of the continent.

The third question we posed at the beginning of this chapter was whether or not the African people understood the implications of independence? I think the bewitching potion of "uhuru" [freedom] was hard to resist for many but was there really a "struggle" for independence on the part of ninety percent of the people of what was then British Africa? Most of them were more concerned with their everyday lives than the wide constitutional issues although some of them were misled into believing that cars, houses and servants would be theirs for the taking once the white man had left. As Kenya's independence drew near we would pass laughing groups of Africans in the rural areas raising their index fingers and shouting "Uhuru!" and we would wonder what seductive pictures the word was conjuring up.

David Nicoll Griffith served in Fort Hall in Kenya between 1959 and 1961. He paints a picture of confusion which probably sums up the mood of the Kikuyu, at least.

When we arrived at Fort Hall, once at the centre of the Mau Mau uprising, military operations against the gangs had finished and the Emergency was effectively over. There was, however, still a close administration in the locations and the people were still in the villages which had been set up at the start of the Emergency. There were here and there other reminders of what had gone on in this place but a few years previously: I shall always retain the memory of a wooden cross by the roadside not far from Fort Hall; with Mount Kenya in the distance as a backdrop, the inscription commemorated a District Officer killed by terrorists at Gakurwe. Even at the height of the troubles the number of terrorists had not been large and not all Kikuyu had supported them. Indeed, we all admired the courage and strength of character of the Kikuyu who remained loyal to the Government; many were killed for their refusal to aid the gangs, their families massacred and their homes burned. Not that they may not have wanted to move towards Independence, but they saw that the bestiality and violence of Mau Mau were not the way to achieve anything. The Anglican Church at

273

Fort Hall was the cathedral church of the Fort Hall diocese and its bishop was himself a Kikuyu, the Rt. Rev. Obadiah Kariuki. The church, dedicated to St. James and All Martyrs, had been built as a memorial to the loyal Kikuyu who had fallen, many of their relatives and those who survived having contributed towards the cost. There is in it a set of superb murals, painted with an African motif by an African artist and depicting events in the life of Christ.

The ending of the Mau Mau Emergency heralded the beginning of a more acceptable expression of political aims, namely the formation of African political parties properly constituted. As far as Fort Hall was concerned this meant the Kenya African National Union (KANU); at the outset it was exclusively Kikuyu in membership, and there followed many months of campaigning by Kikuyu politicians. The theme was, of course, independence for the country with KANU forming the Government, and this message was promoted by all kinds of cajoling and propaganda at large public gatherings. Kikuyu would come from all parts of the District to attend these, and the Police were fully extended in covering them.

One day I was returning to Fort Hall in our car with my wife and two-year old son. As we rounded a bend we found the road blocked by a huge crowd of Kikuyu who were making their way to a political gathering. They were already in an excited state, evidenced by their dance-like movements and ululations from the women. We edged our way through at a very slow pace, the entire car surrounded by the crowd; I knew full well that if a wheel went over somebody's foot we would have been in serious trouble. We emerged without mishap, but the experience was unsettling.

We would get reports of what was said at these meetings, and it was distressing whenever we learned of instances of those simple people being duped by false promises. 'You see those nice houses over there? If you vote for us you will all get to live in houses like that after Independence' was one such example. There were also cases of tribesmen from the Reserves being accosted on the streets of Nairobi and asked to select a car they would like from those parked nearby. The number of the car was then written on a piece of paper and handed to its new 'owner' in exchange for 10/=, with the promise that when Independence came he could claim it. Anything we might have said on the matter would of course have fallen on deaf ears, since we were labelled as the cause of all life's woes, and our position had not been improved by 'fact-finding' visits from British socialist politicians. These rarely lasted more than a week or so and one cannot even begin to form a judgement of a country and its people in a couple of weeks, for in such a time it is only the most vociferous of agitators who are likely to leave their impression; I personally did not get the 'feel' of Kenya until I had been there several years. Yet on the basis of such visits articles appeared in the British press with such titles as 'Kenya under the Iron Heel' and a photograph of

274

Nazi jackboots alongside. All of us in the Service had in fact spent our entire working lives, and a great deal of energy, in trying to help the indigenous people to a better and more rewarding life; to educate them, indeed, to the point where they could safely manage their own affairs in the face of the complicated world outside. It was therefore particularly depressing to realise that the 'facts' as 'found' were not designed to present a balanced view at all, but only to gain political capital.

On a lighter note, Elspeth Huxley, with her vibrant descriptive powers, describes in her book 'Four Guineas', how in The Gold Coast she spoke to *a mammy who wore a large straw hat on the back of her head and put her arms akimbo on wide hips wrapped in a cloth patterned in orange, claret and sea-green. Her close-waisted bodice had flounces over the shoulders and buttoned tight over generous dusky breasts. Her laugh was deep and masculine, shaking her whole body; there was about her a generosity like that of good burgundy, yet a hardness too; beside such an amazon I could but feel synthetic, bloodless and deeply conscious of an empty quiver - like a discarded icecream cone beside a cornucopia.*

She spoke very little English, and roared with laughter at everything I said. We soon got on to politics; they permeate the air.

'CPP' she said, striking her bosom with joy. 'All the market - all CPP! All SG! All Free Dom.'

These are magic passwords, SG for self-government and now Free Dom. Once again she roared with laughter and slapped her thigh. 'SG makes us all rich!' SG swam before us like a vision of a mighty god or emperor in cloth of gold and purple, pledged to endow us all with joy, wealth and Free Dom - surely some ambrosial, cockle-warming mead - with Kwame Nkrumah as his chancellor.

Alluring as it might be to believe it now, there never was a struggle, no epic fight for freedom such as that, for example, of Moses leading the Hebrews out of Egypt. In order to justify the word 'struggle' there must be opposition. But more, there was a ripple to presage the changing tide which increased in vigour and intent and which, willy nilly, caught up many people as it began to rush along. The British allowed the tide to flow and indeed helped to direct and harness it but they never opposed it.

In many places the atmosphere of friendship scarcely altered as people became aware of what was ahead. Sir Arthur Richards was greatly impressed by the *unswerving loyalty to the Government shown by all Native Authorities* in the northern Emirates. In the Sudan in 1953 Brian Carlisle wrote to his fiancée: *The Sudanese are a wonderfully friendly and well mannered nation and although there is a very small minority that want us to go in a hurry even they are charming to meet and have no personal animosities at all against any of the British. The political situation has deteriorated and it is more obvious than ever that we have not got much longer in this country but there is really no danger of any unrest or violence...it is very natural that a young nation should want to run its own affairs.*

Of course there were dreams, aspirations and ambitions. Nnamdi Azikwe, Editor of the West African Pilot voiced those dreams with thrilling eloquence; *The Ibo giant is waking from his stupor... A mighty nation shall rise again in the West of Sudan [and] the Ibo shall emerge ... to rewrite the history written by their ancestors...The God of Africa has willed it.*

Others felt a sense of foreboding. One farm hand, Machemi, who had joined the Mau Mau (see Chapter 17: We and They) spent an hour begging me to persuade our parents not to leave Kenya. After his experiences as a member of the Mau Mau, he was not optimistic about a life without the DC as arbitrator and, besides who, when my parents went, would mend that tractor or know how to treat that sick calf?

There was also disquiet amongst the weaker groups and tribes about who would dominate and how would the less strong and less politically astute fare without the white man to hold the ring? In 1953 Eric Downton wrote from South Sudan in *The Daily Telegraph*:

None of the political parties now so active in Khartoum, can claim to represent the South. This applies also to the recently formed Socialist Republican Party which, despite a very limited connection, claimed to be the 'party of the South'. ... In the past few days I have met many Southerners. Among them were representatives of the Dinka tribe, the South's largest with a million members. They come from Nuer, Bari and Latuka tribes. I talked also with educated officials and merchants who are concerned with their lack of political organisation. ... Among southerners there is a renewal of the old distrust of the North. Memories of brutal Northern Moslem slave traders are still much alive.

In the Gold Coast the deeply conservative Muslims feared the power of the southerners and in the television series "*End of Empire*", made many years after independence, an elderly northerner in Ghana admitted that in the north they had wanted independence to come some years later than it did. This was because the north had not been prepared for self-rule and the consequence was that the southerners had been able to steal the advantage.

In Nigeria Malam Aliyu Bidu, an influential Northerner, was concerned that if independence came too quickly the North there would also be at the mercy of the more progressive South.

What can be done now? The North is poor, the south is wealthy. The south has its own home-born lawyers, doctors and engineers. The North has produced, as yet, no lawyers and engineers, and only one doctor. There are twenty schools in the South for everyone in the North. The South has its own newspapers and even the railway and the post and telegraph offices are staffed by Southerners. More important still, the Southerners have learned to organise themselves in unions and political parties.

Nevertheless the tidal race was running and more and more people were being swept into it. The Nigerian Youth Movement tried to stir the country into an heroic struggle. Sir Bryan Sharwood Smith wrote:

Already events in India and in Southeast Asia had encouraged sincere and serious minded politicians in Lagos and the south to hope and plan for freedom from British rule within a measurable span of years. But there were also those same parts of the country, small groups of men, less well equipped with wisdom and .... who, having drunk over-deeply of the heady wine of nationalism, were talking wildly of violence and of arson and hinting darkly of plots to massacre Europeans in their beds. The great mass of the population, however, remained unimpressed and responsible politicians agreed with the Governor's [Sir Arthur Richards] comments on the prevalent 'glib talk about dying for Nigeria. ... Nigeria,' he said 'needs men who will live for her, a far harder and more exacting task.'

In the Sudan Brian Carlisle who had been DC Gezira wrote to me:

Political activity in Khartoum and to a lesser extent in other towns, hotted up again in 1952-53 and it was felt by the Governor that a more rapid policy of Sudanisation was necessary. I had become engaged on my 1952 leave and was taking leave early in 1953 to go home and get married. I had of course done my best on my leave and in my letters to describe Hasaheisa to my fiancée and to laud the fine house and garden. Then to my great surprise only a few weeks before I went on leave, I heard that my very capable Sudanese No. 2, Aly Hassan Abdulla, was to take over from me and that I was to be transferred to Rumbek in the Southern Sudan - a completely strange place to me. But I was sorry to leave Gezira and am immodest enough to believe that so were some of the parishioners. The Hasaheisa merchants, all card carrying Ashigga Party members, came to ask why I was being moved so soon and I responded that it was the policy of Sudanising posts being executed: they looked a bit blank so I said that this was the aim of their Sudanese Political Parties to which they responded that this might be alright for a policy but they did not expect it to be executed in their district. That was the way of things.

Politics was the in-thing throughout all the British colonies and protectorates. We have seen how there was dissent between the traditionalists and new young thrusters when Christopher Dodwell worked on his papers at a desk in the road to keep them apart [See Chapter 14: Service in the Outposts.] A mixed mood of jitters and elation prevailed. Into Nicoll Griffith's office in Mombasa at the beginning of the sixties would appear:

gentlemen wearing sunglasses and carrying briefcases; they would walk in unannounced, lean over the desk and tell me of all the wonders that would occur once Independence had been gained. One informed me that they would do away with many of the unnecessarily restrictive laws which hampered the people's freedom; when I asked him to give me an example, he said: 'Why, for instance, do you insist on vehicles keeping to only one side of the road? We would allow them to use as much of the road as they wanted'.

A few years earlier - 1953 - elections were held throughout the Sudan for a new Parliament. Brian Carlisle wrote:

The Northern Parties (N.U.P. and Umma) mounted political campaigns in the South. The old administration had to hold the ring and see that the elections were conducted fairly without intimidation and without largesse being distributed to the voters. We warned the politicians that they were not to give bribes and that excessive entertainment of the voters fell into this category. In Rumbek the NUP were running a Northernised Dinka called Abdulla Adam and on the day before polling, the Police Officer reported that despite the warnings Abdulla Adam was holding a large party and that large stocks of beer had been assembled. I ordered the Police to bring a charge against Abdulla Adam and the stocks of beer were seized as evidence. Abdulla Adam was tried by a magistrate from the adjoining district, found guilty and fined £100 but on appeal the sentence was quashed on the grounds that beer drinking had not got started (my Governor's comments on hearing of the quashing was that Guy Fawkes should have been exonerated on the grounds that he had not lit the gunpowder). Despite the lavish entertainment Abdulla Adam got very few votes and I think it was really because of this that the Chief Justice took such a lenient view. We were pleased with the two candidates who were elected and thought they would both stand firm for Southern interests in Parliament but when they got to Khartoum they came under intense pressure from the NUP and in the following April they crossed the floor and joined the ranks with the NUP as did many other Southern members. Once this had happened any possibility of some special interim arrangements for transfer of power in the Southern Sudan evaporated. The Sudan had moved down the road to the eruption of violence in 1956 and the sad long Civil War between the two parts.

The trouble is that South and North really ought to be two different countries but the

278

South is really too poor and too remote to stand on its own feet. Up to 1947 the two parts were really being developed separately but this became politically impossible. After that whenever the British tried to come up with constitutions or administrative arrangements that were some sort of safeguard for the South, the rug was pulled from under their feet by the leading Southerners caving in to Northern blandishments. Looking back it is very sad to think that all we did in the South fell down like a pack of cards in the long Civil War. The only thing that has survived is the Christian Church which despite oppression and persecution is now flourishing. In a letter to his fiancee Mr Carlisle asked her to pray for the Sudanese. and he reported to her that one of his colleagues, Ranald Bayle, had resigned because he felt so strongly that we had let down the Southerners.

E.H. (Ted) Nightingale who had been Governor of Equaoria in 1954 wrote in his memoirs. The blacks were not in favour of immediate independence, as they realized it would mean being dominated by the northerners, whom they hardly differentiated from the Egyptians, still regarded as potential slave raiders. A good number of Southerners had a grandparent, or even a parent, who had been taken away into slavery. Northern Sudanese, in private conversations, often automatically and without malice, referred to the blacks as 'the slaves'.....It was obvious that independence was not going to be to the advantage of the Southerners and the few of them capable of thinking politically realized this. I was frequently approached by these leaders, who said 'You simply must not leave us like this. You must stay and look after us until we are better able to look after ourselves.' A possibility which found favour with the thinking Southerners was for Britain to obtain a United Nations mandate to administer the Southern Provinces, perhaps for fifteen or twenty years, until such time as they were able to catch up sufficiently with the North to hold their own politically.

This is what I recommended, but it was turned down by the Foreign Office, presumably for reasons of international politics, no doubt connected with Egypt and the Suez Canal agreement, which Britain was keen to conclude, though, to many of us in the Sudan, it seemed unlikely to be worth the paper it was written on.

The Southerners' fear of being dominated by the North was so great that some of their leaders warned me that their people would revolt rather than submit to rule by the North. I reported to Khartoum that the chance of this happening after independence was a risk that I considered too great, but the Foreign Office decided *to ignore it.*

In early 1954, Ted was summoned to Khartoum to meet Selwyn Lloyd, the Foreign Secretary, and to give him the Southerners' view. *We all spent a hot and busy day telling Selwyn Lloyd in no uncertain terms what we thought about the situation. Came sunset and, as was customary, the palace major domo brought out the whisky and offered the Foreign Secretary a drink. He accepted with alacrity, remarking that it was the only kind word that had been addressed to him that day. It was disappointing that the meeting seemed to have no influence on the Foreign Office's plans, which, I think, were already fixed. In the event it took only eight months from the introduction of self-government for this to happen, starting at Torit, with a mutiny of the black troops against their Arab officers in August 1955.*

In 1964, Ted Nightingale was sitting on his verandah on his farm at the Kinangop in Kenya enjoying the twilight darkening in the sky. He had retired from the Sudan Political Service. Four men, dressed in shukas and sandals, walked quietly into the garden. Mr Nightingale recognised them as Dinka men from Southern Sudan. He greeted them.

They told him they had walked all the way from South Sudan. They said, "Things are very bad there, Sir."

"So I hear." Mr Nightingale responded.

"Please will you come back, Sir? We need you to return. We cannot manage things without you."

"I cannot return. That would be impossible. The Sudanese people wanted us to leave and I am afraid you must now run your own affairs.

At about the same time in Northern Rhodesia, soon to become Zambia, a 27 year old newly promoted DC, Jonathan Lawley, was also having doubts about the wisdom of rushing the naive and trusting Tonga tribe into the sharks' pool of venal politics.

I asked him to write me a piece about his experiences and views on independence in October 1964 from the point of view of a young DC:
I had just been promoted to District Commissioner and they were exciting and busy times. My district was a large and important one: Gwembe, taking in the whole of

the north side of Lake Kariba and down the Zambezi to its confluence with the Kafue. There were two sub-districts with a population of 65,000 which had benefited from a lot of Kariba resettlement money and, until the Kariba dam was built, had been largely left to itself and its traditional way of life in the valley cauldron at 1,600 feet. In 1964 I was 27 and this was a return posting to Tonga country where I spoke the language. My spirits were high and I considered myself both fortunate and privileged.

About three months before independence, the Prime Minister and President designate, Kenneth Kaunda, came to stay. I had met him a few months earlier when he had come to talk to expatriate civil servants in the Luapula Province. He had arrived by small aeroplane at Fort Rosebery airfield and had been greeted by the Provincial Commissioner with a handshake and by the Chief of Police with a salute which raised a great cheer from the crowds of Africans. He had impressed me then when he promised that Zambia would not be like Ghana and he had told us all that nobody who did not want to would need to leave as a result of independence. One policeman asked for an assurance about this pledge and got it.

Now at Gwembe as a bachelor, I needed all the help I could get from the boma ladies who came up trumps with meals and entertainment. Kaunda was highly appreciative of all our efforts and he impressed everybody with his courteous and gracious manner.

His objective on this visit was to win round the local people to the idea of independence and rule by UNIP. This was something they associated with domination by the Bemba tribe from the North. Kaunda did very well and was received with courtesy if not enthusiasm but when he spoke with local tribesmen with no English I had to translate. He came across as a good man, high principled and passionately dedicated to Zambia's future pride and prosperity. I wished that the rest of the UNIP leadership were the same. Nonetheless I found him naive. He was clearly imbued with the idea that racism was foremost amongst evils but he did not seem to understand us or our culture. He was, however, incredibly open and keen to learn but he gave the impression that he could be deeply influenced by the last person he had talked to. He told me that one of his main worries was about who he was going to be able to trust after independence. I said that surely he should trust the British who no longer had any particular ambitions in Africa and who retained a greater dispassionate understanding than any other nation.

The fact was that in August 1964 everything was happening at once. A few months earlier we had had the very first rural local government elections and as with the earlier national elections the best way to get your particular party elected was to promise everything that had hitherto been associated with white privilege in the minds of the local people.

281

The essence of democracy and tolerating the other man's viewpoint was simply not understood and thus democracy did not seem to be destined to last. More worrying, though, was the fact that although there had been some progress towards preparation for independence through training for responsibility in the civil service, the fact was that before independence Africans had minimal responsibility. They actually ran almost nothing at all where there was not a white veto or supervisory power. At the eleventh hour, the very year of independence, a number of supposedly promising people were suddenly plucked out of lowly positions and required to "shadow" senior British officers. Simultaneously there were vast over-promotions which were bound to fail. All this triggered a scramble for status and money amongst African civil servants who thought they were being deprived if they did not see a gigantic leap in their fortunes. The sad fact was that the country had received totally inadequate preparation for independence to the point of gross irresponsibility on the part of the British Government. Everything had seemed to happen at once and at the last moment. Even if drastic action had begun at the time of MacMillan's "winds of change" speech in 1960, Zambia might have had more of a chance. Now clearly there was nothing that could be done to extend the period of preparation. In Luanshya in 1963 I told Sir John Moffat, David Livingstone's descendent and a prominent local liberal, that Britain's policy of moving headlong towards independence seemed to me to be courting disaster. His response which I was reluctant to accept at the time but which I see now to reflect the truth, was that come what may Britain was determined to divest itself of its African responsibilities. There was nothing we could do about this even if we knew that the policy was misguided. We would just have to come to terms with it and make the best of it. I think I did accept it and I think my age made this easier: many older colleagues merely accepted their golden handshakes and pensions and left.

I felt particularly sad after having spent most of my childhood in southern Africa and having seen at close hand the evils of racism in South Africa and the missed opportunity in Southern Rhodesia, due to the greed and lack of foresight of Europeans, to build a multiracial society within a new Central African Federation. Many of those Europeans who had opposed and thereby blocked a joint participation were recent immigrants from the UK after the war and they tended to vote for politicians like Ian Smith who had promised to preserve their privileged position. For me, however, joining the Colonial Service represented faith in Britain's long term role in Africa and her ability to steer much of the continent down a middle course which would not only be a positive example for South Africa but would catch on over a huge swathe of southern and eastern Africa to counterbalance the extremes of black and white nationalistic fears and aspirations. But this was not to be. During the fascinating and hectic run up to independence in Northern Rhodesia I came to terms with the inevitable, though I had little truck with dressing up as something noble Britain's act of abandonment of responsibility by politicians such as MacMillan and Macleod.

It was particularly difficult to deal with the bewilderment of all the good loyal, mature African District Messengers or those manning the local courts or even simply the ordinary people who could not understand why we were so determined to give way to people whom they saw even more clearly than we did as self-seekers who were corrupt and ignorant to boot. All the really good people, or nearly all of them, seemed to be begging us to retain the status quo and of course we let them down. A saving grace however was the fact that the new powers that be were seldom bent upon settling old scores or taking revenge. The ability to forgive and forget is one of the great strengths of Africa and so it was in Zambia.

I think that underlying everything for me and my colleagues in the Provincial Administration was our deep love of the country and its people and the sense of impending loss. All of us, whether people such as me who had served for less than five years or others who had seen a working lifetime, had been deeply involved with local people in a job where it was essential to understand and to empathise. You had to like and respect the people you were working with. If you did not the job would have been intolerable.

We were set apart fundamentally from the administrators in the white dominated south because we were in no way working to any racial agenda or for the preservation of white privilege, dressed up in the name of "standards". Although we were sometimes accused of not understanding the wider picture, our lack of a personal axe to grind meant that we understood the issues far better than those "settlers" whose main fear and preoccupation was to lose their privileged position. We never lost touch with ordinary people. Village to village touring was a main part of a DC's job and through it we remained in touch and retained their

trust. (I remember being so struck years later when I was helping to supervise the independence elections in that same Zambezi valley but on the southern bank in Southern Rhodesia when it became Zimbabwe, that the new administration had totally lost touch with the people.)

Looking at my diary of just before independence 33 years ago my preoccupations were mainly over the future, on the British role in Africa and how it related to culture. I wrote 'we have not created black Englishmen in Africa. ... Certainly they do not want to embrace our culture;. they want to develop their own culture and personality. Britain is stepping out at a time when with the cut and thrust of the modern world she should be doing all she can to maintain her strength and position here. Colonial people will have contempt for our weakness, and our enemies in the 'wings' will rub their hands gleefully and shout 'neo-colonialism' at our future efforts.' We could have done so much more and finished off the job, being proud of our imperial role and by making it a Commonwealth effort. The deep underlying concern was that independence was coming far too soon and that the consequences were going to be dire. On independence eve, 23rd October 1964, I telephoned my opposite number a hundred miles away at Mazabuka to ask him how the sword fitted in with the DC's uniform. I had inherited it from a portly retiring deputy Provincial Commissioner on the Copperbelt a couple of years before and I had never worn it. I was determined that it should see the light of day for the first and last time. He said, 'Jonathan, you're not going to wear it are you?' I said I jolly well was, so he said, 'Well be it on your own head' and gave me the appropriate instructions. That night I set off by car with my DO to the nearby Chikuni mission where we were invited to the midnight flag lowering and raising ceremony. During the preceding days we had been preoccupied with borrowing loudspeaker equipment for our main ceremony the next day at the native authority HQ, and I had been very busy with no time to think and reflect. Then came midnight, and there was the brand new Zambian flag flying for the first time at the top of the floodlit flagpole to the strains of the new stirring Zambian national anthem. I was suddenly hit hard by the significance of it all. One had to feel hope for the new nation even if in the background there was trepidation and, almost simultaneously, sweeping over me a feeling of immense sadness. To quote from my diary, 'I found myself more deeply moved than I have ever been, also sadder. It was like losing somebody who had meant a great deal to you. I was not ashamed to shed a tear for everything that this country and the Empire had stood for and for all that so many good men had put into it - not for personal gain but especially because they believed in what Britain stood for.'

I felt that the new masters would simply not understand and care about what we had stood for, whereas the ordinary people certainly did. There was the feeling that we were letting down these people, both the population and the loyal civil servants such as the District Messengers who had total faith in us and had shown us exceptional loyalty.

I felt personally that I was lucky that I was likely to be in a position to continue to preserve our relationships with the local people for at least a year or two. In the event though, after independence the role of the District Commissioner - or District Secretary as he was now called - changed and there was little time to devote to getting out into the district on village to village tours and messages started coming in to the boma asking what had happened to the DC.

On independence day itself I remember that it was stinking hot at Gwembe Boma as it usually is at the end of October before the rains. But, 90 degrees or so was cool compared to what it would be down in the valley at Munyumbwe where the main celebrations were going to be held. There was to be a massive beer drink, the roasting of oxen and lots of Tonga dancing; this took the form of everyone jumping up and down in unison blowing cow horns. Before going down to Munyumbwe, however, there was my own little ceremony to perform involving the uniform and the flag. Most of the messengers were already at Munyumbwe so there was a turn-out of only five or six when I arrived at the Boma, sword clanking and uniform white topee just about obscuring my features. There was a small gathering including my faithful secretary, Jean Nixon, with a cine camera to record the event. As I prepared to inspect the messengers I looked up to see the union jack on the flagpole was flying at half mast. I had been determined that if a flag was to be raised another had to be lowered. No doubt the duty messenger had thought that it might be considered politically incorrect to fly a union jack in the normal way on independence day, even just for a brief ceremony and he was probably right.

Down at Munyumbwe it was like stepping into a furnace. There was a lot of traditional beer around and everyone was happy. African National Congress and United National Independence Party Councillors walked hand in hand and an atmosphere of immense goodwill prevailed. I think also that the ordinary people were reassured - the chiefs certainly were - that the district still had a British DC. The valley Tonga were a backward people who had had little contact with so-called civilisation before the Kariba dam was built. Their women used to knock out their front teeth. This was considered to be a sign of beauty which probably had its origins in trying to discourage slave traders. They also continuously smoked great gourd, water cooled pipes and went about bare-breasted. Before the white man came at the beginning of the century they lived with the continual threat of attack from stronger tribes like the Matabele and the Lozi who stole their cattle. All these factors made them pro-government and fearful of independence.

After it was all over I devoted myself to twenty months of change and helping the district to adapt to new realities. Then the long-awaited notice of my transfer to Lusaka came through. My successor, a recently promoted clerk, was a most unhappy man. Far from considering that he had had bestowed upon him an honour and privilege to be given charge of one of the most important districts in the whole of Zambia, he felt that he deserved promotion to even higher echelons such as Assistant Secretary or Under Secretary in a Ministry in Lusaka, like many of his friends. He did not hesitate to make his feelings known. My own friends, the Head Messenger Mwene Falls and driver Benjamin Shipopo, were philosophical but the local UNIP Secretary came to tell me of his disappointment and disgust at the appointment. It seemed to dash all the hopes he had cherished for Gwembe when the time came for the

285

district to have a Zambian DC.

Meanwhile I packed up my goods and chattels which a gang of prisoners from the gaol loaded on to the boma lorry and I left the lovely old house with its wide verandahs from which one could gaze across the immense views over the Zambezi Valley; the little guest house under the huge avocado pear tree which bore delicious but tiny hens' egg-sized fruit and the flagpole on the brown lawn.

When we arrived in Lusaka we headed for the block of government flats in Birdcage Walk and the bachelor accommodation which I rated. I could hear the prisoners remarking, when they saw the three-storey building, that the bwana must be coming up in the world judging by the size of his new house!

Thus wrote Jonathan Lawley in Zambia.

In Kenya A.W Horner, CMG, TD was Director in charge of the Kenya Independence celebrations. The design of the flag, the new national anthem and the ceremonial itself were all his responsibility. He answered to Tom Mboya who was Minister for Legal and Constitutional Affairs. He had been landed with the job when he was Permanent Secretary to Mboya. The Acting Governor, Eric Griffith-Jones, had called a meeting of Permanent Secretaries to discuss who would run the independence ceremonies which were to take place some eight months hence. He looked enquiringly around the table but there were no takers. Griffith Jones then looked at Horner and said, "Actually, Arthur, the Africans have asked for you."

Horner was wise enough to hesitate and asked for time to think about it but one of the other Permanent Secretaries said to him as they were leaving the meeting, "Do you realise that this is an enormous compliment to you, Arthur?" Flattery won the day and he decided to do it. But *it nearly drove me mad* he told me with feeling. After it was all over and he had returned to England, he found it difficult to forget that Tom Mboya had been publicly rude to him on the day of the ceremony. The main problem for Horner was that the African regard for the finer points of formality was, at best, unreliable. The stands built round the ceremonial arena were marked off into areas for general guests and, of course, a special area for VIP's. Arthur had wanted the boys from the Technical College to be ushers in order to ensure that everyone was courteously guided to the correct seat but Mboya vetoed this idea and said that he wanted personnel from KANU (Kenya African National Union - the governing party) to do it. Arthur conceded but he could not get any African to take charge of them. Not even an African

Policeman was sufficiently brave to take on such a responsibility. In the event, therefore, he had had to get a Captain from the British Army to do it. The day before the ceremony there was to be a meeting of the ushers at 2 pm. They turned up at 3.15 pm, many of them slightly tiddly from lunch and said, "We're not going to do this sort of European thing." On the day of Independence not one usher turned up in the VIP stand. Despite each guest having a numbered ticket, chaos ensued and people who were not supposed to be there, such as two Chinese with no English, settled themselves in the VIP seats. This caused Mboya to turn on Horner and publicly swear at him, reducing Mrs Horner almost to tears. Arthur gave a spirited response and the Bishop of East Africa, the Rt Reverend Leonard Beecher who was sitting nearby, intervened to try to diffuse the situation. In the event it was, to his everlasting gratitude, a large, powerful Kikuyu lady and a friend of Arthur's, who took charge in a cheerfully bossy way and sorted it all out to everybody's satisfaction.

Arthur's troubles were not, however, over. Unseasonally, for mid-December, it poured with rain and many of the guests' cars became bogged down in mud on their way to their stands. Horner had sent the Public Works Department to the arena prior to the ceremony to patch the soft places but the Police had been told not to let anybody into the arena and so they stopped the PWD too. The quagmires therefore remained.

The Ugandan Prime Minister, Milton Obote had not actually been invited: the invitation had gone out to the President of Uganda which was the Kabaka. But word had reached Horner a few days beforehand that Obote had confiscated the Kabaka's Rolls Royce and had forbidden him from going. He planned to attend himself.

On his arrival in Nairobi Obote telephoned the Police and demanded a posse of despatch riders. They had not been briefed and had no idea that he had to be deposited at the back of the stands. They therefore duly escorted him into the arena with the intention of allowing him to alight at the foot of the VIP stand. When a black Rolls Royce with flag fluttering came into sight, Arthur said to the President, Jomo Kenyatta, "Here comes Prince Phillip and the Governor" and together they went down to greet them. But it was Obote's car. However, instead of reaching the foot of the stands it sank into the mud up to its axles. Mrs Obote, a delightful Bagandan lady, thought it terribly funny but Obote was like a *storm cloud*.

The crises, Horner told me, were legion but nonetheless, at Midnight on 12 December 1963 the Union Jack was lowered and, after Prince Phillip's famous question, "Are you sure you won't change your mind?" had been declined, the green flag with a shield and crossed spears signifying the nation of Kenya, was raised and the new national anthem 'O God You Are Our Strength' was played.

Arthur also told me how the national anthem tune was chosen. Two tunes for the anthem were submitted to Jomo Kenyatta for consideration. One was written by a Kenya African studying music in Britain and it was on the lines of a traditional hymn tune. The other was a coastal Pokomo tune which had been adapted by a European and his students at a music school at Ngong. When Kenyatta had listened to them both played by the Police band, he was hesitant. Someone said to him, "Watch the totos Mzee." The band played both tunes again. During the hymn tune the children stayed still but when the Pokomo tune was played they began to dance. Mzee wisely settled on the latter. And so it was that small matters such as whether or not the children chanced to dance helped to shape the new nation of Kenya.

Independence achieved, the administrative officers filtered back to Britain and if they were not ready for retirement, they tried to find jobs in commerce, education or in Government. Many were successful and were able to live fulfilled and useful lives but none of them ever forgot their extraordinary work in Africa. Unfortunately, the tide of anti-empire was running strongly and they were judged, not by their peers, but by politicians, journalists and academics who had scarcely any idea of Africa, its complexities and the remarkable service the administrative officers had performed for its delightful but raw people. This has sometimes saddened many of them:

WESTMINSTER ABBEY REVISITED

by J.S. Templeton

This day I came not here to see
Where kings were crowned in all their majesty;
But just a plaque in memory of me
And other tens of thousands like myself
Who served the Crown in lands beyond the sea.
Surely this shows what once made England great
That of her sons so many risked their fate
In undiscovered corners of the world
Where they took British justice and unfurled
The Union Jack, that symbol of fair rule.
'Take up the White Man's Burden' was the call
And answer it they did and gave their all
In building roads and railways and withal
Taking their culture to the alien scene
And turning deserts into pastures green.
The natives were not hostile, it is true
Some even helped with what we had to do
Now they have independence there's no word
Of thanks for all the aid so freely given
They point with pride to cities in the sun
And proudly tell the world 'Look what we've done.'

AFRICAN DISTRICT COUNCIL'S OFFICE,
SOUTH NYANZA,
KISII. 2nd November, 1956.

C.H.Williams Esq., O.B.E., C.M.G.,
Provincial Commissioner,
Nyanza Province,
KISUMU.

Dear Williams,

I have taken this opportunity for writing to you because I have received information that you are retiring during this month. Myself I think that you have not reached the retiring age. The news of your retirement is being known gradually in South Nyanza District, and the people who have heard of it are taken by surprise.

I greatly appreciate your being in Nyanza Province for a long time and I think you have spent most of your life in this Province. I will not forget the period when you were District Officer in South Nyanza and how you were cycling in Karachuonyo Location, teaching people how to grow fruits and how to put manure in the gardens. It was in 1934 and early in 1935 when you did so. You left the Province for a certain period, and later you joined it as the District Commissioner of Kakamega, North Nyanza, after which you were appointed the Provincial Commissioner of Nyanza.

Your being in Nyanza Province for 7 years as the Provincial Commissioner, has brought immeasurable blessings to the inhabitants of the Province. You have been leading us peacefully, gently and happily. You have been always kind to the people of South Nyanza. The only example which I have learnt from you and also which pleased me is your seeking advices from African leaders at the time of crisis. You prevented Mau Mau from entering the province because you were calling people and talking to them together in order to find means of preventing it. Not only for Mau Mau that you did so, but also when the Province confronted with any serious trouble.

You have been organizing things peacefully because you did not like force. I believe many people like myself will be surprised to hear that you have gone without biding them good-bye, although this is due to shortage of time.

Through good leadership with which you have led our Council, we have now improved conditions of the South Nyanza African District Council because you very kindly considered and recommended our petitions which we were submitting to you from time to time through our presidents. You have been doing the same with Central Government because you have had the Africans' welfare in your mind. I believe even the Europeans would state the same thing. We greatly miss you, as we do not know as yet whether we shall have another Provincial Commissioner of your type.

I pray God to be with you until you come back to Kenya in your Farm where you are going to settle.

Remember me to Mrs. Williams and inform her that I hope to see you again when I shall have an opportunity of paying you a friendly visit at your farm.

Your sincerely,

PAUL MBOYA,
SECRETARY, SOUTH NYANZA AFRICAN DISTRICT COUNCIL.

BIBLIOGRAPHY AND NOTES

Chapter 1
Kenya by Norman Leys
Early Days in East Africa by Sir Frederick Jackson KCMG, CB
A Vivid Canvas. Margaret Collyer. Artist and Pioneer previously *Life of an Artist*
The Lunatic Express by Charles Miller
Kenya by Norman Leys
"*Recollections of British Administration in the Cameroons and Northern Nigeria 1921-1957: But Always As Friends*" Sir Bryan Sharwood Smith KCMG, KCVO, KBE, ED
"*Lugard The Years of Adventure*" by Margery Perham CBE (Collins)
"*Kenya Diary*" by Richard Meinertzhagen
The Last Slave Market by Alastair Hazell
The Nigerian Handbook 1953 published by the Crown Agents for the Colonies.
Early Days in East Africa by Sir Frederick Jackson KCMG, CB
A. McCall in a letter to me
Ladder of Bones by Ellen Thorpe
Stirling Library Archive
"*Kenya Diary*" by Richard Meinertzhagen
Heavens, Command by James Morris
The Camel's Back by Reginald Davies
Nigerian Kleidescope by Sir Rex Niven
Chapter 3
Africa View by Julian Huxley
The Lunatic Express by Charles Miller
"*The British in The Sudan 1898-1956*" edited by Robert O. Collins & Francis M Deng
Chapter 4
From "*A Nosegay of Cacti*" collected by J.S.S. Rowlands)
The value of the pound sterling was fifteen or twenty times what it is today.
Bwani Karani by Mervyn Maciel
Sir Richard Turnbull in forward to *'Bwana Karani'*
J.A.G. McCall CMG
Patrick O'Dwyer
G.C.M (John) Dowson
Blamer & Maciel
Set Under Authority by K.D.D.Henderson
Brian Carlisle

Chapter 5
Named after Col Eric Smith CB. Known as ' The Major', he held the record for the most caravans led from Mombasa to Uganda. He was the brother-in-law of Olive, Margaret and Arthur Collyer.

Chapter 6
Sir Rex Niven

Kirwan

But Always as Friends by Sharwood Smith

Set Under Authority by K.D.D. Henderson

New: Before the Dawn in Kenya (page 29), Wilson

Orde Brown quoted in *Before The Dawn in Kenya* by Christopher Wilson

A Vivid Canvas. Margaret Collyer. Artist and Pioneer."

D.N. March 1935

Memoirs of Henry Rangeley

Chapter 7
Kenya by Norman Leys

I make no apology for drawing heavily from Norman Leys' book *Kenya* (first published in 1924.) This is Arthur's own story and his friend and contemporary wrote about it well.

African Afterthoughts by Sir Philip Mitchell GCMG, MC

Early Days in East Africa by Sir Frederick Jackson KCMG, CB

Arthur Collyer's notes and Minutes

Chapter 10
"The Slave Trade and The Scramble by R. Coupland

"East Africa: A New Dominion" by A.G. Church.

Chapter 11
Last Chance in Africa by Negley Farson

So We Used to Do by A.F. Bridges

Gender, Culture & Empire by Helen Calloway

Chapter 14
On The Camel's Back by Reginald Davies

Lugard. The Years of Adventure by Margery Perham

Jack Flynn

Last Chance in Africa by Negley Farson

Set Under Authority by K.D.D.Henderson

Chapter 15
Unfortunately I have lost the reference relating to the first paragraph of this chapter. I believe it came from a report of Lt Col Oscar Watkins CBE who was give the task of raising the Carrier Corps in 1919.

African Afterthoughts by Sir Philip Mitchell GCMG MC
Lt Col Watkins CBE
Nigerian Kleidescope by Sir Rex Niven

Chapter 16

Uganda Protectorate by Sir Harry Johnston GCMG KCB
Corfield Report page 250
Bwana Karani by Mervyn Maciel
The Camel's Back Reginald Davies
An African Life by M.C. Atkinson
The Camel's Back Reginald Davies
Patrick O'Dwyer
Africa View Julian Huxley
LUGARD The Years of Adventure by Margery Perham CBE. Collins 1956
Set Under Authority K.D.D. Henderson
So We Used To Do by A.F.B Bridges
Nigerian Kleidescope Sir Rex Niven
Canon Harry Leakey in a letter to his wife.
Flame Trees of Thika by Elspeth Huxley
The Zambia [Northern Rhodesia Journal] published from Livingstone Museum
The Camel's Back - Davies
African Afterthoughts by Sir Philip Mitchell GCMG MC

Chapter 17

Early Days in East Africa by Sir Frederick Jackson KCMG, CB
The story of the Dini ya Msambwa was contributed by Edwin (Teddy) Eggins who was a DO in Nyanza Province with responsibility for the Kitosh area.
Last Chance in Africa – Negley Farson
The Origins and Growth of the Mau Mau by FD Corfield. This was the official Government paper known as the Corfield Report.
A.W. Horner CMG, TD
African Afterthoughts by Sir Philip Mitchell GCMG, MC. Former Governor and C in C, Kenya

Chapter 18

Burke – to stifle the truth

Chapter 19

Graphite Powder Plumbago for Coating Sand Casting Moulds.
Baringo District is in Kenya today but in 1902 the area known as Uganda stretched as far into present day Kenya as the foot of the Rift Valley escarpment.

293

Mr AlexanderWhyte is referred to in Sir Harry Johnston's book *The Uganda Protectorate* (pub 1902) as a botanist who cleverly transformed the forested eastern side of Entebbe into a botanical garden.

By 1909 Uganda was considered to be in East Africa, while the Congo was in Central Africa

'*Enigmatic Proconsul*' by Richard Frost

Last Chance in Africa by Negley Farson

So We used To Do by A.F.B. Bridges

Recollections of British Administration in the Cameroons and Northern Nigeria 1921-1957: But Always As Friends" Sir Bryan Sharwood Smith KCMG, KCVO, KBE, ED

The Mottled Lizard by Elspeth Huxley

Chapter 20

African Afterthoughts by Sir Philip Mitchell GCMG MC

Chapter 21

Old Sinister a biography of Sir Arthur Richards by Richard Peel

I once heard on the radio an interpreter of Stalin's tell the story of how, privately, during the Yalta talks, Roosevelt and Stalin came to an understanding that the British Empire must go.

Sir Arthur Richards

Recollections of British Administration in the Cameroons and Northern Nigeria 1921-1957: But Always As Friends" Sir Bryan Sharwood Smith KCMG, KCVO, KBE, ED

Edward Humphrey Nightingale, born 1904, died 1996. He was with the Sudan Political Service from 1926 to 1954. His decorations: 1940 Order of the Nile Fourth Class, awarded by the King of Egypt, and in 1955 he was awarded the CMG.

Years later, after independence in Kenya, our cousin, James Dowson, returned for a visit. When talking to an African who had worked for them, he was taken a-back to be told that independence had not been a good thing. James said, "But you voted for it." The man retorted "Yes, but we did not know that we would lose the DCs."

Mzee: affectionate name for Kenyatta, meaning "Old One"

ISBN:10: 1502713497
ISBN-13: 978-1502713490

If you have any comments or queries do write.
veronicabellers@gmail.com

Printed in Great Britain
by Amazon.co.uk, Ltd.,
Marston Gate.